Questions & Answers

EU Law

Questions & Answers Series

Series Editors: Rosalind Malcolm and Margaret Wilkie

The ideal revision aid to keep you afloat through your exams

Q&A Company Law
Stephen Judge

Q&A Criminal Law
Mike Molan

Q&A Employment Law
Richard Benny, Michael Jefferson, and Malcolm Sargeant

Q&A Equity and Trusts
Margaret Wilkie, Rosalind Malcolm, and Peter Luxton

Q&A EU Law
Nigel Foster

Q&A Evidence
Maureen Spencer and John Spencer

Q&A Family Law
Ruth Gaffney-Rhys, with Chris Barton, Mary Hibbs, and Penny Booth

Q&A Human Rights and Civil Liberties
Steve Foster

Q&A International Law
Susan Breau

Q&A Land Law
Margaret Wilkie, Peter Luxton, and Rosalind Malcolm

Q&A Law of Contract
Adrian Chandler with Ian Brown

Q&A Law of Torts
David Oughton and Barbara Harvey

Q&A Public Law
Richard Clements and Philip Jones

- **advice on exam technique**
- **summary of each topic**
- **bullet-pointed answer plans**
- **model answers**
- **diagrams and flowcharts**
- **further reading**

Questions & Answers

EU Law

EIGHTH EDITION

Professor Nigel G. Foster
Dean of Business and Law
The University of Wales
Visiting Professor, Europa Institut Saarbrücken

2011 and 2012

OXFORD
UNIVERSITY PRESS

OXFORD
UNIVERSITY PRESS

Great Clarendon Street, Oxford OX2 6DP

Oxford University Press is a department of the University of Oxford.
It furthers the University's objective of excellence in research, scholarship,
and education by publishing worldwide in

Oxford New York

Auckland Cape Town Dar es Salaam Hong Kong Karachi
Kuala Lumpur Madrid Melbourne Mexico City Nairobi
New Delhi Shanghai Taipei Toronto

With offices in

Argentina Austria Brazil Chile Czech Republic France Greece
Guatemala Hungary Italy Japan Poland Portugal Singapore
South Korea Switzerland Thailand Turkey Ukraine Vietnam

Oxford is a registered trade mark of Oxford University Press
in the UK and in certain other countries

Published in the United States
by Oxford University Press Inc., New York

© Nigel G. Foster, 2011

The moral rights of the author have been asserted

Crown copyright material is reproduced with the permission of the Controller, HMSO
(under the terms of the Click Use licence)

Database right Oxford University Press (maker)

Fifth edition 2005

Sixth edition 2007

Seventh edition 2009

British Library Cataloguing in Publication Data

Data available

Library of Congress Cataloging in Publication Data

Data available

Typeset by Laserwords Private Ltd, Chennai, India
Printed in Great Britain
on acid-free paper by
Ashford Colour Press Ltd, Gosport, Hampshire

ISBN: 978-0-19-959992-9

10 9 8 7 6 5 4 3 2 1

Contents

The Q&A Series

Key Features

The Q&A Series provides full coverage of key subjects in a clear and logical way. The book contains the following features:

- Questions
- Commentaries
- Bullet-pointed answer plans
- Diagrams
- Full model answers
- Further reading suggestions
- Bibliography

online resource centre
www.oxfordtextbooks.co.uk/orc/qanda/

Every book in the Q&A series is accompanied by an Online Resource Centre, hosted at the URL above, which is open access and free to use.

The Online Resource Centre for this book contains revision and exam advice, a glossary of EU law terms, and links to websites useful for the study of EU law.

Preface

This new edition of the book comes at a time in the life of the European Union when at least we seem to have some calm clear water. Having said that, no doubt some other unforeseen crisis will show its ugly head and upset the relative stability of 2010. The Lisbon Treaty was finally ratified by all 27 Member States after the yes majority in the second Irish referendum on Lisbon, the German constitutional challenge was not successful and the Czech and Polish Presidents gave in to the inevitable and ratified the parliamentary approvals of the Lisbon Treaty in their states. All of this happened in late October and November 2009 and the Treaty entered into force on 1 December 2010. Anyone familiar with the European Union will be used to having things change often and sometimes radically. It is what teachers of EU law have to be used to. However, most of you consulting this book will not of course be used to things changing because you will have come to EU law fresh this year. Hopefully though your lecturers will have stressed the dynamic nature of the European Union and EU law and have explained the numerous changes and the reasons for them. The changes brought about by the Lisbon Treaty have been fully taken into account in this book.

The Lisbon Treaty aside, I have made other amendments to take account of new secondary legislation, new case law and generally to review the material contained within the chapters and the handling of that material.

In 1994, in the first edition I wrote:

Whilst, in some quarters, questions and answers books are not regarded too highly and they are fraught with danger in the wrong hands, they do fill an increasing gap in legal education as we struggle to keep up standards in the face of ever higher numbers. Consequently, there is not as much time today to see individual students and provide them with exam coaching or to go through or mark model questions which they have prepared. Hence, a book such as this, if used intelligently, can make up for less personal tuition and assist the student, not only in identifying the correct material and structure to provide in an answer but also to provide a method to test knowledge for exam revision and preparation and hopefully then to boost confidence before the exam itself. I hope therefore the comments and answers provided will succeed in these aims. I would be grateful to receive from any readers, comments on the range of topics, the contents of the answers and the style and presentation of the material in the book.

This is probably as true if not more true today!

Whilst this new edition does not introduce a large number of new questions, it does thoroughly revise the existing answers to questions in the light of the Treaty revision. Some of the questions are amended quite considerably as a result of these changes.

For errors and omissions in this material I am alone responsible. My continued thanks go to my former colleagues; Robin Churchill and Phil Fennell of Cardiff Law School for permission to use a number of questions formulated jointly and severally for tutorial, essay and exam questions used on the courses on European Community law over the 22 years I spent at Cardiff. I now have the additional experience of teaching EU law to students in Buckingham Law School for five years and on the Masters Degree Course in EU Law at the Europa Institut at the Universität of the Saarland in Saarbrücken for the last four years. Thanks also to the staff of OUP, in particular Helen Swann, Suzy Armitage and Emily Uecker for their background efforts in ensuring the continued success of the Q&A series and for their work in the production of this eighth edition. Thanks also to the now countless thousands of students to whom I have directly taught EC and EU law who have helped develop my approach to law teaching. Thanks again to research staff and secretarial staff who assisted on the previous editions and whose contribution survives in this edition. Thanks as ever to my family for continuing support and now to Lynsey my daughter who continues to hone up her editorial and research skills which have assisted the production of this volume.

Nigel Foster
Buckingham
September 2010

Table of Cases

Cases are listed numerically in chronological order within each year. ECJ cases are listed ahead of CFI cases. CFI cases are prefixed T-

Commission Decisions

French Courts

German Courts

Italian Courts

UK Courts

Table of Primary Legislation

Table of EU Secondary Legislation

Abbreviations

AG	Advocate General
CAP	Common Agricultural Policy
CFI	The Court of First Instance of the European Communities
CMLR	Common Market Law Reports
Court of Justice	The European Court of Justice
CT	Constitutional Treaty
EC	European Community/ies
ECA	European Communities Act 1972
ECB	European Central Bank
ECHR	European Convention on Human Rights
ECJ	European Court of Justice
ECR	European Court Reports
ECSC	European Coal and Steel Community
EEC	European Economic Community
EFTA	European Free Trade Area
EMU	Economic and Monetary Union
EP	European Parliament
ERTA	European Road Transport Agreement
EU	European Union
GATT	General Agreement on Tariffs and Trade
IGC	Intergovernmental Conference
NATO	North Atlantic Treaty Organisation
OEEC	Organisation for European Economic Cooperation
plc	Public Limited Company
QMV	Qualified Majority Voting
SDA	Sex Discrimination Act
SEA	Single European Act
TEU	Treaty on European Union
ToA	Treaty of Amsterdam
WHO	World Health Organisation

1

Introduction

This book is written to provide a number of example questions on EU law which should be fairly typical of those met on degree level courses on EU law. The questions are then followed by a few sentences or paragraphs of comment on the type of question, the main aspects to be considered in the question, advice on particular issues to be aware of and advice on structuring your answer. The commentaries are then followed by bullet points of the most important elements of each answer and then the suggested answers. These are designed to demonstrate how the particular questions should be answered to get a good mark, ie an upper second or better. Note, however, that the writing and marking of law questions (EU law included) is not a simple arithmetic process whereby, once you have written a sufficient number of points, you automatically qualify for a particular grade. Whilst that is one of the elements taken into account, it is also a qualitative assessment of what has been written. In other words, how you have written what you have written. This in turn refers to the style and structure of your answer, the clarity and precision with which you express yourself and the accuracy of your statements and application of law to fact. Furthermore, if you are able to demonstrate wider reading in your arguments this will also help you achieve a better mark. So there are more factors taken into account than just writing a list of the points that arise and a simple answer to each. The presence of this extra quality will enhance your mark, so its absence, will not allow you to obtain the higher marks. Furthermore, the answers in this book are not model answers which can be learnt by heart and applied to answer any question on a particular topic, although I have often seen this attempted. It doesn't work because for the most part the person attempting the question simply fails to answer the question set. There is no harm, however, in being able to adapt parts of these answers to particular questions providing you are still answering the question. The answers have been designed with the idea in mind that they are exam-type answers rather than answers for assessed course work, which would require far more detail.

Furthermore, this book is not a replacement for work, either for preparation for tutorials or seminars or for revision for the examination. If used carefully, it will help you prepare answers but will not help you learn the material in the first place. It does not present EU law in a systematic way but instead selects particular issues within questions on which to concentrate. It is also worth pointing out that the choice of example cases provided within some if not most of the answers is rather limited, especially in comparison with textbooks and some cases and materials books. This is deliberate because for the most part, one case will be sufficient authority for the points of law you wish to convey in answer to the question set and this is also a realistic approach bearing in mind that in an examination, you will simply not have time to reproduce the numbers of cases in the books and by necessity must concentrate your attention on a smaller number of clearly relevant cases. For the most part I have sought to use as example cases, the leading and more popular cases in EU law. Don't worry, however, if these do not coincide with the cases you have read, learnt or have been referred to in your course on EU law. As long as they cover the same issue or point, they are perfectly acceptable alternatives in an examination. It is the legal point at issue and not necessarily the particular case authority although there are certain leading and classic cases which should be cited such as *Van Gend en Loos* in relation to direct effects.

A brief mention will be made here in respect of the terms European Union and European Community, although these have been unified now following the entry into force of the Lisbon Treaty as the European Union, both will be found in older textbooks and in previous case law. The term European Union was brought in by the Treaty on European Union (TEU) (also known and referred to as the Maastricht Treaty) and describes the extension by the Member States into additional policies and areas of co-operation. Following the entry into force of the 2007 Lisbon Treaty, it is correct to refer only to the European Union. The three pillar structure has, effectively, been dismantled. Provisions relating to the Common Foreign and Security Policy will remain within the TEU, whereas, all aspects relating to Freedom, Justice and Security, including judicial and police cooperation, previously spread over both Treaties, will be located entirely within the revised EC Treaty (named the Treaty on the Functioning of the European Union (TFEU)).

It must be assumed in a book of this nature that you have already completed your course or in the case of particular topics that you have completed those topics before consulting the suggested answers here. It is also assumed that you are already familiar with the statutory provisions of Union law and the case law of the Court of Justice so that references to a case by one name or by a short title will be enough for you to identify the case. Therefore, in order to avoid cluttering up the text, the references to cases will be to the name of the case and the case docket number as given to it by the European Court of Justice (C) or the General Court (previously the Court of First Instance) (T). This number identifies a case uniquely, although it is not often used to identify cases for the purposes of examinations. However, by adopting this method it does allow you to look the case up in either the alphabetical or case number numerical case lists in textbooks for further details.

Furthermore, because you will be working directly from the text of this book, ie you will be reading each question and answer as a complete whole, you will be unlikely to enter the book via the case references, and so it was considered appropriate only to include one set of case tables. Given that some cases are often known by more than one name or the case names can commence with different words and letters, it seems safer to offer the numeric list, especially as these identify the case uniquely and are also contained in the text.

As far as the choice of topics included in the book is concerned, this is becoming slightly more difficult as EU law extends its scope and degree courses change to reflect this or to reflect the particular topics of interest to those examining the course. There is, however, an irreducible minimum largely because EU Law is a core subject for the Law Society and the Bar. So, whilst the subject matters contained in this volume cover all of the reduced Law Society and Bar Council requirements, it may not cover all the topics on your particular course or, indeed, the particular approach taken.

The Treaties are abbreviated to the TEU and TFEU and to avoid confusion these will always be employed after the article number, where appropriate the predecessor EC and EEC Treaties may be referred to using those abbreviations. As previously with the entry into force of the Treaty of Amsterdam on 1 May 1999, the original Treaties have been renumbered following the Lisbon Treaty. Although new numbering now applies, it is necessary to be aware of the old numbering as previous case law will refer to old numbering only and as some cases take up to 13 years to final judgment on appeal before the ECJ, the problem will remain a current one for a while yet. The policy adopted in this book is to refer predominantly but not exclusively to the new numbers only and occasionally, where this is relevant, to include the old numbers in brackets, eg, Art 267 TFEU (ex 234 EC) and very occasionally back to the old EEC Treaty (ex 177 EEC). For the most part, even when referring to pre-Lisbon or Amsterdam case law or legislative provisions, the new number will be given first although this may not be technically correct. Occasionally, when close attention to the old numbers and content of provision is essential, the old numbers will be retained but this will be made clear, eg old Art 12 EC (now 18 TFEU). It is hoped confusion may be avoided. Similarly, the terms 'Union' and 'EU' will be employed unless discussing old case law where the court itself, of course, used the terms then valid of Community and EC law. In those instances the new terms will be placed in brackets. Quotes will use the terms current at the time without adding the new terms afterwards. I realise this may cause some confusion but this is the consequence of the changes agreed by the Member States and we just have to live with it and through it, until the years bring some familiarity and stability with the new numbering and terms.

It may be useful here to make one or two comments in respect of the use of statutory materials in the examination room if these are permitted on your course.

Most institutions allow reference to statutory materials during the examination. One real advantage is that there is no need to concentrate too heavily on memorising statutory provisions whilst revising. It leaves you more time to consider the application and interpretation, rather than having to waste time on the regurgitation of particular provisions. It also makes it pointless to reproduce the whole of a legislative provision in an answer if the examiner knows that you have it in front of you during the examination. Indeed, there is no need for the reproduction even if statutory materials are not allowed to be used in the examination. However, to ignore completely the legislative provisions prior to the examination means you will be unfamiliar with them and will probably waste time finding the relevant provisions, eg some candidates, when provided with material, seem to spend an inordinate amount of time browsing or flicking through them during the examination. If you can, try to treat these materials as a last resort or a mental crutch to which you can refer should your memory fail you. There is no compulsion to look at them at all, but you may still need to cite specific parts of provisions to support your answer.

Open-book examinations, where you are able to take in other materials as well, are less common and vary considerably as to the materials that the candidate is allowed to use during the examination and the time allowed to complete the examination. You still have to revise and prepare thoroughly for the examination and not try to rely on finding the information whilst in the exam hall. They are a hybrid between the closed-book examination and assessed work in the form of extended essays or dissertations, but still require a structured answer at the end of the day.

Many of the changes agreed for the Constitutional Treaty (CT) were incorporated into the 2007 Lisbon Reform Treaty which has not replaced the existing Treaties but has amended and revised them, the main changes are highlighted here.

The Union obtains legal personality, the EC Treaty has been renamed the Treaty on the Functioning of the Union and the term 'Community' has been replaced throughout by 'Union'. The proposed Union Minister for Foreign Affairs has instead been called the High Representative of the Union for Foreign Affairs and Security Policy and appears thus far to be referred to as the 'High Rep'.

The new European Council form has been established as envisaged by the CT.

The names and types of secondary law 'Regulations, Directives and Decisions' have been kept but new definitions for them have been introduced, taken from the CT.

The Charter on Fundamental Rights has become legally binding but with an opt out for the UK and Poland and one effectively negotiated for the Czech Republic and contained in Declaration 53 which, like for the UK and Poland, confirms that the Charter does not apply to domestic law.

The TEU has been turned more into an overview Treaty with the EC Treaty, now named TFEU being converted more into a treaty dealing with substantive issues, both, however, will concern the institutions.

The OUP Q&A series online resource centre: www.oxfordtextbooks.co.uk/orc/qanda/ will contain links to EU portal web pages and further useful information.

The *Blackstone's EU Treaties & Legislation,* 21st edition, contains the consolidated versions of the EU and TFEU Treaties as revised and amended by the 2007 Lisbon Treaty.

Finally, and I hope this advice is not too late, the best preparation for an examination is to have worked consistently over the period of your course. If you have, some of the questions and answers suggested here might actually make sense to you and not be the first time you have come across the issues, cases or law involved. Apart from that, I wish you 'all the best' in the examination.

2

The Origins, Institutions and Development of the Union, the Legislative Processes and Budgetary Process

Introduction

Questions on the topics in this chapter cover a number of related subjects and can consequently give rise to a very wide range of questions, the exact form or content of which will be determined by the emphasis given the topics in your courses. Given that this topic might be covered by introductory lectures rather than tutorials or seminars, it is most likely that most of the questions posed will be of the essay type rather than problem questions. Therefore, a range of questions and framework answers to cover these areas has been included. However, because the coverage of this topic can vary significantly between courses, it is consequently more difficult to predict with accuracy the range and type of questions which may be encountered. Direct questions on the history and development of the Communities and how it has developed into the Union would be rare because the answers could only be very descriptive and not therefore particularly suitable for the level of examination you are taking. Questions therefore tend to be concentrated on the institutions and in particular on the inter-relationship of these institutions in the legislative and other processes of the Union.

Other exam questions may concern the role and legality of the Management Committees and procedures, the budget or legislative procedures in further detail or questions may focus on the powers and rights of the European Parliament (EP), the Council or the

Commission separately. Following the considerable institutional reform brought about by the Lisbon Treaty, questions focusing on this might also be expected.

The first questions will, however, concern the more general aspects of EU law courses.

Question 1

'The United Kingdom has been described as a reluctant partner as far as its attitude to the European Union is concerned.'
   Discuss this statement in the light of the development of the European Union.

 Commentary

This question is looking for a historical analysis, not just of Britain's attitude but also of the general developments of the Communities and now Union as it should be called following the entry into force of the Lisbon Treaty. This is because Britain's attitude was originally a direct response to the setting up of the European Economic Community and as further developments took place in the EEC and the other two Communities, so further reactions from Britain were prompted.

   The answer could be divided into time periods to help in the presentation, however such divisions are often artificial and the facts may not always fit comfortably. The answer should thus include a brief outline of the setting up of the Communities and in particular, the reasons for this. Periods could, however, include the 1950s and the setting up of the Community, the attempts of the UK to enter in the 1960s and the reasons for this, the 1970s when Britain entered, but had second thoughts, and the 1980s to date. The latter period includes the at times hostile relations of the UK with the rest of Europe and also a seeming change in attitude as a result of the landslide Labour Party victory in the May 1997 General Election, although subsequent developments have cast doubt on this change of attitude, especially following the 2010 change of government.

   Much of the explanation for Britain's attitude lies in the realm of politics rather than law, in a strict sense. The degree to which this is then covered in your course will determine whether such questions will be set in an examination and the amount of discussion expected in your answer.

   Finally, you could provide a paragraph summarising Britain's attitude to the EC and now EU.

 Answer plan

- The reasons for the establishment of the Communities and Union
- The UK's original reasons not to participate and change of mind in early 1960s
- Two failed and one successful entry attempt
- Membership, budget renegotiations and the opt-outs at Maastricht
- A change of heart from 1997 under Labour?
- The 2007 Lisbon Treaty and latest developments

Suggested answer

Although there had been ideas to unify Europe before the Second World War, it was only afterwards that they found peaceful fruition. This was prompted by the horrific events and the devastation of Europe in the Second World War which left much of Europe in economic and political ruins. Political and economic co-operation and development between nations were regarded as crucial to replace the economic competition which was viewed as a major factor in the outbreak of wars between European nation states. Thus, plans were put forward to eliminate harmful national jealousies and to promote economic and political stability, especially in the face of the rising soviet threat. The first forms of cooperation concentrated on these aspects and led to the setting up of the United Nations in 1945, the Organisation for European Economic Cooperation (OEEC) in 1948 and the North Atlantic Treaty Organisation (NATO) and the Council of Europe in 1949.

The direct impetus for the Communities came in the plan proposed in 1950 by the French Foreign Minister Robert Schuman, based on the research and plans of Jean Monnet, to link the French and German coal and steel industries. The Schuman Plan would not only help economic recovery but also remove the disastrous competition between the two states. It was aimed to make future war not only unthinkable but also materially impossible. It was left open for other European countries to join in the discussions and Italy and the Benelux nations (Belgium, the Netherlands and Luxembourg) took full part. The establishment of the Communities was not intended to exclude Britain which was invited to participate in negotiations but took no further role than that of observer, despite the seeming enthusiasm of Churchill and many in the UK about the unification of Europe and the apparent leading role that Britain might play. Britain, however, did not envisage a role as a key participant and was reluctant to involve itself further in the negotiations.

To try to explain some of the reasons for this attitude it must be pointed out that Britain had at the time a historical legacy which involved quite different economic and social ties, including the Empire and Commonwealth and the Atlantic alliance, which were the result of both historical colonisation and the alliances which had found victory in the war. These ties of security and common language are often overlooked but played no small part in the attitude of Britain to Europe in the immediate post-war years. Britain also regarded its status as remaining a world power whose sovereignty and independence could not be compromised by membership of such an organisation.

Hence, six nations went on without the UK to sign the European Coal and Steel Community Treaty (ECSC) in 1951. As a result of the success of this first Community, the six Member States decided to extend the scope of their cooperation. The Spaak Report was prepared to consider the establishment of an Economic

Community and an Atomic Energy Community for energy and the peaceful use of nuclear power. Britain was again invited to participate fully but again declined. On 25 March 1957 the two Treaties of Rome were signed establishing the European Economic Community and the European Atomic Community. Britain instead embarked on what might have seemed the potentially wrecking path of establishing in 1958, with other non-EC States, a European free trade area (EFTA); a free trade area but with no further political aims and no desire to create a supranational organisation capable of superseding the Member States in any way.

Following this initial reluctance, a change of mind by the UK occurred in 1961 when the Conservative Government, under Prime Minister Harold Macmillan, applied for membership. The previous reasons for not joining included the view that because Britain retained its world power status and direct links with most of the world, membership was neither desirable nor necessary. However, these had been weakened by the economic demise of the UK, the Suez débâcle and continuing conversion of the Empire into the Commonwealth of independent states. Trade patterns were shifting towards Europe, the Atlantic alliance was less prominent and the Commonwealth started to appear as not such a promising long-term trading relationship. Britain had also observed the much faster economic improvements taking place in the EEC of six and was envious of this. It was clear that this certainly provoked the main interest in membership. Whether the UK had now become fully supportive of the entire package and aims of the Community is less clear. However, Britain had now to bargain from the outside and the application was in any case vetoed by President De Gaulle of France. The second attempt, the 1967 application by the Labour Government, under Prime Minister Harold Wilson, was also vetoed by De Gaulle.

The third attempt in 1970, under the Conservative Government of Edward Heath, was successful and in 1973 the UK joined the Communities with Ireland and Denmark, mainly because of their trade dependence on the UK. This was regarded by some as a panic measure spurred on by the view that if the UK was unable to get in at this stage Europe would leave the UK behind.

The timing of this entry was in fact unfortunate. Instead of the UK being able to participate equally in the post-war boom and recovery, the economy of Europe had received a setback and Britain along with the rest of the western world became the hostage of oil price increases. Instead of a period of economic prosperity, the 1970s witnessed high inflation and economic stagnation. To aggravate matters still further, the high and arguably inequitable level of the British budget contribution became the focus of attention. It did not take long before disquiet with the terms of entry arose. It seems that we paid too high a price to join the club and that the budget wrangles that polarised opinion both in Europe and the UK were inevitable, given the pattern of trade in the UK which initially favoured imports from Commonwealth non-EEC countries, and having to pay the higher CAP regulated food prices, all of which added to the economic problems.

In 1974, a new government was elected in the UK and a renegotiation of the terms of entry was started. This was climaxed by the approval of the British public in the then unprecedented 1975 referendum which not only approved membership but also the renegotiated terms regarding budget contributions. However, it was only a partial cure for the level of contributions, and this dispute was later reopened by Margaret Thatcher. Its effect was, however, to cast the UK firmly in the role of the reluctant partner and as a troublemaker in Europe.

Viewed politically, the UK had decided to cast its lot with the EC, aware that some loss of sovereignty was involved and that a potentially high monetary contribution was required. One side of the bargain was not, as with other Member States, the security of nationhood or the stamp of approval and stability of the democratic political system that membership gave. The fact that the UK had won the war and had centuries of stability meant that these were so well secured in the UK that the EC could never seriously be considered for these advantages, or to keep the peace, which Britain had secured with its allies by victory in the last war. The other side of the bargain was to share in the spoils of European economic progress. Given the changing circumstances, this proved to be a dubious economic gain. No wonder that there was a feeling by some, which still remains, that membership had sold Britain short.

In the 1980s, the first part of the decade was occupied with further wrangles over the British budget contribution and reluctance to reform the Communities which hindered progress on other matters in the Community and did not engender relaxed relations with Britain's partners in the Community. The budget contributions were settled in 1984, only to be questioned again in the 1990s and again in 2002 and 2004 and since then.

Furthermore, the discussions and agreements made in Maastricht in 1991 to 1992 demonstrate how Britain continued to be out of line with its other partners by its reluctance to fully participate. Part of the agreement reached in Maastricht was that the UK opted out of the Social Policy but all other Member States went ahead with this. Maastricht also agreed to a process and timetable for moving towards economic and monetary union. The UK negotiated another opt-out here in respect of the decision of whether to join the final stage in which a single currency would be established.

The change of government in the United Kingdom on 1 May 1997 saw a change in the relationship with Europe with the new Labour Government announcing soon afterwards the intention to sign up to the social chapter, which was carried through shortly afterwards, and generally to take a more participatory role in Europe. The UK opposition to monetary union seems to have been removed although uncertainty as to when and even if the UK might join continues to this day.

The Treaty negotiations for the Amsterdam and Nice Treaties, the Convention and IGC for the Constitution for Europe, the expansion to 27 States in 2007 and the changing political relationships between the leading EU States (notably France, Germany and the UK) have led to a far more complex Union now than a few years ago. The UK's attitude remains somewhat ambivalent, expressing on the one hand to be at the heart of Europe and on the other, showing a reluctance to commit as deeply as other Member States, notably to the Euro. The proposed UK referendum on the Constitution, abandoned as a result of the Dutch and French rejection of the CT and the 2007 Lisbon Treaty was ratified but without a referendum in the UK. The 2007 Lisbon Treaty witnessed, though, a return to reluctance to fully commit by the UK by securing an opt-out from the binding application of the European Charter on Fundamental Rights in domestic matters. The 2010 coalition Government in the UK appears to have taken a neutral stance on the EU which is no surprise given the different positions on the EU the Conservatives and Liberal-Democrats expressed in the election campaign.

Trying to summarise Britain's attitude over the five decades is no easy matter, as it is a complex of many concerns and influences. Whether Britain is a reluctant or just hesitant partner is itself still unclear. The fact that the UK up to the end of 2010 has still not committed itself to adopting the Euro must still leave room for doubt. There is, however, certainly no serious talk of withdrawal these days by any of the political parties likely to be members of a UK Government.

Question 2

'European integration is initially a wholly political concept whose implementation proceeds by the formulation of economic policies and decisions.'

Comment on this statement by the European Commission from the 1960s.

 ## Commentary

This question basically addresses the questions of why the Communities and now Union were set up and how they were designed to achieve their aims. This question focuses initially on the original reason or reasons for setting up the European Communities, ie the initial impetus which prompted moves to pursue European integration. Hence, the answer must commence with a review of these reasons. The fact that these reasons find their base in politics is stressed and must be addressed in the answer in contrast to suggesting that the reasons were based purely or merely on economic grounds, although it is very difficult to distinguish the two terms completely.

This in turns leads you on to considering the form of integration envisaged, ie the process by which the implementation of the political concept was to be achieved. This brings in considerations of initial theories of European integration including federalism and functional integration.

Next, you should look at how the implementation was to be achieved. This will involve you in considering the overall objectives of the original EEC Treaty and the way in which further laws and decisions could be reached to assist integration.

Since you are informed that the quotation arises from the 1960s you will be aware that it pre-dates the discussions for the various treaty revisions including the Treaty on European Union and the 2007 Lisbon Treaty about where the Union is heading and how it should be reformed to assist it in getting there (wherever that is). However, don't limit your answer to an intention as viewed in the 1950s and 1960s. You should also include in your answer a discussion on developments since that time including the Single European Act (SEA), the Treaty on European Union, the Amsterdam Treaty, the Nice Treaty, and the 2007 Lisbon Treaty. You could consider the further question of whether the arguable eventual goal of the Communities, and now Union, that of political union to be achieved by progressive economic integration, will ever be reached.

Answer plan

- Reasons for establishing the European Communities
- Ultimate goal of integration?
- Objectives of the Treaty of Rome
- Developments since the 1950s
- No longer just economic but also social policies
- The significance of recent reform attempts

Suggested answer

The term 'European integration' is taken to refer to the European Communities which were set up in the 1950s. What were the reasons for setting up these Communities by treaties between nation states? The Communities were a political response to the Second World War and the massive destruction that had taken place in Europe as a consequence. They represented both an attempt to ensure that such a war could not occur in Europe again and to provide a better and hopefully more stable means by which the reconstruction of Europe could take place. They aimed to remove the rivalries between nation states by legally binding them together in economic communities. So, the reason for setting up the Communities was the result of entirely political motives to eliminate war and provide a new basis for economic reconstruction of Europe. Thus the primary motivations were political but economic reasons were also inevitably involved.

What was then the political concept of European integration? At the time the Communities were being contemplated and even after the establishment of the Treaties, different views were adopted on the form of integration. These ranged from the view that a European Federal State was envisaged to the view that the

Member States were only participating in the erection of a common market concerned only with economic cooperation.

It was, however, originally widely considered that because there was success in certain policies this would automatically lead to a spillover from one area to another to lead to increasing integration and that the whole process of integration was a dynamic and not a static process. This process is termed functional integration. In fact, it was considered that in order for the original policies to work properly there must be continuing integration. Thus sector-by-sector integration and the process of European integration were regarded as inexorable. For example, common tariffs and the establishment of the Common Market would lead to exchange rates being stabilised to ensure that production factors and costs in the Member States were broadly equal. This in turn requires monetary union to be established to ensure exchange rates do not drift apart and this requires full economic union to be achieved so that the value of different components of the common currency is not changed by different policies in different countries. This economic integration would also mean that the political integration would eventually follow. Whilst the above is a rather simplistic account of the theories of integration, it also helps understand the suggestion that any decision on the part of the Community, and now Union, to go no further in terms of integration would in fact not maintain a stable position but would ultimately be regressive as it would start to undermine or undo the previous successes and integration achieved.

Federalism or some form of federal state may therefore be the argued goal of the Communities, and now Union, if the aims are not limited to the distinct policies thus far agreed. In order to make the goal of the Communities and Union more acceptable the term 'a closer union' has been used in both the old EC and EU Treaties. The post-Lisbon TEU expresses this again as the Member States being 'Resolved to continue the process of creating an ever closer union.' Its exact meaning is unclear as to whether it refers to federalism or something short of that. The UK's view on this during the negotiations for the Treaty of European Union was that it falls somewhat short and whilst the Community does operate on the supra-national level, the UK maintained that it does not signify an inevitable move to federalism, a view now shared by other countries such as Denmark, Poland and the Czech Republic.

Secondly, the way in which these fundamental political objectives were to be converted into economic and social integration must be considered. This was initially by the agreement to establish a treaty providing the legal basis for economic and further integration. The aims and objectives of the Community were clearly set out in the EC Treaty. The Preamble and Arts 2 and 3 set out in general terms the type and range of policies the Community was to pursue to achieve the general objective of European integration.

Article 2, for example, set the general goals as the establishment of a common market and an economic and monetary union. This was to be achieved by the implementation of the common policies or activities referred to in Arts 3 and 4. Article 3 notably includes policies on customs duties, a common commercial policy, free movement of goods, persons, services and capital, agriculture and fisheries, transport, competition. Newer developments include activities and policies in the social sphere, economic and social cohesion, the environment, research and technological development, trans-European networks, health protection, education and training, culture, development cooperation, overseas policies, consumer protection and energy, and civil protection and tourism.

Those objectives and policies outlined in Arts 2 and 3 are expanded upon in specific parts of the Treaty, for example, free movement of workers in Art 39 (now 45 TFEU) and competition law in Arts 81–82 (now 101–102 TFEU). The Treaty Articles were not to be the only source of legal provisions formulating the economic policies and decisions. The Community institutions, notably the Council, Commission and to an at first very limited extent, the European Parliament, were also empowered by the Member States with their own law-making powers to establish further laws to achieve European integration and the objectives of the Treaties. These powers were summarised in Arts 250–252 EC (now 293–294 TFEU). Furthermore, a European Court of Justice was established for the Community to adjudicate on Community law and provide rulings binding on the Member States. These further help to implement the concept of European integration.

Thus, whilst it would be true to agree that the original concept was a political one, which has and is being implemented by economic policies, the debate continues and it is clear from the intense discussions surrounding the Single European Act, the Treaty on European Union and the further changes in the 1990s to date that the eventual goal of the Union is far from clearly or definitively determined. European integration is still dependent on further political impulses. Implementation of European integration can only proceed by further political policy and not just by economic decisions. Indeed it can be observed from the very modest scope of social policy in the original EEC Treaty, Art 119 (now 157 TFEU), that considerable advances or inroads have been made into other non-purely political or economic areas of the Member States' economies. See the policies noted above from Art 3 of the EC Treaty. The underlying political nature of the EU was clearly seen during the negotiations at the Nice 2000 IGC and more recently in gaining the ratification of all 27 Member States for the Lisbon Treaty, where only after very hard political bargaining was sufficient agreement reached to provide for continued European expansion and integration. The political impetus for new policies to assist integration and indeed the wide-ranging political debate as to the future of the EU continues with the 2007 Lisbon Treaty. These events show quite clearly that European integration is indeed a wholly political concept because without the political agreement, there will be no further economic integration.

Question 3

'The Council of Ministers is by its very nature the federal institution of the Community.' (Walter Hallstein).
   Discuss.

 ## Commentary

This question appears to be quite simple but in order to get a respectable mark, it would involve you in more work than meets the eye. In order to answer this fully, a little lateral thought is required rather than just simply describing or analysing the position and the work of the Council. However, it clearly involves the Council as the central element in any answer. The term 'federal' is also a decisive element of the question. In order to provide a meaningful answer there should be a definition of what is meant by federal, both generally and in particular respect to the European Union. If your answer only included those aspects it would be adequate but only just and probably not attract more than a 2(ii) mark. To get more you would have to place these central elements of your answer in context. The relevant context here would be in relation to other institutions of the Union as the question implicitly requires an answer to this point, ie that the Council is 'the' federal institution as opposed to, or in contrast to, the others. You would need therefore to consider the position and role of the Commission and the European Parliament and compare these with the Council. Whilst this is a historical quote, it should now be discussed in view of the fact that the Communities have now evolved into the European Union and following the **Lisbon Treaty** has added the European Council as one of the main institutions of the EU. Its position in relation to the Council should also be considered.

   First of all you should describe the pertinent features of the Council and its main tasks.

 ## Answer plan

- The Council of Ministers and its main tasks
- The meaning of 'federal', generally and in respect of the institutions
- The European Parliament and federalism
- The European Commission and federalism
- The European Council and federalism
- Final comparison

Suggested answer

The Council of Ministers (now simply termed the Council) is governed by Arts 13 and 16 TEU and 237–243 TFEU and is the principal legislative organ of the Communities. Its composition is outlined in Art 16 TEU and consists of representative government ministers of the Member States depending on the subject matter under discussion. Foreign ministers attend the General Council and the agriculture or finance ministers, for example, attend the specialist Councils. In total, there have been nine different configurations of the Council, although this is not fixed and can be determined by the European Council under Art 236 TFEU.

Article 16 TFEU imposes on the Council the power to carry out policy making and coordinating functions and confers upon it the power to take decisions. Article 290 TFEU allows it to delegate decision-making powers to the Commission.

The Council has the final power of decision for the adoption of legislative proposals made by the Commission. Depending on the Treaty requirements it may have to consult the EP, the Economic and Social Committee or the Committee of the Regions and, by numerous later amendments to the Treaties, share the law-making process with the EP. Formally, it reaches its decisions by voting, but whether this must be by unanimity or the majority required, differs according to which Treaty Article the legislative proposal is based on. In combination Arts 16(4) TEU and 238 TFEU provide three different proceedings consisting of a simple majority, qualified majority or unanimity voting. The qualified majority provides a means whereby decisions can be made without having to get the agreement of every Member State. The expansions in 2004 and 2007 have meant that finding the appropriate balance in terms of voting rights of each country has been difficult but the underlying principle remains that it provides a way for the Council to function by majority voting, but that this has to represent a certain proportion of the Union in terms of both the number of countries and a majority of the population of the Union.

Next, the term 'Federal' needs to be analysed. Whether the Council can be considered to be the Federal institution first requires a consideration of what is meant by federal. Federalism is defined as a form of government in which two or more states constitute a political unity while remaining independent in respect of their internal affairs. It involves the construction of political institutions which oversee integration on many fronts as agreed by the constituent states. A federal state is usually achieved by democratic means and can be otherwise referred to as a confederate state. Examples of federal nations are the USA, Nigeria, Switzerland, Germany, Australia and Canada. These consist of federal and state governments with appropriate spheres of power.

Is this applicable to the Council of Ministers? The Council is federal in that it consists of representatives of the Member States who meet together to act in a legislative capacity, creating rules binding on the constituent Member States. However, it is more often the case that national interests are pursued by the individual members rather than the Council acting collectively first and foremost in the interest of the Union. Furthermore, it is not the equivalent of a federal government as other institutions in the Union play a part in the legislative and executive processes, namely the European Parliament and the Commission. Thus, to describe it as federal was perhaps too optimistic. By its method of action, it is more intergovernmental and was described so by the Italian member of the European Parliament, Spinelli, largely responsible for the Parliament's Draft Treaty on European Union published first in 1984.

However, before you can conclude that it is not the only federal institution, you need to look at the other institutions.

The Commission, the executive of the Community, was given the sole right as the proposer of legislation under Art 155 (now 17(2) TEU) of the original EEC Treaty, although this has been in effect partially circumvented by the Council and European Council. It has its own powers of decision and is able to exercise powers delegated to it by the Council. This is now subject to the measures under Arts 290–291 TFEU.

The tasks and composition of the Commission are now determined by Art 17 TEU and Arts 244–250 TFEU. It consists of members appointed by common accord of the Member States. Commissioners are required to act independently (Art 17 TEU). The Commissioners are required under oath to act in the interest of the Union rather than in the interest of their host Member States. The Commission is, however, described as multinational or supranational, and not federal, because the Commissioners are not representing or acting for the constituent states but for the Union.

The European Parliament, originally called the Assembly and consisting of members nominated from the Member State governments, is now directly elected. It is arguably more aptly named an Assembly, consisting only of one chamber, whereas a Parliament usually consists of two chambers and a Head of State.

Before the SEA, the Parliament had largely advisory and consultative powers, which under Art 137 EEC (now Art 14 TEU) provided that the Assembly shall 'exercise the advisory and supervisory powers which are conferred on it by this Treaty'. The Treaty specified only 17 instances where the EP had to be consulted. Under its advisory role, certain provision of the Treaty required that the EP be consulted before a decision could be adopted by the Council, see old Arts 54 and 235 EC. The participation in the legislative process was increased by the Conciliation procedure of 1977 and the introduction of the cooperation procedure by the SEA. The Maastricht Treaty introduced a co-decision procedure by which the EP enjoys an ultimate power of veto over proposed legislation, which was extended into more areas by the Treaty of Amsterdam and the Treaty of Nice and was significantly further increased by the 2007 Lisbon Treaty.

However, despite these improvements, the legislative role of the EP is still not fully on a par with the Council, and the term 'democratic deficit' is used to describe this state of affairs. Parliament at the moment thus lacks the power to really be described as federal. It is federal in as much as, in limited circumstances it participates in the legislative process to create binding legislation on the constituent Member States, but this is very limited. It does consist of representative members from each of the constituent states but they are elected to represent regional constituencies and political parties and not state governments.

Following the Lisbon Treaty, the European Council has now been established as a full main institution with a European Council President appointed for 2½ years (Art 15 TEU) to provide political impetus. Whilst this body does have certain powers in relation to the appointment of the Commission and determining the powers of the other institutions, it does not have legislative powers as such. Its composition is very much intergovernmental and although it can take some decisions by QMV, it is regarded as representing more the governmental interests of the Member States at the top of the EU institutions and thus would not seem to be a federalist rival to the Council, in terms of answering the question.

Thus, of the four political institutions, leaving the Court of Justice to one side, it may be true to say that the Council by its nature should be the federal institution. However, because the Council does not act in that manner and the other three have at present little capacity to do so, it cannot therefore be truly described as such.

Question 4

'As far as its legislative procedures are concerned, the EU is neither efficient nor democratic.'

(a) Discuss this statement in the light of the powers and the decision-making procedures of the Council, Commission and European Parliament.

(b) What reforms would you advocate which would overcome these criticisms?

Commentary

This question is quite complex because it is in three parts. The first part can be broken down to determine what issues must be considered. You must consider the legislative procedures, ie they must be described as concisely as possible because there is a lot more of the question to answer and because specific features of these procedures will be considered in the answer to (a), thus they need only briefly be outlined at the outset. Having basically described the two types of procedure, you must then address the issues that, in respect of the two procedures, the EU is neither efficient nor democratic in respect of the powers and activities of the three political institutions in the second sentence of the question.

This final section is probably the hardest to prepare for in that it really requires you to have read particular advocated reforms during your course on top of those already put into effect following the entry into force of the 2007 Lisbon Treaty, rather than try to consider reforms in the exam. Although good original suggestions will pick up a few extra marks it is not the major part of the answer and is not worth spending an excessive amount of time trying to think up reforms, if you have not previously prepared such suggestions. In other words, in order to do well in this question, you must have at least prepared for the possibility of a question on institutional reforms in your revision. If you have not, it would probably be better to find another question to answer.

Answer plan

- Legislative procedures
- Roles of the Council, Commission and European Parliament
- Efficiency and democratic deficit
- Reforms undertaken
- Possible future reforms

Suggested answer

At present all the legislative procedures commence with a proposal from the Commission although following the entry into force of the Lisbon Treaty, suggestions and recommendations for legislative acts may also come from the EP, the European Council, the Member States, the ECB, the ECJ, the EIB and EU citizens. Following the Lisbon Treaty there are now effectively just three procedures: the ordinary legislative procedure, the special legislative procedure and the consent procedure. The special procedure though incorporates a number of different procedures as will be discussed. In addition, the Commission and the Council have limited go-it-alone powers.

Under its initial advisory role a limited number of EEC Treaty Articles (17) provided that the Council was required to consult the EP as to its opinion before coming to a decision on Community secondary law; see, for example, old Arts 54 or 56 EC. The *Isoglucose* cases (Roquette Frères) (Cases 138–9/79) confirmed that the EP had to be consulted. However, on receipt of that opinion the Council could proceed to ignore it and override any view given by the EP. In two cases, *EP v Council* (C-65/91) and *Parliament v Council* (C-392/95), the Court annulled two Regulations which had been substantially amended by the Council without a further consultation of Parliament taking place when the Council had amended its draft legislation. This still exists within the special legislative procedure but only in limited instances as will be considered further below.

The two readings cooperation procedure (Art 252 EC) was introduced to establish a form of first and second reading in areas largely affecting the internal market but following the Lisbon Treaty has been completely discarded.

Article 289 TFEU (ex 249 EC) has been amended over the years to provide that the EP act more extensively with the Council and Commission in the legislative process notably by the introduction of the co-decision procedure and its renaming as the ordinary legislative procedure, detailed in Art 294 TFEU (ex 251 EC). It provides for the enhanced participation of the EP to the extent that ultimately, the EP can reject a legislative proposal at a second reading. The EP cannot impose its own will on the content of a legislative proposal, thus parliamentary veto might be a better description of the process. Note that in the procedure, the Council votes mainly by QMV but at times, according to some Treaty Articles and parts of the procedure itself, it must vote unanimously. The following description takes into account the amendments made to the procedure by the Treaties of Amsterdam and Lisbon which ironed out some of the initial teething troubles and delays originally experienced in the operation of the procedure.

The EP gives its opinion on a legislative proposal. The Council can adopt this by a qualified majority if it agrees or if the EP has made no amendments to the Commission proposal. If not, the Council can adopt a common position which the EP can, within three months, either approve or take no decision, in which case the Council can adopt the measure. Alternatively, the EP can reject or amend the proposal by an absolute majority, in which case the Council can, within three months, approve those amendments by a qualified majority. However, if the Commission has issued a negative opinion on the amendments, the Council can only approve by unanimity. If the Council does not accept the amended proposal, the matter is referred to a Conciliation Committee to attempt to achieve a compromise within six weeks. If a joint text is approved, the Council and EP may adopt the provision together within six weeks. If there is no agreement the Council must confirm its position within six weeks and the EP may finally reject it within six weeks by an absolute majority.

The efficiency and democracy of these procedures must be considered in the light of powers of the institutions which support or contradict the view expressed in the question.

The powers of the Council are basically set out in Arts 16 TEU and 238 TFEU (ex 202 EC). The Council disposes of Community legislation which must be initiated by the Commission. The power of the EP is set out in Art 14 TEU (ex 192 EC) which provides that the EP shall exercise legislative functions which are detailed in Arts 289 and 294 TFEU and by giving consent (previously known as assent).

The Commission's powers are to initiate the legislative procedure by making proposals and to act under powers delegated to it by the Council. The Commission's right to act under delegated powers is extremely restricted by the management committee structure by which the Council retains overall much of its original powers.

Features that support the first statement are the limited role played by the EP in the legislative procedure and the fact that the main procedure is quite convoluted and slow. Finally the most fundamental feature is that even with the ordinary legislative procedure, the EP's ultimate power is only that of a negative veto.

Addressing the criticism concerning the lack of efficiency, the delays that were often and still are experienced in the legislative procedure can be cited and that there are still a number of different procedures according to the Treaty. The procedures are also becoming more complex and, as evidence, the stagnation of the legislative process in the 1970s and 1980s could be highlighted. Further evidence is that the Council could not cope with the amount of work necessary and has had to devise ways in which decision-making power could be delegated but that control could nevertheless be retained by setting up a number of complex management committees. The Council by its nature acts in the interests of the Member States and not the Union, hence compromises must be reached which has delayed some legislation by very many years.

The question of democracy is easier to address and clearly points to the role of the EP as the only directly elected body but only having a minor role in the legislative process and the question of delegation to Committees controlled by the Council and not the EP. This whole argument is described as the democratic deficit in the EU, ie because the EP is the only directly democratically elected element, in order to maintain the democratic right or justification of EU laws, the legislative process must be more in the hands of elected bodies. If this democratic deficit is real then something needs to be done.

Finally to move on to reforms. To help you in this part, the reforms already put into effect under the Maastricht, Amsterdam, Nice and Lisbon Treaties should be considered to determine whether these have answered the criticisms before suggestions for further reform are made.

The criticisms of the Maastricht and subsequent reforms are that the power of co-decision still only gives the EP a negative power of veto and Art 294 TFEU (ex 251 EC) is not comprehensive and still only applies to limited specific areas, although this has been expanded significantly by the Treaties, especially the Lisbon Treaty to some 40 more Treaty Articles. The ability under Art 225 TFEU (ex 192 EC) to request the Commission to make legislative proposals in areas of EU policy is also unclear as to whether it can insist that a proposal is made. However, these do not actually increase the ability of the EP to insist on particular measures and thus do little to reduce the democratic deficit and make the Union more democratic. Also, the amendments by the Nice and Lisbon Treaties were more limited in scope than hoped and planned for, particularly in view of the changes proposed originally for the Constitution for Europe which originally would have provided for one single legislative procedure featuring the co-decision process. However, the cooperation procedure which was used less and less was scrapped in favour of the co-decision procedure which became the 'ordinary' procedure under Arts 289 and 294 TFEU. And, whilst this procedure was extended again into new areas, certain areas such as Tax and Social Security retained the use of unanimous voting, indeed, as have over 50 other legal bases. Whether this addresses the concerns about democracy and efficiency will only be measurable after the passage of time. The Lisbon Treaty also introduced a role for the National Parliaments in the legislative process which is now referred to in Art 12 of the amended EU Treaty and is contained in a Protocol on the role of National Parliaments. This requires that draft legislative acts of the Union are forwarded to National Parliaments for their opinion. Whilst this could be argued to increase democracy, it might be at the expense of efficiency as another body (or collection of bodies) is introduced into the law-making process and apart from the in-built extra time required may simply slow or prevent the Council from reaching a consensus on a particular issue if hindered by an unfavourable National Parliament or Parliaments' opinion.

Whatever other reforms you suggest will depend on your views as to whether the Union is inefficient or undemocratic or, whether previous reforms have improved the situation, ie does it answer the democratic deficit? Your suggested reforms might be to increase the EP's powers to give equal power of decision-making as now enjoyed in the approving of the budget, and generally to speed up the procedures, but it would not do simply to state this. You must say how this is to be done and the consequences for the other institutions. Any increase the powers of the EP have is to be at the expense of some other organisation, not the National Parliaments but the Councils of Ministers and/or the Commission.

Question 5

'The choice of legal base of an EU legislative provision can become a matter of dispute.' Discuss.

Commentary

First of all you need to consider exactly what a legal base is, so a definition must be provided and the relevance of its choice must be explained, as must the consequences for the various parties involved in the legislative processes. The use of different legal bases in the Treaty determines which particular legislative procedure is employed in enacting the provision. This in turn determines the extent of the role played by the various institutions. You should determine which institutions are concerned and why. The choice of a certain legal base is important to the Member States, the Council, the Commission and the EP. Each of these could be considered briefly in turn. Then the reasons why it can and does give rise to legal disputes must be provided. Better candidates will be able to refer to decided cases to help them and to demonstrate how the Court of Justice has resolved these disputes.

Answer plan

- Definition and choice of 'legal base'
- How it affects the Commission
- How it affects the EP
- How it affects the Council and Member States
- Decisions of the ECJ
- Consequences of Treaty Reform

Suggested answer

The legal base or authority for the enactment of EU secondary legislation is initially determined by the subject matter of the legislative proposal. This can be seen in the area of free movement of persons which provides a legal base for the Council and European Parliament to enact further secondary legislation for the free movement of workers. Article 45 TFEU (ex 39 EC) provides the basic policy and Art 46 TFEU (ex 40 EC) provides the legal base to enact secondary legislation in support of the policy. Article 46 TFEU requires that the ordinary legislative procedure (previously known as the co-decision procedure) under Art 294 TFEU (ex 251 EC) be used. Hence, the legal base of each particular proposal for a Regulation, Directive or Decision determines the procedure to be used. This in turn then determines which participants (eg Council plus European Parliament or Economic and Social Committee or the Committee of the Regions) take part in the legislative process and also the level of their participation. The choice of legal base therefore is fundamental to the relative powers and ability of the institutions to affect the content of EU law.

The Member States and each of the major institutions are affected in the following ways. It should be noted here that this is less of an issue following the 2007 Lisbon Treaty entry into force because of the revision of the legislative acts reducing the number of law-making procedures. It remains though an important issue with regard to the residual and general law-making powers in Arts 114, 115 and 352 TFEU because of the different participation levels of the EP in particular and the requirement of unanimity in two of those articles by the Council.

The Commission

The Commission is concerned because the use of qualified majority voting in the Council of Ministers is extremely important to the Commission which stands a greater chance of having proposals accepted by a majority rather than by all Member States. The extreme views can thus be ignored rather than taken into account at the draft stages and in the legislative proposal put forward by the Commission.

The Commission may wish to see a proposal go through on a majority vote if it was of the opinion that one or two Member States may object. Thus, the Treaty base may affect the precise content or formulation of the proposals, in that, if they know a qualified majority vote applies, then they can ignore the objections of the extreme views in Council as these will be outvoted. Hence, they need not water down proposals to take into account all views. See *Commission v Council* in the *Erasmus* decision (case 242/87).

The European Parliament

The EP is clearly concerned as the legal base is also vital to the level of participation of the EP in the legislative process, ie whether it can participate only by being consulted, which gives the final say to the Council or whether it can participate in the co-decision process in which case the EP has marginally more say in the process. Its opinion in the consultation procedure can be ignored by the Council whereas, for example, under Art 114 (ex 95 EC, ex 100a EEC), measures for the single market, the co-decision procedure is more likely to reflect the views of the EP.

The Member States and the Council of Ministers

The Member States are represented in Council by the relevant ministers of the national governments. As such they are subject to whatever political pressures are present in the Member States and the degree to which this is important depends on the strength of the government concerned and the strength of the pressure groups and lobbies who might object to certain legislative proposals. In some Member States the farming lobbies are very influential and the governments in these Member States may therefore wish to take into account their protests. If these states are a minority in Council, the consequence for the Member States is that if a legal base is used which does not require unanimity to enact legislation, they would not be able to veto the measure or at least water down the requirements significantly. An example of where a Member State has taken an action to try to protect such an interest is the *UK v Council* (the Hormones case 68/86).

The Council might therefore continue to prefer to use a base requiring unanimity because as a body it retains full unshared power in the legislative process, other bases weaken its position as an EU institution.

Hence, differences of opinion can arise as to the correct legal bases and the institutions and Member States have often fought over legal base, because it is possible to base measures on more than one Treaty Article due to the fact that the subject matter can straddle more than one Treaty Article. Measures in support of the single market require majority voting rather than unanimity in the Council and because this makes life easier for the Commission, it has tried to exploit this by introducing as much legislation as possible under Art 95 EC (now 114 TFEU), whereas one or more Member States and/or the Council have argued the proposals should have as their legal base other Articles requiring unanimity. Looking at it from the other side, a single Member State which objects to a particular measure would wish to veto it and would want unanimity in Council to have that chance. It would object to the Council deciding to adopt the measure under a legal base requiring QMV. The subject matter may simply lend itself to both and thus give rise to a genuine dispute. The EP has not refrained from challenging the Council for the use of the incorrect legal base and regularly brings cases before the ECJ (see, eg, *EP v Council* (Data Exchange C-22/96)) claiming that by using a legal base which gives it less participation, its prerogatives are being eroded. An early example of the many cases which have reached the ECJ on legal base is the case of *UK v Council* (the Hormones case (68/86)) concerned with a ban on growth producing hormones. It was argued that an earlier Art 100 EC, an internal market measure, which required unanimity was more suitable than old Art 43 EC (the Common Agriculture Policy measure) under which the measure was actually adopted and required only a qualified majority. The adoption by qualified majority was objected to by the UK. The Court of Justice was required to consider whether the subject matter more concerned the free movement of goods and thus a single market measure or really agricultural policy and thus the CAP. The use of the qualified majority procedure under the CAP was held to be appropriate by the Court of Justice.

In the 1992 case of *European Parliament v Council* (Students Residence C-295/90), Parliament successfully challenged the adoption of Directive 90/366 on the free movement of students which the Council adopted under old Art 235 EC requiring only consultation rather than under an earlier Art 7 EC, which would require the cooperation procedure to be used, thus giving the EP a greater role in the legislative process. The Directive was annulled and was re-enacted.

A further case to focus on the issues raised above is *Commission v Council* (Re: Titanium Dioxide Directive C-300/89). The Council adopted a Directive on the basis of old Art 130s EC as an environmental measure which then required unanimity and only consultation of the EP, despite the protests of the EP at the time. The Commission argued it should have been adopted using an earlier Art 100a EC as a single market measure, which then required QMV and the co-operation procedure instead. Whilst the Court acknowledged that both could be a valid base, the use of Art 130s EC instead of Art 100a EC deprived the EP of its greater role in the legislative process. Even if both were used, as suggested by the Council, it would still have to decide unanimously and thus overrule any opinion objections of the EP.

In a similar challenge, in case C-155/91 *Commission v Council* (Waste Directive), to a Directive (91/156) on waste disposal, adopted under old Art

130s EC by the Council, the Commission challenged it on the basis that old Art 100a EC in respect of the internal market should have been used as the legal base. On this occasion, the Court disagreed and held that the protection of the environment stated in the Directive was the real reason and not the free movement of waste. Therefore the challenge by the Commission was rejected. The view of the ECJ was that it was not so much the right to move waste around but the promotion of the most efficient way of dealing with waste to protect the environment, ie by not preventing its movement to the most efficient waste disposal operators.

A further case concerned the adoption by the Council in June 1993 of a Directive specifying a minimum working week, albeit with the ability of workers to work longer voluntarily. The UK which was opposed to this was unable to veto the proposal as it was introduced under the health and safety of workers provision under the old Art 118a of EEC Treaty (social policy) which requires only a qualified majority in the Council. The UK requested the annulment of the Directive in case C-84/94 *UK v Council*, arguing that it would have been more appropriate to base the measure on Arts 308 (old 235 EEC, now 352 TFEU) or 94 (old 100 EEC, now 115 TFEU), either of which would have required unanimity on the part of the Council thus allowing the UK the chance to veto the measure. The Court of Justice was, however, satisfied with the choice of Art 118a EEC.

The view of the Court of Justice is essentially that the democratic process which now involves the EP demands that where two legal bases are available requiring differing procedures, the one allowing the EP the greater role must be used so as not to deprive the EP and the Community of its democratic right, unless it can be shown the matter is primarily more concerned with a particular Treaty base. In contrast, in Case C-376/98 *Germany v Council* (Tobacco Advertising), the ECJ held that the ban on tobacco advertising was mainly based on health grounds and not the internal market. It was, however, adopted under old Art 100a EC (now 114 TFEU), the internal market harmonisation measure. It was held to have been outside the Community competence to enact it because the correct public health article did not allow for harmonisation of laws (old 129(4) EC), which was precisely what the Directive did.

Given the simplification of the legislative procedures by the Treaties of Amsterdam, Nice and even more so under Lisbon and the change of legal procedure for many provisions in favour of the EP, it will become less of an issue following the 2007 Lisbon Treaty entry into effect. This has reduced the types of legislative procedures in use by removing the cooperation procedure entirely and relying less on the consultation procedure. Qualified majority voting in the Council will be increased and unanimity on the part of the Council of Ministers will be restricted to taxation, social security and foreign policy. As a result there should be less scope for disputes about the legal base.

Question 6

In the light of the roles of the Advocates General and the European Court of Justice and with reference to the jurisprudence of the Court, consider whether the ECJ possesses law-making powers in the EU legal order.

Commentary

This is a relatively straightforward question dealing generally with the Court of Justice and the Advocates General and their impact in the EU legal order. The question can be broken into easier sections. First, you clearly need to outline the position and function of the Advocate General and the role and powers of the European Court of Justice. The place to start for both of these is with the Treaty.

You have then to decide whether the role played by the ECJ in the decisions it reaches constitute a law-making power and thus whether it adds to the body of EU law, or whether it merely interprets and applies existing EU law. The reference to the jurisprudence of the ECJ is simply asking you to refer to the case law of the ECJ where necessary to support your arguments and answer.

The amount of detail you include for the first part of the answer will depend on the coverage in your course and whether, for example, you have considered in detail the Protocol on the Statute of the Court of Justice or the Rules of the Court of Justice. If not, then supply as much detail as you can.

Answer plan

- Treaty Articles concerning the European Court of Justice
- The role and powers of the ECJ
- The role and function of the Advocates General
- Temporal effect of judgments
- Development of Community principles of law

Suggested answer

As an introduction, it would be useful to state that the Court of Justice presently consists of 27 judges and eight Advocates General, nominated and appointed by unanimous agreement by the governments of the Member States. They must be chosen from persons whose independence is beyond doubt and who possess the qualifications required for appointment to the highest judicial office in their own countries (Arts 221–223).

The position of the Advocates General is established under Art 222 of the EC Treaty. The role of an Advocate General is to assist the Court by giving an opinion, in complete independence and impartiality, on the issues of a case.

In doing so the Advocate General will examine the legal issues in depth and critically review the jurisprudence of the Court on the subject. The reasoned submissions of the Advocates General are to be made in open court. It is a general requirement that the opinion of the Advocate General be heard before judgment is given unless the case raises no new point of law (Art 20 of the Statute of the Court of Justice). The Advocate General can therefore take the public view of things and consider the submissions of all the parties but cannot be bound to present or represent any particular view. Additionally, the opinion of the Advocate General is not binding on the Court but it acts like a sort of persuasive precedent. Alternatively, it can be considered that the opinion of the Advocate General acts like a first instance decision subject to an automatic and instant appeal. The Advocate General plays no part in the actual decision of the Court and once the Advocate General has delivered an opinion it brings to an end his or her role in the case.

Whilst not having the formal impact on EU law that the Court has, the Advocates General have nevertheless also helped in the development of EU law. This arises indirectly from their detailed research for cases often involving comparative research of the laws of Member States. At times this has led to a direct influence by the introduction of national legal principles into the EU legal order, eg in the case of *Transocean Marine Paint Association v Commission* (17/74), the principle of *audi et alterem partem* (the right of the other party to be heard) was introduced by the Advocate General and adopted later by the Court. An opinion of an Advocate General may be referred to in later cases as a sort of persuasive precedent as in the case of *Prodifarma v Commission* (T-3/90) when the Advocate General's opinion in a previous case was taken up by the Court of First Instance (CFI) (now called the General Court following the Lisbon Treaty).

Article 19 TEU (ex 220 EC) outlines the general function of the Court of Justice. It states 'It (the Court of Justice) shall ensure that in the interpretation and application of the Treaties the law is observed.' Originally it had exclusive jurisdiction over EU law but was joined by the Court of First Instance and judicial panels (now the General and Specialised Courts under Arts 256–257 TFEU (ex 225a EC)). The Court has been divided into chambers to help expedite the business of the Court. The jurisdiction and tasks of the Court are laid down in Arts 258–281 TFEU (ex 226–245 EC).

As a result of the fact that the European Treaties and some of the secondary legislation are framework measures, they often require considerable amplification and interpretation. This, coupled with the style of interpretation which has been adopted by the Court to give effect to the aims of the Treaties, has given a wide scope to the Court of Justice to engage in judicial activism.

A primary form of interpretation is described as teleological in that the Court tries to determine in the light of the aims and objective of the Treaties and legislation what was intended and what result would assist those goals. These methods are applied in addition to the usual array of methods of interpretation found in the Member States, legal systems. The Court often refers to the spirit of the Treaty and Community (now Union) to come to a particular conclusion. See in particular the leading case of *Van Gend en Loos* (26/62) at para 71 and the case of *CILFIT Srl v Ministro della Sanita* (283/81), concerned with the necessity of national courts to refer a question under Art 234 EC (now 267 TFEU). This form of interpretation allows the Court to be more adventurous in its decision-making than could be assumed from a literal reading of the legal provisions. For example, in certain circumstances it has been held that persons who are unemployed or studying can be classified as workers under EU law, see the case of *Lair v Universität Hannover* (39/86).

Past decisions are often cited in Court, however, they are only persuasive rather than have any formal authority. For example, the *CILFIT* case can also be observed to give rise to a form of precedent in that the ECJ stated that it was possible for national courts to refer to previous judgments of the ECJ in identical cases to achieve a solution without the need for reference to the ECJ. However, it must be stated there is no formal system of precedent but the Court, as do courts in civil law jurisdictions, tries to maintain consistency in its judgments. An example of a reversal of the Court's decisions is in the case of *EP v Council* in the *Comitology* case (302/87) in which the EC was denied the right to take action under Art 230 EC (now 263 TFEU), but it was later allowed in the case of *EP v Council* (C-70/88) concerned with a Euratom decision Treaty base by Council to protect Parliament's prerogatives.

One aspect which may hinder a law-making role is the requirement to give a single judgment of the Court. This is because a single judgment is at times difficult to interpret later because it does not reveal whether the decision was reached on a unanimous or majority verdict. Hence it can be confusing and terse and thus difficult to apply in future cases as 'established' law.

It can be observed that the Court has played a crucial role in the establishment and development of the EU legal order by the establishment and development of leading principles of EU law. Notable judgments are those concerned with what are now fundamental decisions of the Court including direct effects and supremacy and case rulings in actions concerning the rights of the EU institutions, notably the EP. In the case of *Les Verts v EP* (294/83), an action against the EP under Art 230 EC (now 263 TFEU) was admitted despite the lack of any mention in the Article that the EP could be a defendant and in *EP v Council* (C-295/90) concerned with the Treaty base, the extension of the rights of the EP to take action under Art 230 EC (now 263 TFEU) was confirmed despite not being given the right under the provision of the Article itself.

A number of cases could then be cited to provide evidence that the ECJ enjoys some form of law-making role but it would be best to rely on leading cases in which the ECJ has established the fundamental principles of EU law of direct effects and supremacy of Community law; *Van Gend en Loos* (26/62) and *Costa v ENEL* (6/64). Quotations from these cases could be employed to great effect. In *Van Gend en Loos* the ECJ held:

> . . . the Community constitutes a new legal order of international law for the benefit of which the States have limited their sovereign rights, albeit in limited fields, and the subjects of which comprise not only Member States but also their nationals.

From *Da Costa* it was held:

> By contrast with ordinary international treaties the EEC Treaty has created its own legal system which became an integral part of the legal systems of the Member States and which their courts are bound to apply. By creating a Community of unlimited duration, having its own institutions, its own personality, its own legal capacity and more particularly real powers stemming from a limitation of sovereignty or a transfer of powers from the states to the Community the Member States have limited their sovereign rights and have created a body of law to bind their nationals and themselves.

Also:

> It follows . . . that the law stemming from the treaty, an independent source of law, could not because of its special and original nature, be overridden by domestic legal provisions, however framed, without being deprived of its character as Community law and without the legal basis of the Community itself being called into question.

These cases must demonstrate more than the simple interpretation and application of law as there is nothing in the Treaty to expressly establish these two fundamental principles of EU law. Furthermore, the introduction of new principles to the EU legal order also establishes new principles and rules of EU law.

Inevitably, in reaching conclusion an answer to such a question depends on how you define 'law-making'. I consider it to be at least arguable that given the width of the scope that the ECJ enjoys it would not be incorrect to describe it as having law-making powers. Indeed, during the Intergovernmental Conference in 1996–1997, some of the Member States had expressed their dissatisfaction with the high degree of judicial activism exercised by the ECJ in cases such as *Barber* (C-262/88). No changes resulted from this but it may be regarded as evidence that the Member States consider the ECJ to be doing more than just interpreting law.

Finally, in view of the severe difficulties the EU has had in reforming itself, the last question in this chapter is one on this reform process which may well be examined in your course.

Question 7

The 2007 Lisbon Treaty, having eventually being ratified by all 27 Member States, is a much poorer substitute for the 2004 Constitutional Treaty whilst essentially making the same institutional and other changes to the European Union.
  Discuss.

Commentary

This question is a topical one which is designed to highlight not only the changes which have been proposed but also the difficulties the Member States have been experiencing for the last few years in trying to reform the European Union.

   You must consider not only what the 2004 Constitutional Treaty and its substitute, the 2007 Lisbon Treaty, contain and make a comparison of these contents but also in order to make sense of the latter part of the question, you must outline why these Treaties were considered desirable or necessary in the first place. So you need to go back to the previous decisions of the Member States in the European Council which launched the Union on this tortuous and still unsuccessful reform path. Finally, you need to address the fact that both attempts to reform the EU have been undermined by rejection in one or more states at some stage. The CT was rejected by the Dutch and French electorates in May and June 2005 and although 18 states eventually ratified the CT, it was abandoned in June 2007. Its replacement, the 2007 Lisbon Treaty was initially rejected by the Irish in June 2008, but again a clear majority of the states had already or subsequently ratified it but the Irish electorate went on to approve it in 2009 and it entered into force on 1 December 2009. You must try to sum up the latest position on the consequences of these developments for the future of the reform of the EU.

Answer plan

- Outline the decisions of the Member States which provided for a reform process
- Sketch out the main steps of this process
- Consider and compare the main changes proposed under both the CT and the 2007 Lisbon Treaty
- Discuss the consequences of the rejections in 2005 and 2008
- Revisit and re-evaluate the need for and possible chances for further reform

Suggested answer

In order to consider why significant changes were proposed in both the Constitutional Treaty (CT) and the 2007 Lisbon Treaty, it is necessary to review the period immediately preceding these Treaties.

In preparation for the planned future expansion of the EU, in 1999, the then 15 Member States convened an intergovernmental conference to discuss institutional change and which concluded with the signing and eventual ratification of the Nice Treaty. The key provisions of this Treaty included amendments to the organisation and operation of the European Courts, temporary changes to the composition of institutions for future enlargement and re-weighting of the votes in Council. These changes were contained in a protocol rather than as amendments to the Treaty. The Nice Council Summit also saw the agreement of the Member States as to how to move on to the next stage of Treaty amendment and further integration. It was further agreed to do this in a different way to make Treaty reform more inclusive and transparent. The Nice Council Summit provided, a 'Declaration on the Future of the Union' which was to address a number of issues for the next IGC, planned for 2003. The details were finalised at a later summit of the Member States in Laeken in December 2001, which saw the start of an ultimately unsuccessful attempt to put the EU on a new constitutional footing. The Laeken Summit formally set up and prepared the agenda for a 'Convention on the Future of Europe' which was headed by a Praesidium of 12 members, led by Valéry Giscard d'Estaing, a former French President. It further consisted of representatives of the heads of state and government of the 15 Member States and the 13 candidate countries, 30 representatives of the National Parliaments and 26 from the candidate countries, 16 members of the EP, and two members from the Commission. It laid out in a declaration the goals for making the European Union more democratic, transparent and efficient. In particular, attention would be paid to the governance of the Union, institutional preparations for the forthcoming expansion, the division of competences and democratic participation in decision-making processes of the Union. The Convention worked until June 2003 when it wrote up its report and a draft CT was finalised and presented to the European Council in Greece on 18 July 2003. This was subsequently considered by the IGC which commenced in October 2003 and the draft CT was presented to the Heads of State and Government Summit in Rome in December 2003.

The main features of the CT included a new longer 2½ year term for the President of the European Council, a foreign minister, a smaller Commission, the formal inclusion of the Charter of Human Rights into the Treaty, new simplified legislative tools and more involvement for National Parliaments in law-making. After some very hard bargaining on voting numbers in Council and the number of Commissioners in 2003–2004, the CT was signed in October 2004 by all the Member States in Rome and handed over to each of the Member States to ratify it by parliamentary approval or referendum or both according to the constitutional or legal requirements of each state. However, in referenda, the CT was rejected by the electorates of France and the Netherlands in 2005. After an agreed period of reflection during which some states continued the ratification process, taking the total to 18, the process was abandoned. After a period of so-called reflection, in

June 2007, a further summit was held to see if the CT could be rescued or replaced. The German Presidency had the task of either making the CT more palatable or coming up with something in its place which nevertheless addressed the institutional challenges of enlargement. However, after another late night of Summit discussions, it was agreed to abandon the CT entirely and replace it. Even though the CT was abandoned, it is worthwhile listing the agreements reached in that Treaty because most of these matters ended up in the new Reform Treaty although in slightly altered or different form.

1. The transfer of a number of Article bases from unanimity to qualified majority.

2. Making the Charter of Fundamental Rights a legally binding part of the Treaty.

3. Providing the EU with the status of a legal person.

4. Establishment of the European Council as a main institution and the appointment of a President for the European Council (with 2½ years term of office).

5. A smaller Commission comprising two-thirds of the number of Member States.

6. Creation of a common EU foreign minister to lead a joint foreign ministry with ambassadors.

7. An express statement that Union law shall have primacy over national law.

8. Procedures for adopting and reviewing the Constitution, some without the need for another IGC.

9. An exit clause for Member States.

The 2007 Lisbon Treaty, which did not replace the existing Treaties but amended them, has retained the following features of the CT. The Union did get its legal personality, the proposed Union Minister for Foreign Affairs is instead called the High Representative of the Union for Foreign Affairs and Security Policy (the High Rep). The European Council with President was established as envisaged by the CT. The Commission size was also to be reduced as planned, but this was revised again as a part of the deal to get Ireland to hold a second referendum on the Lisbon Treaty. The names and types of secondary law 'Regulations, Directives and Decisions' will be kept.

The Charter on Fundamental Rights will become legally binding but only through a Declaration attached to the Treaties and with an opt-out for the UK and Poland. Primacy of Union law was removed as an express statement in the Treaty and instead placed in a declaration which merely affirmed the settled case law establishing primacy. The transfer of a number of articles to QMV and the co-decision procedure proceeded largely as planned.

The aspects of the CT which were not retained in the Lisbon Reform Treaty were those more of a symbolic nature which were perceived by the Member States to be a large part of the reason for the rejection by the French and Dutch electorates although studies have failed to establish this with any authority. The items completely abandoned were the references to a European flag, anthem, a motto and reference to a Europe day celebration which were argued to suggest too strongly of statehood.

The Lisbon Treaty was supposed, by stripping away the offensive parts of the CT and retaining most of the institutional changes, to make the changes more palatable to the Member States and their electorates. However, as the question suggests, the end result is less than satisfying despite making most of the changes considered necessary to allow the union to operate effectively in the future. This is because of the way the changes were made. Rather than contained in a single document, as was with the CT, the Lisbon Treaty does this by complicated and extensive amendments to the EC and EU Treaties. The TEU will be turned more into an overview Treaty with the EC Treaty being converted into a treaty dealing with substantive issues, called the Treaty on the Functioning of the European Union and the term 'Community' has been replaced throughout by 'Union'. Both Treaties, however, concern the institutions and a number of Articles in both Treaties are concerned with the same subject matter. In addition, rather than tidying up and reducing the protocols and declarations attached to the Treaties, more have been added.

At this stage it is clear that the Union Treaty architecture remains complicated, but having been ratified by all Member States, it is progress. As the questions suggests, this could have been done better perhaps in a single document and still have removed those elements considered offensive and which did not contain the word 'Constitutional' or similar, by just calling it, for example, the 'Consolidated EU and EC Treaty'.

The final part of the question draws attention to the fact that not only was the CT rejected by the electorates in two Member States, but its supposed much more palatable replacement, the Lisbon Treaty, was rejected by the Irish electorate in June 2008. Indeed, all but one state considered that the changes were insignificant enough not to have to subject the Treaty to a referendum at that time. It was generally assumed it would be ratified with less difficulty than the CT. Following a period of consideration and negotiation after the Irish rejection, in exchange for the agreement by Ireland to hold a second Referendum, EU leaders agreed to provide legal guarantees respecting Ireland's taxation policies, its military neutrality and ethical issues. More controversially they also agreed that each state should maintain one Commissioner each, contrary to the Treaty itself, thus keeping the present total at 27. Constitutional challenges in other states such as Germany, the Czech Republic and Poland were resolved and the deliberate delay by the Czech President in completing the Constitutional ratification process was withdrawn. The Treaty was finally ratified by all 27 States in November 2009 and entered into force on 1 December 2009.

In conclusion, I would suggest that with only, for the most part, the symbolic aspects having been removed and because most substantive changes remained, the Lisbon Treaty is a poorer substitute, especially because of the way that the changes have been made.

Further reading

Arnull, A, *The European Union and its Court of Justice* (Oxford: Oxford University Press, 2006).

Bache, I and George, S, *Politics in the European Union* 2nd edn (Oxford: Oxford University Press, 2006).

Blair, A, *The European Union since 1945* 2nd edn (Harlow: Pearson Longman, 2010).

Devuyst, Y, *The European Union Transformed: Community Method and Institutional Evolution from the Schuman Plan to the Constitution for Europe, revised and updated edn* (Brussels: Peter Lang, 2006).

Hallstrom, L, 'Support for European Federalism? An Elite View' (2003) 25(1) Journal of European Integration 51.

Kokott, J-RA, 'The European Convention and its Draft Treaty Establishing a Constitution for Europe: Appropriate Answers to the Laeken Questions?' (2003) 40(6) CML Rev 1315.

Peterson, J and Shackleton, M, *The Institutions of the European Union* 2nd edn (Oxford: Oxford University Press, 2006).

Richardson, J (ed), *European Union: Power and Policy-making* 3rd edn (Abingdon: Routledge Press, 2006).

Temple Lang, J, 'How Much do the Smaller Member States Need the European Commission? The Role of the Commission in a Changing Europe' (2002) 39(2) VML Rev 315.

Wall, S, A *Stranger in Europe: Britain and the EU from Thatcher to Blair* (New York: Oxford University Press USA, 2008).

Ward, I, *A Critical Introduction to European Law* 3rd edn (Cambridge: Cambridge University Press, 2009).

3

The Sources, Forms and Individual Remedies of EU Law

Introduction

This chapter includes questions on a wide variety of often overlapping points concerned with the sources of EU law. The sources of law are the Treaties which are regarded as primary sources and secondary legislation which can be enacted by the institutions of the Union by virtue of the powers given by the Member States and which are contained in the Treaties. Additional sources of law in the EU legal order are agreements with third countries, general principles and the case law of the ECJ establishing, amongst other case law developments, the doctrine of direct effects, supremacy of EU law and state liability. Note that under the 2007 Lisbon Treaty, the same forms of law will be retained but with distinctions provided in new Arts 288–291 TFEU for legislative, delegated and implementing acts.

The prime candidate for questions in this area, because of its far-reaching ramifications, must be the doctrine of direct effects. Questions about this topic will be posed in all manner of forms and mixed with more general questions on the sources of law so that you may also be required to consider, for example, the direct effects, if any, of international agreements entered into by the EU. A sample of such questions is included in this chapter.

Question 1

Identify the sources of law (other than Treaty provisions and secondary EU legislation) invoked by the European Court of Justice. What is the justification for the recognition and application of such sources in the EU legal order?

Commentary

This question bypasses a consideration of the prime sources of EU law, namely the Treaties and Regulations, Directives and Decisions, to consider other sources of law and legal rules which have had an impact in the EU legal order. First of all then you need to identify those other sources according to different types, if it is possible to categorise them conveniently. You will most likely concentrate on the provisions of international agreements, general principles of law and fundamental rights provision, the latter two categories extensively developed by the ECJ. Having identified other sources of law, you must then account for their recognition and application in the EU legal order. This requires you consider this, both from the point of view of whether there are any direct or indirect legal justifications arising from the EU Treaties for the ECJ to employ these other sources in its judgments, and whether there are any non-legal arguments which would either justify or demand their application.

Answer plan

- Identify non-Treaty based sources of EU law
- Status of international agreements and general principles
- Case law of the ECJ
- Rationale for the acceptance of non-Treaty based sources

Suggested answer

The EU Treaties and the secondary forms of EU law sanctioned by those Treaties, in particular Regulations, Directives and Decisions under Art 288 TFEU (ex 249 EC), are not the only sources of law or legal rules which have an impact in the EU legal order. Whilst the Treaties and secondary EU legislation are clearly the most important and abundant sources, other sources have been recognised and employed by the ECJ. These other sources can be broadly classified into two categories.

A first additional source of law arises from the international agreements entered into by the EU on behalf of the Member States, or those, such as the European Road Transport Agreement or the North-East Atlantic Fisheries Convention, the EU has taken over the competence of the Member States as agreed. Most notable are the WTO and GATT agreements on import duties and trade, association agreements with other European states and the Lomé and Cotonou Conventions between the Member States and many Third World nations.

The second major source of law includes the categories of general principles and fundamental rights. General principles of law have been used to assist the Court of Justice in the interpretation and application of EU law and by the parties to assist them in challenging the EU institutions or law and the actions of the Member States in the application of EU law. These principles are also referred to in Arts 263 and 340 TFEU actions against the Community institutions.

General principles from external sources can arise from particular provisions of other legal systems, in particular the constitutions of Member States, principles of natural law or justice found in common law or in written form in some Member States or international law and agreements, for example, the European Convention on Human Rights (ECHR). Sometimes, the actual articles of the ECHR are referred to directly as in the *Hauer* (44/79) and *Kirk* (63/83) cases. The public law and legal systems of Germany, France and now the UK have all had a considerable impact on the supply of general principles for the EU legal order. The principles which form a source of EU law need not be present in all of the Member State legal systems nor indeed in a majority. The Court of Justice will often conduct a comparative review of whether or in what form the principle exists in some or all of the Member States. In particular now, Art 6 TEU provides that the Union shall respect fundamental rights, as guaranteed by the ECHR and those human rights common to the Member State as general principles of EU law. Furthermore, any applicant states joining the European Union are now obligated by Art 49 TEU to have respect for human rights. At the Nice Intergovernmental Conference (IGC) in 2000, the Parliament, Council and Commission agreed a European Charter of Fundamental Rights which has now been incorporated by Declaration (No 1) attached to the 2007 Lisbon Treaty and will be binding in the European Union with the exception of Poland and the UK who have negotiated an opt-out Protocol and the Czech Republic by agreement.

Often too, the Advocate General or judges in the case may be particularly influential in the introduction of a certain principle into the EU legal order. The Advocates General from particular countries are more easily able to identify the principles, which may be common in one form or another in a number of the Member States and thus more likely to introduce these principles to the Court of Justice. For example, the Latin maxim *audi alterem partem* was introduced by the Advocate General in *Transocean Marine Paint Association* v *Commission* (17/74). He argued that in the absence of Transocean being allowed to present their views on the matter, the Commission's Decision would be in breach of a general principle of law, clearly applicable in the UK and other legal systems.

When it comes to considering the rationale for these additional sources of EU law, it is to be noted that the justification for the recognition and application differs according to the type of other source.

The conclusion of agreements with countries associated with the Member States and agreements with other third countries are specifically catered for under Arts 217–218 TFEU (ex 300 and 310 EC). In the *Haegemann* v *Belgium* (181/73) case, an agreement between the Community (now Union) and Greece was held to be binding on the Member States even though such agreements are not envisaged by ex Art 249 EC (now 288 TFEU). Furthermore, although there is no statement in the Treaty that such agreements entered into by the Union or by the Member States can give rise to direct effects, the Court of Justice has held that they may give rise to direct effects providing they satisfy the criteria established in the leading case of *Van Gend en Loos* (26/62). These criteria tend, however, to be more strictly applied. To this extent an investigation of one of the GATT provisions in the case of *International Fruit (No 3)* (21–22/72) was held not to be directly effective. However, provisions of the Yaoundé Convention and the EEC-Portugal association agreement were held to be directly effective in the cases of *Bresciani* (87/75) and *Kupferberg* (104/81).

With regard to general principles, whilst some are clearly imported into the legal system from external sources, others have been developed by the Court of Justice from the Treaty. There are three Treaty Articles which provide some justification for the Court of Justice to introduce general principles into the Community legal order.

Article 19 TEU (ex 220 EC) is a general guideline set by the Treaty for the functioning of the Court of Justice. It provides that the Court of Justice shall ensure that in the interpretation and application of the Treaties the law is observed. This is taken to mean the law outside of the Treaty. Ex Art 220 EC has been invoked to introduce very many different general principles of law, most notably human rights. More specifically, two further articles of the Treaty mandate the court to take account of general principles of law. Article 263 TFEU (ex 230 EC) refers to the infringement of any rule of law relating to the application of the Treaty as one of the grounds for an action for the challenge to the validity of EU law and Art 340 TFEU (ex 288(2) EC), concerned with damages claims, specifically allows the settlement of claims against the EU institutions on the basis of the general principles of the laws of the Member States. The latter two are specific to the claims raised under those Treaty Articles but they do serve to reinforce the Court of Justice's claim that it can rely on general principles as a source of law in the EU legal order.

The EC Treaty (Arts 12 and 141) (now 18 and 157 TFEU) has also supplied the basis for non-discrimination which applies both in relation to nationality and sex and has been further developed into a general principle of equality and non-discrimination.

More widespread and logical arguments for the inclusion of general principles are that the EU and Court were morally and socially, if not legally, obliged to observe fundamental human rights especially those upheld in the constitutions of the Member States. No self-respecting legal system in Europe could ignore, or be seen to be ignoring, such ideologically important rights such as these. Failure to observe them might lead to serious clashes with Member States' constitutional law, which might have led to severe strains on the EU legal system. The *Internationale Handelsgesellschaft* ([1974] 2 CMLR 540) case showed the potential for conflict and ultimate harm to the EU legal order if the EU fails to uphold human rights provisions.

Another argument stems from the fact that the Treaties are only framework Treaties and require completion by reference to other laws. For the most part this is done by the specific secondary legislation of the EU, but this only provides the substantive law rules which also often require interpretation by the Court of Justice. The EU legal order was established anew and does not have the traditions of the Member States' legal systems to rely on which are rich in developed principles of law. Therefore, something is needed to assist the Court of Justice in its task, and general principles, many of which are borrowed from the Member States' legal systems, do just that.

The European Union now has a much stronger base for fundamental rights because the 2007 Lisbon Treaty entered into force with the Charter of rights attached by a Declaration (No 1) which provides it with legally binding force. Whilst this would not prevent the ECJ from continuing to look at other sources of fundamental rights, clearly the rights Charter should be its first port of call.

Question 2

Article 288 TFEU provides that Regulations shall be directly applicable in all Member States. Does this mean they are also necessarily directly effective?

Commentary

This is a seemingly straightforward question but one which can be deceptive and thus difficult to answer. Clearly, the starting point for the answer to this question lies with Art 288 TFEU and a definition of 'directly applicable' and, furthermore, an explanation of the consequences of this concept. Once that has been set out you need to define the concept of directly effective and decide whether Regulations, by virtue of the fact they are directly applicable, are by necessity directly effective.

Answer plan

- Article 288 TFEU: definition of Regulation
- Meaning of 'directly applicable' and consequences thereof
- Meaning of 'directly effective' and whether Regulations are automatically so

Suggested answer

Direct applicability refers to a means or mode of incorporation, or the way in which international law finds validity in national legal systems. This is recognised in international law and means that international law is automatically binding (otherwise described as self executing) in national states.

Article 288 TFEU (ex 249 EC) declares that Regulations shall have general application and that they shall be binding in their entirety and directly applicable in the Member States. They are designed as general provisions of legislation applicable to all rather than specific individuals or groups and are often termed normative acts (see case 16 & 17/62 *Fruit & Vegetable Confederation* v *Council*). Regulations are detailed forms of law so that the law in all Member States is exactly the same. They are also described as self executing because of the way they obtain legal validity in the Member States without the need for any implementation or transformation into national law by the Member States. Article 288 TFEU carries an obligation that the Member States are not to transform EU Regulations into national legislation. It was held in the case of *Commission* v *Italy* (Slaughtered Cows) (39/72) that Member States cannot subject a Regulation to any implementing measures than those required by the act itself. There may, however, be circumstances where the Member States are required to provide implementing measures to ensure the effectiveness of the Regulation as in the case of *Commission* v *UK* (Tachographs) (128/78). This obligation also applies to Treaty Articles as these also satisfy the requirement of directly applicable law by automatic validity in transformation and that they are also generally binding because they can obligate individuals.

The special elements or criteria, therefore, are that Regulations are automatically binding and general, because they apply also to the citizens directly and not just to nation states.

In contrast to the above definition it is now necessary to define and explain the concept of directly effective. Directly effective is the term given to judicial enforcement of rights arising from provisions of EU law which can be upheld in favour of individuals in the courts of the Member States. It may also be referred to as 'direct effects' and it describes the right to rely directly on EU law in the absence of national law or in the face of conflicting national law.

Direct effects can apply to Articles of the Treaty, Regulations, Directives and Decisions, in fact any binding law in terms of Art 288 TFEU and in some circumstances outside of Art 288 TFEU as with international agreements. However, in contrast to provisions of law which are directly applicable such as Regulations, certain criteria have to be fulfilled before the ECJ can declare a particular EU law provision to give rise to direct effects. The criteria for directly effective were determined by the ECJ in a series of cases commencing with the leading EU law case of *Van Gend en Loos* (26/62). In *Van Gend en Loos*, a private legal individual company challenged an import duty imposed by the Dutch authorities and claimed it was contrary to Arts 12 and 13 of the EEC Treaty (now 30 TFEU). The Dutch authorities in their defence claimed that the obligation was one imposed by the Treaty on the Dutch state alone and could not be invoked by an individual of that state. The Court of Justice held that the institutions of the Community are endowed with sovereign rights, the exercise of which affects not only Member States but also their citizens, and that Community law was capable of conferring rights on individuals which become part of their legal heritage. For a particular provision of Community (now EU) law to be upheld before a national court in the face of non-implementation, or incorrect implementation of national law, the provisions have to be:

- clear and precise;
- leave no discretion to the authorities of the Member State;
- unconditional; and
- require no further implementation by either the Union institutions or the Member State.

Hence in the *Van Gend en Loos* case the company could rely directly on the Treaty Article to avoid paying the unlawful duty imposed by the Dutch authorities.

Thus, to contrast these two concepts: direct applicability is a mode of incorporation, whereas direct effects is a judicial development for the enforcement of rights. Another difference is that direct effects can apply to all forms of EU law whereas directly applicable applies just to certain types. Directives are not, for example, directly applicable but only apply to persons to whom they are addressed. They are not self-executing and in most cases must be transformed by national legislation into national law. Directives can, though, give rise to direct effects.

Direct effects was sometimes considered to be a sub-concept of direct applicability or direct applicability a pre-requisite for direct effects. The Court of Justice has spoken in the *Verbond van Nederlandse Ondernemingen* (51/76) and *Grad* (9/70) cases of Regulations which are directly applicable but which by their very nature can have direct effects, which suggests this is automatically the case. In *Grad* the Court also stated that the ability of an individual to invoke a Decision before a national court leads to the same result as would be achieved by a directly applicable provision of a Regulation, again as if to suggest the concepts are the same.

The question whether Regulations which are directly applicable are necessarily directly effective is essentially asking if it follows that directly applicable provision must, without exception, be capable of direct effects. The answer must be no, because direct effects are not automatic. For example, individual provisions, including those of Regulations and Treaty Articles, still have to satisfy the criteria laid down by the Court and do not do so in all instances, whereas direct effects can arise from all forms of legislative provision.

Therefore, whilst generally Regulations are capable of direct effects, it is not necessarily the case that individually they will give rise to direct effects capable of enforcement by an individual; see, eg *Eridania v Ministry of Agriculture and Forestry* (230/78).

Finally, to emphasise that the 2007 Lisbon Treaty has not changed the designation of Regulation.

Question 3

While the TFEU suggests that Regulations and Directives are very different types of legislative instrument, in practice, as a result partly, but not exclusively, of the doctrine of direct effect, the distinction between Regulations and Directives has become blurred.

Discuss.

Commentary

A question which concentrates on the debate which ensued and continued for a long time following the ECJ's gradual development of the doctrine of direct effects. It was considered that the establishment and development of direct effects by the ECJ was undermining the distinction between the two forms of secondary EU legislation established by the Treaty along the lines that if both Regulations and Directives could give rise to direct effects then no real difference any longer existed between the two. To some extent these concerns were answered by the first *Marshall* (152/84) case to reach the ECJ which decided that Directive could not give rise to rights capable of enforcement by individuals against other individuals, the so-called horizontal direct effects, thus a distinction remains as Regulations are capable of horizontal direct effects. Nevertheless, the issue is still relevant and topical.

In answering the question you clearly need first to outline both forms of law from their Treaty base and then to explain that they were intended as having different functions. You then need to consider why in practice the distinction has been undermined. The question itself indicates that you should concentrate your answer on the influence of the doctrine of direct effects on this practice. This requires therefore a definition and explanation of direct effects.

Answer plan

- Article 288 TFEU: Regulations and Directives
- Definition and functions of Regulations

- Definition and functions of Directives
- Regulations and Directives in practice
- Direct effects of Regulations and Directives

Suggested answer

The question concerns Regulations and Directives which are at present the two most important forms of secondary law that can be enacted by the institutions of the EU under the power granted by Art 288 TFEU (ex 249 EC). This provides the following:

A regulation shall have general application. It shall be binding in its entirety and directly applicable in all Member States.

A directive shall be binding, as to the result to be achieved, upon each Member State to which it is addressed, but shall leave to the national authorities the choice and form and methods.

Regulations are general or normative provisions of legislation applicable to all legal persons in the EU rather than to specific individuals or groups. They are usually very detailed forms of legislation to ensure that the law in all Member States is exactly the same.

Regulations become legally valid in the Member States without any need for implementation and this process is sometimes described as self executing. In fact it was held in the case of *Commission* v *Italy* (Slaughtered Cows) (39/72) that Member States cannot subject the Regulation to any implementing measures than those required by the act itself. There may, however, be circumstances where the Member States are required to provide implementing measures to ensure the effectiveness of the Regulation as in the case of *Commission* v *UK* (Tachographs) (128/78).

Directives, in contrast, set out aims which must be achieved but leave the choice of the form and method of implementation to the Member States. This was done to ease the way in which national law could be harmonised in line with EU law and give the Member States a wider area of discretion to do this. If, for example, a Member State considers that the existing national law is already in conformity with the requirements of a new Directive then it need not do anything, apart from the requirement now in Directives that the Member State inform the Commission of how the Directive has been implemented. Member States are given a period in which to implement Directives which can range from one year to five or more, depending on the complexity of the subject matter and the urgency for the legislation.

It may be useful at this stage to try to summarise the notable differences in the forms of legislation. Directives are aimed at the Member States or named individuals, whereas Regulations apply to everyone. Regulations were designed to be directly applicable but it would seem from Art 288 TFEU that Directives require some form of implementation in order to take affect or have validity in the EU legal order. Directives were designed with the harmonisation of different national rules in mind whereas Regulations were aimed to be prescriptive by providing one rule for the whole of the EU. Hence Regulations would be detailed and precise and Directives more likely to be framework provisions laying down general guidelines and are therefore less precise by nature.

Thus, by design, these are very different forms of legislation. The answer can now consider why the distinction seems to have been blurred in practice. This can be covered in two parts, first generally and then with specific attention to direct effects. In practice a less rigid or distinct division has been observed.

It is not always the case that Regulations are precise and complete, as noted above in the case of the Tachographs, and further action was required on the part of the Member States. Regulations should be normative but they are often used in respect of specific individuals: eg anti-dumping regulations and others in the area of competition law. On the other hand, directives can often be very detailed, see eg Directive 2004/38 concerning now quite detailed provisions in support of the free movement of workers and members of the worker's family, which has consolidated a lot of previous case law on the topic.

The biggest assault on the distinction arose when the ECJ held that it was not only Treaty Articles and Regulations which could give rise to rights which could be directly enforced by individuals before the national courts but also other forms of EU law could also give rise to such rights. These have come to be known as 'direct effects' in the EU legal order. This is the term given to judicial enforcement of rights arising from provisions of EU law which can be upheld in favour of individuals in the courts of the Member States. The term 'directly effective' may also be used and it describes the right to rely directly on EU law in the absence of national law or in the face of conflicting national law. The cases of *Grad* (9/70) and *Van Duyn* v *Home Office* (41/74) confirmed that Directives could also give rise to direct effects, providing they also satisfy the criteria required of Directive effects as initially laid down in the case of *Van Gend en Loos* (26/62) and that the time limit given to the Member State has expired (case 148/78 *Pubblico Ministero* v *Ratti*). Therefore, although Directives are not directly applicable in that they are not automatic and general in application and give rights without further implementation, Directives have been held to give rise to directly enforceable rights in specific circumstances, ie where they have not been implemented or have been incorrectly implemented (case 51/76 *Verbond van Nederlandse Ondernemingen*).

The argument then arises as to whether the distinction has been eroded in that both Regulations and Directives can be enforced by individuals in the national courts and that in practice there is really not a great deal of difference between them. This might have been, or become, more likely if the Court of Justice had not decided in the case of *Marshall* (152/84) that Directives could not give rise to rights which could be enforced against other individuals, the so-called 'horizontal direct effects'. To date, the Court has upheld this position, although there is a line of case law developing which suggests that in an action between private parties, a Directive may be relied on incidentally. In the case of *CIA Security* v *Signalson*(C-194/94), CIA was able to rely on the Directive's requirement that Member States notify the Commission to get clearance for national technical standards, in an action by a competitor accusing them of not meeting legal requirements. Belgium had not notified the Commission, thus their standards were held to be inapplicable. These incidental direct effects cases do not, however, blur the distinction.

Thus, whilst it may be argued that in practice the gap between Regulations and Directives has narrowed, clear distinctions remain and they are still used for different purposes as the occasion demands, ie either a harmonising rule to accommodate different previous positions or a new rule entirely. Furthermore, even when it comes to considering direct effects, Directives are only enforceable by individuals in a limited number of cases where approved by the ECJ and not universally and they do not provide rights directly enforceable between individuals.

Question 4

Does the distinction between vertical and horizontal direct effects cause difficulties for individuals in actions involving EU law? If so, what has been done to mitigate these difficulties?

Commentary

This question picks up the detail where the last one left off, in that it asks you to consider the arguments in respect of horizontal direct effects and whether this causes problems for individuals in certain circumstances. The circumstances are those in respect of the consequence that the ECJ ruling in *Marshall* (152/84) and subsequent case law denied individuals the ability to enforce Directives against other individuals.

The answer requires a definition of what is meant by both types of direct effect and requires you to know and explain that it is impliedly referring to the direct effects of Directives which cause the difficulties. The distinction was highlighted by the *Marshall* case which should be discussed along with the consequences of the decision which have given rise to difficulties, if you agree that this is the case.

The final part asks you then how the difficulties have been avoided or circumvented. This requires you to refer to the developing case law of the ECJ which has already provided some alternative solutions where individuals are deprived of the protection of horizontal direct effects from Directives. In particular, the development of the principle of state liability has come to the aid of individuals who might otherwise have suffered from a lack of legal redress against other individuals.

 ## Answer plan

- Definition of direct effects as developed through case law
- Direct effects of Treaty Articles, Regulations and Directives
- *Marshall* v *Southampton AHA* (152/84) and consequences
- *Von Colson* and *Harz* cases (14 and 79/83) and indirect effect and the *Mangold* (C-144/04) judgment
- *Francovich* (C-6 and 9/90) and state liability
- *Factortame III* and subsequent cases
- Incidental horizontal effects cases

Suggested answer

Direct effects is an EU concept developed by the Court of Justice to apply to Treaty Articles, Regulations, Directives and Decisions. It is the term given to judicial enforcement of rights arising from provisions of EU law which can be upheld in favour of individuals in the courts of the Member States. To be capable of direct effects a provision must satisfy the criteria established by the Court of Justice, initially in the case of *Van Gend en Loos* (26/62), that the provision:

  should be clear and precise;

  should be unconditional;

  should not require implementing further measures by the state or Union institutions; or

  should not leave room for the exercise of discretion by the Member State or Union institutions.

In *Van Gend en Loos* it was held that the institutions of the Community (now Union) are endowed with sovereign rights, the exercise of which affects not only Member States but also their citizens and that Community (now EU) law was capable of conferring rights on individuals which become part of their legal heritage.

Direct effects have been found to arise from many Treaty Articles, which often obligate not just organs of the state as in a vertical relationship but other individuals, in particular in the EU context, employers.

It was confirmed by the Court of Justice that employers are obligated to comply with the requirements of a Treaty Article and other individuals may enforce corresponding rights directly against the obligated party who has failed to comply with EU law. In this case the resultant rights are termed horizontal direct effects. The first case to confirm this was that of *Defrenne* v *Sabena (No 2) (43/75)* in which the rights of an air hostess for equal pay guaranteed under Art 119 (now 141) were upheld against the employing state airline, Sabena, who were in breach of the obligation. That Directives could also give rise to direct effects was confirmed by the ECJ in the cases of *Van Duyn* (41.74) and *Ratti* (148/78).

VERTICAL DIRECT EFFECTS

STATE (OR STATE BODY)

INDIVIDUAL (NATURAL OR LEGAL PERSON)

HORIZONTAL DIRECT EFFECTS

INDIVIDUAL v INDIVIDUAL

For a considerable time the question of whether Directives could be held further to give rise to horizontal direct effects and thus be enforceable against other individuals was open to speculation. However, the Court of Justice decided in the case of *Marshall* (152/84), which concerned a claim for equal treatment in retirement against the Health Authority, that Directives could only be enforced against the state or arms of the state and not against individuals. The Health Authority was held to be a part of the state. A claim against private employers would fail in the same circumstances.

Marshall decided there could be no horizontal direct effects of Directives mainly as a result of the fact that Directives are not addressed to individuals, therefore individuals should not be obligated by them. The result of this decision is that the scope of the concept of public service as opposed to a private body is crucial. Rights contained within Directives cannot be enforced by individuals against other individuals. This has the result that there is not a uniform application of EU law either in a Member State or between Member States. There is no uniformity in the application of EU law between public and private and employers within Member States and between Member States, because there are different concepts of what is the state and what are private and public employers. Furthermore, this position can be further complicated by the movement of utilities and companies in and out of public ownership. Certain individuals are thus denied rights that employees in the public sector can enforce in the face of non-compliance by Member States. The uniformity of the Union is undermined in important areas of law dealing with employment rights, where many Directives are relevant to private employers and the protection of individuals and their rights; eg Art 157 TFEU can create horizontal direct effects but the Directive providing other rights cannot (Directive 2004/38). An example of the dire consequences for individuals is the *Duke* case ([1988] 1 CMLR 719) in the UK, which considered the same question as in the *Marshall* case (152/84). However, in *Duke* a private employer was involved and the House of Lords held that Mrs Duke could not uphold her claim for equal treatment in retirement because Directives could not give rise to direct effects which could be relied on horizontally. The decision has thus led to an arbitrary and uneven protection of individual rights (see more recently the case of *Dori* (C-91/92)).

There are various arguments for and against having horizontal direct effects of Directives but these go beyond the required answer for this question and should not be rehearsed here.

Once you have identified that in certain circumstances the decision concerning Directives is unfortunate, case law which mitigates the harsh consequences can be considered.

One way pursued by the ECJ is by expanding the concept of public sector in the case law and thus including more individuals capable of protection of Community law, see, eg, the cases of *Johnson* v *RUC* (222/84) and *Foster* v *British Gas* (C-188/89) which showed that, although the concept was wide enough to include nationalised industry and includes any form of state control or authority, a distinction nevertheless remains between public and private employers. Although it may be considered that tinkering with the scope of what is meant by an 'emanation of the state' will broaden the concept and protect more people but this does not get to the heart of the matter. It still allows a variation as between public and private employees and between the Member States. The difficulties and limits to this approach are demonstrated in the UK case of *Rolls Royce plc* v *Doughty* ([1992] 1 CMLR 1045), in which the Court of Appeal considered that the nationalised Rolls Royce was not a public body for the purposes of the claim to direct effects. Privatisation of once nationalised companies also affects the rights of individuals. In *Rieser Internationale Transporte GmbH* v *Autobahnen- und Schnellstraßen Finanzierungs AG* (C-157/02), it was held that the provisions of a directive capable of having direct effect may be relied upon against a legal person governed by private law where the state has entrusted to that legal person the task of levying tolls for the use of public road networks and where it has direct or indirect control of that legal person. Thus, private companies undertaking a public duty also come within the scope of the *Foster* ruling.

Another line of case law has developed, however, which may provide an alternative for individuals defeated by the absence of horizontal direct effects. The first cases in this line which is referred to as indirect effects but also the sympathetic or harmonious interpretation principle, are *von Colson* (14/83) and *Harz* (79/83). Both cases concerned Art 6 of the Equal Treatment Directive (76/207) respectively, concerning a public and private employer; thus the contrast of available remedies was starkly visible. Rather than highlight the unfortunate results of the lack of horizontal direct effects of Directives, which would have helped *von Colson* but not *Harz*, the Court of Justice concentrated on Art 5 EC (now 4(3) TEU) which requires Member States to comply with Union obligations. The Court held that this requirement applies to all authorities of Member States including the courts, and so the courts are obliged to interpret the implementing national law in such a way as to ensure obligations of a Directive are obeyed. The difficulty with the *von Colson* line of argument is that it requires there to be national law to interpret, or rules with which the national court can, and is willing to, construe to achieve the correct result. Further cases which develop the boundaries of this principle are *Marleasing* (C-106/89), which required the national courts to apply Community law regardless of whether the national law was based on any particular Directive and regardless of the intent or even existence of national law, and *Kolpinghuis* (80/86) which held that a Member State which has not implemented a Directive cannot invoke it against an individual, ie direct effects not to be used to worsen the position of an individual. Neither goes as far to protect the rights of individuals to the same extent as would be achieved by the extension of horizontal direct effects to Directives. More recently, in the case of *Pfeiffer* v *Rotes Kreuz* (cases C-397–401/01) the ECJ has confirmed that national courts are bound to interpret national law so far as possible to achieve the result sought by a directive taking into account national law as a whole. That is, as opposed to narrowly looking at a particular national provision. The denial of horizontal effects of Directives by the ECJ has though been confirmed in the case of *Dori* (C-91/92). A case which appeared to introduce horizontal effects is *Mangold* (C-144/04) but it is suggested that this merely extends the *von Colson* sympathetic interpretation principle to general principles of the EU, which concerned in the case itself, the general principle of no discrimination.

A significant alternative development by the ECJ is the use of general provisions of the Treaty, Arts 5 and 189 EC (now 4(3) TEU and 288 TFEU) originally in the *Francovich* case (6 and 9/90) to impose liability on the state for the non-implementation of Directives. This has been extended to other breaches of EU law obligations by Member States. In *Francovich*, the relevant Directive was held to be not capable of giving rise to direct effects, but the requirements of the effective and uniform application of Community (now EU) law gave rise to a liability on the part of the state to compensate for its failure to implement the Directive where the Directive had conferred rights on individuals and that there was a link between the breach and the damage caused. It does, however, take the emphasis away from the difficulty caused by the lack of horizontal direct effects of Directives. *Francovich* has now been followed by the *Brasserie du Pêcheur* case and *Factortame III* (46 and 48/93) in which the ECJ held that all manner of breaches of Community (now EU) law by all three arms of state could lead to liability to individuals. Thus it expands the circumstances which might give rise to liability in cases where there would be no rights because either there are no horizontal direct effects or even no direct effects at all. But the focus has been moved to the seriousness of the breach. *Factortame III* introduced the revised criteria that the breach must be analogous to that applied to liability of the EC (now EU) institutions under Art 288 EC (now 340(2) TFEU). This is known as the Shöppenstedt Formula and in order for liability to arise on the part of the Member State, there must have been a sufficiently serious breach of a superior rule of law designed for the protection of individuals. This has provoked further case law to help decide how serious a breach is required for Member States to incur liability. *British Telecom* (C-392/93) takes a less generous view of what constitutes a breach but this can be contrasted with the *Hedley Lomas* case (C-5/94) where a mere infringement will invoke potential liability. Thus, if there is a breach, Member States must compensate according to the principles established in *Francovich*. Further, the *Wagner Miret* case (C-334/92) creates a bridge or link between *Marleasing* and *Francovich* because the ECJ states that if Member States can't construe national law to read in conformity, which is a distinct possibility as a result either of the court being incapable or unwilling, it must be assumed that Member States nevertheless intended to comply with its EU law obligations. Thus, if there is a breach, Member States must compensate according to the principles established in *Francovich*. In other words, a *von Colson* failure under EU law should not be the end of the litigation line. There is also a development which, whilst not providing rights directly enforceable between individuals, does allow an individual to rely on the provisions of a Directive not implemented by a Member State in a defence action between individuals. In *CIA Security v Signalson* (C-194/94), CIA was able to rely on the Directive's requirement that Member States notify the Commission to get clearance for national technical standards, in an action by a competitor accusing them of not meeting legal requirements. Belgium had not notified the Commission; thus their standards were held to be in applicable and thus CIA did not have to meet them. The case of *Unilever v Central Foods* (C-443/98) confirms this development. In these cases, a Directive which imposes an obligation on the Member States has been used to incidentally prevent reliance on national law not complying with that Directive. The Directive itself is not enforced against an individual.

It may be concluded that the difficulties caused by the *Marshall* (152/84) decision, whilst not overcome, have been mitigated in most other circumstances.

Question 5

As part of its social programme, under Art 157 TFEU , the Council adopted two (fictitious) Directives on 1 January 2009. The first Directive 2009/1 provides inter alia that 'Member States shall take such steps as they consider appropriate to encourage employers to adopt the same pension arrangements for men and women doing the same kind of work'. The second Directive 2009/2 provides that 'Member States shall ensure that employers do not discriminate between men and women doing the same kind of work in respect of holiday entitlement.'

Member States were given two years in which to implement both Directives. At the present time (January 2011) the UK has taken no steps to implement either Directive.

In July 2010, a Local Authority Purchasing Department engaged Mrs Evans and Mr Rees as clerks. Their work is the same and they are paid the same. However, Mr Rees' contract of employment provides that he is entitled to five weeks' holiday a year and is included in the company's own pension scheme, whereas Mrs Evans' contract of employment provides that she is entitled to three weeks' holiday a year and is excluded from the company's pension scheme.

In January 2011, the Local Authority Purchasing Department engaged a further clerk, Mrs Jones, who is employed on the same terms as Mrs Evans.

Mrs Evans and Mrs Jones are unhappy with their contracts of employment. Advise Mrs Evans, who made a claim in December 2010, and Mrs Jones who now claims, whether there are any provisions of EC law on which they could rely in an action brought before an English court or tribunal.

How would your advice be different if the place of employment at which they were working had been privatised?

Commentary

This question concerns the rights provided by two Directives and the ability of individuals to rely on these rights directly before the courts of their own country as a result of the fact that the Member State has not implemented the Directives within the time period for implementation. In this question and questions similar to this which you might be set for term work or in exams, you may ignore the fact that there may be real Directives covering the same ground or providing the same or similar rights. These fictitious Directives are designed to test your knowledge of the principles learned in your studies but it may also be possible that real Directives are actually used on your particular course. Whichever are used, the method suggested below remains the same.

It is necessary to discuss direct effects and the problems associated with the direct effects of Directives and where necessary, the alternative remedies where direct effects are not found to exist and in a novel development in this problem where a claim is made in respect of Directives which do not yet need to be implemented. In order to provide a solution you should identify the issues or particular problems arising as a result of the facts of the case. Then apply the legal rules to the issues and come to conclusions on each issue. Where helpful or necessary you should introduce any relevant case law to come to a conclusion on the problems or aspects of it.

Answer plan

- State relevant/material facts
- Law: **Art 288 TFEU** Directives and doctrine of direct effects
- Satisfaction of direct effects criteria for both Directives
- **Art 157 TFEU** and previous case law on meaning of pay
- Private employers and horizontal direct effects
- Alternative remedies under *von Colson*, *Francovich* and *Mangold*

Suggested answer

The facts here are that there are two Directives which have not been implemented by the UK which provide rights in respect of pensions and holiday entitlement for workers. Both Directives should have been implemented by 1 January 2011. One complaint relates to discrimination from July 2010 and the other from January 2011. In the claims by Mrs Evans and Mrs Jones, they claim discrimination relating to pension arrangements and paid holiday entitlement.

The applicable law for these claims is Art 288 TFEU which requires Member States to achieve a required result when implementing Directives and the doctrine of direct effects which will allow individuals to enforce EU rights before their national courts. The further developments by the ECJ of indirect effects and state liability will also need to be considered as well as the case of *Mangold*, which provides that in certain circumstances Directives where implementation periods have not expired may nevertheless help determine the outcome of a case in favour of individuals before the national courts.

It would be useful to briefly define direct effects and the particular considerations applicable in respect of Directives. Directives can give rise to direct effects providing they satisfy the criteria as laid down in *Van Gend en Loos* (26/62) and subsequent cases. The special concerns of Directives and the time limits given for their implementation were considered in *Publico Ministero* v *Ratti* (148/78) which concerned the prosecution by the Italian authorities for breaches of national law concerning product labelling. Mr Ratti had complied with two Directives; however, the expiry period for implementation of one of which had not been reached. The Court held he could rely on the one for which the time period had expired provided it satisfied the other requirements, but not for the Directive whose implementation period had not expired. So, when the time period has expired an individual can rely on the Directive if it fulfils the criteria. The case of *Verbond van Nederlandse Ondernemingen* (51/76) extended the situation to where a Directive had been implemented but that implementation was not faithful to the requirement of the Directive. The Court of Justice held that to deny the rights of individuals would be to weaken the effectiveness of Community (now Union) obligations and that individuals helped to ensure that Member States kept within the realms of the discretion granted. In the case of *Marshall* (152/84), the ECJ held, however, that Directives could not be enforced against other individuals but could only be enforced vertically against the state to whom they were addressed. The more recent case of *Mangold* (C-144/04) however, suggests that under certain circumstances it may not be necessary to wait for the implementation period to have expired for individuals to obtain help from the rights contained in a Directive.

So, with the facts and law established the claims of the two workers must be considered.

Mrs Evans and Mrs Jones seek to rely on both Directives, Mrs Evans from July 2010 and Mrs Jones from January 2011. It is necessary to know whether in the absence of the UK implementing legislation at the material time they can rely directly on the Directives to give them rights enforceable in the national courts. To determine this the criteria adopted by the ECJ must be applied. Two questions arise, both of which must be answered. They are: have the time limits for the implementation of the Directives expired, and are the provisions relevant directly effective?

Only if the time limit has expired can the Directives be relied on, except in the indirect and narrow circumstances of the *Mangold* decision of the ECJ, discussed further below. So in respect of any claim to rely on either of the Directives before January 2011 the time limits will not have expired and the claim will fail. The UK should have implemented by 1 January 2011. Therefore, applying the *Ratti* (148/78) case, when the first claim was made the time limit had not expired and therefore the Directive cannot give rise to direct effects at that time but only after the implementation period had expired, although the *Mangold* judgment might apply. It will be considered also at the end of the answer.

The time limit had expired for the second claim made in January 2011, ie Mrs Jones' claim, so we can move on and consider whether both Directives can give rise to direct effects.

The claim in respect of equal pensions is covered by the first Directive, but does it satisfy the criteria for direct effects? Is it clear, precise and unconditional, etc? The answer to this is probably that it is not clear enough given the words 'Member States shall take such steps as they consider appropriate to encourage'. Therefore, there will not be direct effects and the Directive cannot be relied upon before the national courts; see generally the cases of *Van Gend en Loos* (26/62) and *Van Duyn* (41/74).

The second Directive relates to the holiday entitlement. Does it satisfy the criteria of direct effects? Yes, the Directive is clear, precise, legally perfect, complete and requires no further legislative intervention or implementation. It imposes a clear and unconditional obligation on Member States to ensure that employers do not discriminate between men and women doing the same kind of work in respect of holiday entitlement. The word 'shall' is a clear obligation. The provision therefore meets the requirements for direct effect, and can be relied on before a national court.

Alternatively it may be argued that as pensions have been held to constitute pay which is covered by Art 157 TFEU, a claim is therefore not dependent on the Directive and can be lodged relying on Art 157 TFEU itself, which is clear and precise and has been held to give rise to direct effects in the case of *Defrenne* v *Sabena (No 2)* (43/75) and applied to pensions in the case of *Worringham* v *Lloyds Bank Ltd* (69/80). Whether holiday entitlements could also be interpreted to be pay is uncertain as there is no previous case which has considered this. The case of *Garland* (12/81) held that low fare travel facilities for the family of ex-workers could be considered to be pay under Art 119 (now 157 TFEU), but whether this would extend to holiday entitlement is not guaranteed although it is likely.

In respect of the holiday entitlements, other remedies may be available using the *von Colson* (14/83) line of case law. The ECJ held in *von Colson* that, although a Directive may not be horizontally directly effective, the Member States' courts should take the provisions of the Directive into account when applying national law. With the second Directive, however, there are no rights in national law, so a national court cannot make an interpretation according to EU law. In these circumstances the *Marleasing* (C-106/89) and *Koplinghuis* (80/86) cases should be applied to state that there are general obligations under Arts 4(3) TEU and 288 TFEU (ex 10 and 249 EC) for the Member States to ensure compliance with EU law. If, for whatever reason, the national courts can not or will not interpret national law to read in compliance, the case of *Francovich* (C-6 and 9/90) might apply to obtain damages for the failure to implement the Directive. If an individual suffers damage as a result of the failure of a Member State to implement a Directive, the Member State may be liable to pay damages, if the Directive itself defined and conferred a right on individuals, the content of which was clear and not open to differing interpretations (*British Telecommunications* (C-392/93)). The fact that the UK has not taken any steps to implement the Directives by the prescribed time has been held by the Court of Justice to be sufficient to find a sufficiently serious breach of EU law (*Dillenkofer* (C-178,179,189 and 190/94)). It may well be, therefore, that both Mrs Jones and Mrs Evans have a claim for compensation against the UK. Any damages they do obtain must compensate them in full for losses directly incurred because of the breach (*Bonifaci* (C-94 and 95/95)). Finally, *Mangold* (C-144/04) suggests that the general principles may give rise to horizontal direct effects but this judgment requires further confirmation and does not apply to Directives.

Two more recent cases lend further support to the sympathetic interpretation of *von Colson* but also mark a further novel development by the Court of Justice. The cases of *Mangold* and *Lindorfer* (C-144/04 and C-227/04) do encourage national law to take any measures they can to provide for the rights in EU law regardless of the state of national law but they also suggest, in particular the

Mangold case, that despite the fact that a Directive's implementation period had not expired it may be possible to nevertheless achieve the requirements of the Directive. In the case, the ECJ held that despite the fact that the Directive was past its implementation date, the principle breached by the Member State was discrimination which was a general principle of EC law. Hence then it could not be affected by the transposition period of a directive which provided a framework in which the general principle was applied. Thus the general principle applied, not the Directive. The argument in the case was that both a strict application of Art 6 of Directive 2000/78 and the application of the general principle would have the same result; therefore, in order to get over difficulties of transition period or the lack of direct effects, it was better to use the general principle. This would help both claims which were premature but also where the Directive for whatever reason gave rise neither to direct effects nor indirect effects. In this case, equality of treatment between men and women is most certainly a general principle stated previously in the preamble to the EC Treaty and now Art 2 TEU which would lead to the claim by Mrs Jones succeeding.

In answer to the final part of the question relating to the status of the Local Authority purchasing department as a private concern it can be generally stated that the Court of Justice has repeatedly emphasised that direct effects of Directives only arise as against the Member States, and not against private individuals (see *Marshall* (152/84) and *Dori* (C-91/92)), thus none of the claims would succeed here. However, whilst Directives cannot give rise to horizontal direct effects, Treaty Articles can, so a claim for equal pensions provisions will succeed if lodged under Art 157 TFEU , as discussed above and in this case also the *Mangold* and *Lindorfer* cases could apply to achieve the same result.

In conclusion, there is such an array of remedies available to individuals under EU law today, that both claims would in all likelihood succeed.

Further reading

Brinkhorst, L, 'Casenote on the *Grad* and *SACE* decisions' (1971) 8 CML Rev 380.

Drake, S, 'Twenty Years after "von Colson": the Impact of "Indirect Effect" on the Protection of the Individual's Community Rights' (2005) 30 EL Rev 329.

Easson, A, 'The Direct Effect of EEC Directives' (1979) 28 ICLQ 319.

Nassimpian, D, 'And We Keep on Meeting: (De)fragmenting State Liability' (2007) 32 EL Rev 819.

Pescatore, P, 'The Doctrine of "Direct Effect": An Infant Disease of Community Law' (1983) 8 EL Rev 155.

Prechal, S, 'Member State Liability and Direct Effect: What's the Difference After All?' (2006) 17 EBLR 299.

Prechal, S and De Vries, S, 'Seamless Web of Judicial Protection in the Internal Market' (2009) 34(1) EL Rev 5.

Schermers, H, 'No Direct Effect for Directives' (1997) 3(4) EPL 527.

Steiner, J, 'From Direct Effects to *Francovich*: Shifting Means of Enforcement of Community Law' (1993) 18 EL Rev 3.

Tridimas, T, 'Liability for Breach of Community Law: Growing Up and Mellowing Down?' (2001) 38 CML Rev 301.

Winter, J, 'Direct Applicability and Direct Effect; Two Distinct and Different Concepts in Community Law' (1972) 9 CML Rev.

4

The Supremacy of EU Law and its Reception in the Member States

Introduction

The subject matter of this chapter is one which should be clear immediately. It is likely that many of you reading this will already have considered this topic from the national point of view in constitutional or public law courses. Inevitably, questions on this topic in EU courses in the UK will most likely concentrate on the relationship between the EU and the UK and many will involve a consideration of the reasons for the supremacy of EU law before looking at the reception of EU law in the UK. Some questions, however, may look at these two aspects independently. Additionally, and depending on whether a consideration of the reception of EU law in other Member States has been covered in your course, a look at the reception in one or two or more other Member States may be undertaken and examined.

Both the legal arguments for supremacy and the political logic will often be considered in establishing the reasoning for EU law supremacy.

The first question in this chapter concentrates on the reasons for EU law supremacy from the point of view of the Union and in the view of the ECJ.

Question 1

Is it the case that 'the doctrine of the supremacy of EU law is a logical if not a necessary inference from EU Treaties'?

Commentary

This clearly concerns the now well-established doctrine or principle of constitutional law of supremacy. As with most questions, a definition of the subject matter of the question would be required. So, with the above question you need to state clearly and concisely what you understand by the phrase 'the doctrine of the supremacy of EU law', ie that established by the Court of Justice in the leading cases, *Van Gend en Loos* (26/62) and *Costa* v *ENEL* (6/64).

You are then asked whether it 'is the case that it is a logical if not a necessary inference' and you have to determine exactly what this cryptic part of the question is demanding for an answer. It suggests the supremacy of EU law is *logical*, but that it is not a *necessary inference* from the Treaties. You must address both these contentions.

Although the word logical appears first I would address the part about the inference first, because this refers you to the Treaty provisions. It also appears to me to make sense to consider whether the Treaties do provide for the supremacy before having to consider the logic of whether EU law is supreme. Then, finally, you must decide, if it is the case, how the Treaties logically provide for supremacy. This should be done with reference to any assistance from the Treaty and from the jurisprudence of the ECJ in which statements on supremacy are made.

Note that if the **Constitutional Treaty** had entered into force, the supremacy of EU law would have been expressly stated (in **Art I-6**); however, such an express statement was toned down for the **2007 Lisbon Reform Treaty** which has simply added a **Declaration (No 17)** to the Treaty referring to the well settled case law on primacy as confirmed by an **Opinion of the Legal Service of the Council (11197/07 of 22 June 2007)**. The declaration on primacy therefore is still not a bold express statement contained within the Treaties but tucked away in an oblique reference. The answer needs to reflect this.

Answer plan

- Definition and Treaties' position on supremacy of EU law
- Consideration of the leading cases: *Van Gend en Loos*, *Costa* v *ENEL* and *Simmenthal*
- Specific aspects of Constitutional law: *Internationale Handelsgesellschaft* case
- A logical if not necessary inference
- Consideration of the *Factortame* cases

Suggested answer

The question has already hinted that the EU Treaties do not expressly provide for supremacy, ie there is at present no Treaty Article which clearly states that EU law is supreme, although this would have been different if the Constitutional Treaty had been ratified by all Member States and brought into force. However, it is still the case that by a direct reading of either of the EU or TFEU Treaties, you might not necessarily infer that EU law is supreme. However, whilst there is no express statement of supremacy in the Treaties, it can be argued that some of the articles of the Treaties impliedly or logically require supremacy. Thus, a conclusion as to whether EU law supremacy is to be inferred from the Treaties depends upon a consideration of some of its provisions. For example, see Art 4(3) TFEU, the good faith or fidelity clause; Art 18 TFEU, the general prohibition of discrimination on the grounds of nationality; Art 288 TFEU in respect of the direct applicability of Regulations; Art 344 TFEU, the obligation of Member States to submit only to Treaty dispute resolution and Art 260 TFEU, the requirement to comply with rulings of the Court of Justice. From these Treaty Articles, you could conclude that EU law infers supremacy but cannot state that the Treaty expressly or categorically imposes it.

It is more through the decisions and interpretation of the Court of Justice that the reasons and logic for the supremacy of EU law were developed. The Court of Justice's view on this is quite straightforward. From its case law, notably *Van Gend* (26/62), *Costa v ENEL* (6/64) and *Simmenthal* (106/77), it is first of all clear that EU law is assumed to be an autonomous legal order which is related to international law and national law but nevertheless distinct from them.

The *Van Gend en Loos* case affirmed the Court's jurisdiction in interpreting EU legal provisions, the object of which is to ensure uniform interpretation in the Member States. The Court of Justice held that the Community (now Union) constitutes a new legal order of international law for the benefit of which the States have limited their sovereign rights.

Further elaboration of the new legal order in *Van Gend* was given in *Costa v ENEL*. The case raised the issue of whether a national court should refer to the Court of Justice if it considers Community (now EU) law may be applicable or, in the view of the Italian Government, simply apply the subsequent national law. The Court of Justice stressed the autonomous legal order of Community (now EU) law in contrast with ordinary international treaties. It held that the EEC Treaty has 'created its own legal system which became an integral part of the legal systems of the Member States and which their courts are bound to apply. By creating a Community of unlimited duration, having its own institutions, its own personality, its own legal capacity and more particularly real powers stemming from a limitation of sovereignty or a transfer of powers from the states to the Community the Member States have limited their sovereign rights and have created a body of law to bind their nationals and themselves.'

The Court also established that Community (now EU) law takes priority over all conflicting provisions of national law whether passed before or after the Community (now Union) measure in question:

> The integration into the laws of each Member State of provisions which derive from the Community, and more generally, the terms and spirit of the Treaty, make it impossible for the states, as a corollary, to accord precedence to a unilateral and

subsequent measure over a legal system accepted by them on the basis of reciprocity. Such a measure cannot therefore be inconsistent with that legal system.

That is, a later national law does not overrule an earlier EU law. As additional justifications, the Court of Justice also invoked some of the general provisions of the Treaty: Art 5 EEC (now 4(3) TEU), the requirement to ensure the attainment of the objectives of the Treaty and Art 7 EEC (now 18 TFEU), regarding discrimination, both of which would be breached if subsequent national legislation was to have precedence. Furthermore, the ECJ considered that Art 189 (now 288 TFEU), regarding the binding and direct application of Regulations, would be meaningless if subsequent national legislation could prevail. The Court summed up its position:

> It follows . . . that the law stemming from the treaty, an independent source of law, could not because of its special and original nature, be overridden by domestic legal provisions, however framed, without being deprived of its character as Community law and without the legal basis of the Community itself being called into question.

Therefore, EU law is to be supreme over subsequent national law.

There are two cases which additionally consider the conflict between EU law and national constitutional law.

The *Internationale Handelsgesellschaft* case (11/70) concerned the claim that Community (now Union) levies were contrary to German constitutional law. The German Constitutional Court sought to reserve this question to itself but the ECJ held that the national courts did not possess the power to review Community (now EU) law. The Court of Justice held that if there were no violation of Community (now EU) fundamental rights, the Community (now EU) measures were acceptable, ie there should be no reference to national constitutions to test the validity of Community (now EU) law.

The second case of *Simmenthal* (106/77) arose from a conflict between the Italian constitution and Community (now EU) law. In Italy the constitutional practice existed that the power to disregard or declare invalid a provision of national law was the sole right of the Constitutional Court. A lower court was faced with inconsistency between a Community (now EU) law provision and a national provision but was aware that the national requirement to refer first to the Italian Constitutional Court would have the effect of subrogating Community (now EU) law to national law, inconsistent with existent Community (now EU) case law on the matter in the *Costa v ENEL* (6/64) case. However, disregarding the national law was contrary to constitutional requirements. The Italian magistrate made a reference to the ECJ and asked whether subsequent national measures conflict with Community (now EU) law and must be disregarded without waiting until those measures are formally repealed or declared unconstitutional.

The ECJ firstly declared that the doctrine of direct effects of Community (now EU) legislation was not dependent on any national constitutional provisions but a source of rights in itself. Therefore, national courts which are called upon to apply provisions of Community (now EU) law is under a duty to give full effect to those provisions including a refusal to apply conflicting national legislation, even if adopted subsequently. The ECJ also ruled that directly effective provisions of Community (now EU) law also preclude the valid adoption of new legislative measures to the extent that they would be incompatible with Community (now EU) provisions and that any inconsistent national legislation recognised by national legislatures as having legal effect would deny the effectiveness of the obligations undertaken by the Member State and imperil the existence of the Community (now Union).

In the *Factortame (No 2)* case (C-213/89), the Court of Justice, building on the principle laid down in *Simmenthal* (106/77), ie that a provision of EC (now EU) law must be implemented as effectively as possible, held that a national court must suspend national legislation that may be incompatible with EC (now EU) law until a final determination on its compatibility has been made. In the case of doubt national law should be suspended. The *Factortame (No 2)* case represents another confirmation that national constitutional practices or rules, in this case the doctrine of parliamentary sovereignty in the UK, must not be allowed to stand in the way of a Community (now EU) law right. In the case, this was the clear understanding of the UK national courts that they had no power to set aside or not apply an Act of Parliament. The ECJ held that even if the Community (now EU) law rule was still in dispute, the national procedure should be changed so as not to possibly interfere with the full effectiveness of the Community (now EU) law right.

Hence, the Court of Justice in the cases of *Van Gend en Loos*, *Costa v ENEL* and *Simmenthal*, amongst others, has held that EU law supremacy is a logical conclusion. It can also be inferred from the EU law doctrine of direct effects that EU law should be supreme both because of the transfer of powers from the Member States and by having its own law-making machinery. It must, therefore, have precedence if the Union is going to work. The voluntary limitation of sovereignty and the need for an effective and uniform EU law requires supremacy. To give effect to subsequent national law over and above the Union legal system which Member States have accepted would be inconsistent and illogical. If the Constitutional Treaty had come into force, supremacy of EU law would have been expressly stated. The replacement 2007 Lisbon Treaty has acknowledged supremacy in a rather roundabout way. In Declaration (No 17) it makes reference to the well settled case law which had established EU law supremacy.

Finally, in this context it is worth mentioning the consequences of a Member State not giving primacy to EU law when it should have done. Liability on the part of the state will be incurred, as first established by the Court of Justice in the *Francovich* case (C-6/90) and later confirmed in *Factortame III* (C46 and 48/93).

Question 2

Consider how the Court of Justice's argument for the supremacy of EU law tempers traditional views of international law implementation and the principle that later laws overrule previous laws.

Commentary

This question requires you to consider the reasons for the supremacy of EU law according to the ECJ and to explain the consequences of this supremacy on previous held or valid international law principles. In your answer you need to outline the view of the ECJ or its grounds for stating that EU law should be supreme over the law of the Member States. The question then requires you to compare and contrast this view with the usually traditional relationship between international law and national law and the generally accepted principle that a later rule overrules a previous law. The answer should thus focus on the new legal order created by the founding of the Union which has upset or altered traditional views.

Answer plan

- Union and ECJ argument for supremacy
- Union case law on supremacy
- Incorporation: monism and dualism
- The effect of EU law on national legal orders

Suggested answer

The first thing to consider is the reason why the Court of Justice has explained why EU law should take priority over conflicting national law. Whilst it is the case that there is no express declaration or specific legal base for the supremacy of EU law in the Treaties, it can be argued that some of the articles of the EU Treaties impliedly require primacy; for example, Art 4(3) TEU , the fidelity clause; Art 18 TFEU, the general prohibition of discrimination on the grounds of nationality; Art 288 TFEU, the direct applicability of Regulations; and Art 344 TFEU, the reservation of dispute resolution. If the Constitutional Treaty had come into force, supremacy of EU law would have been expressly stated but its replacement, the 2007 Lisbon Treaty, only indirectly acknowledges this in a Declaration attached to the Treaty. It is through the decisions and interpretation of the Court of Justice that the reasons and logic for the supremacy of EU law have been developed. The Court of Justice's view on this is quite straightforward. From its case law, notably *Van Gend en Loos* (26/62), *Costa* v *ENEL* (6/64) and *Simmenthal* (106/77), it is clear that EU law is assumed to be an autonomous legal order which is related to international law and national law but nevertheless distinct from them.

The *Van Gend en Loos* (26/62) case affirmed the Court's jurisdiction in interpreting EU legal provisions, the object of which is to ensure uniform interpretation in the Member States. The Court of Justice held that the Community (now Union) constitutes a new legal order of international law for the benefit of which the states have limited their sovereign rights.

Further elaboration of the new legal order in *Van Gend* was given in *Costa* v *ENEL* (6/64) in which the Court held:

> By contrast with ordinary international treaties the EEC Treaty has created its own legal system which became an integral part of the legal systems of the Member States and which their courts are bound to apply. By creating a Community of unlimited duration, having its own institutions, its own personality, its own legal capacity and more particularly real powers stemming from a limitation of sovereignty or a transfer of powers from the states to the Community the Member States have limited their sovereign rights and have created a body of law to bind their nationals and themselves.

The Court also established that Community (now EU) law takes priority over all conflicting provisions of national law whether passed before or after the Community (now Union) measure in question by holding that:

> The integration into the laws of each Member State of provisions which derive from the Community, and more generally, the terms and spirit of the Treaty, make it impossible for the states, as a corollary, to accord precedence to a unilateral and subsequent measure over a legal system accepted by them on the basis of reciprocity. Such a measure cannot therefore be inconsistent with that legal system.

That is, a later national law does not overrule an earlier EU law.

The Court summed up its position:

> It follows . . . that the law stemming from the Treaty, an independent source of law, could not because of its special and original nature, be overridden by domestic legal provisions, however framed, without being deprived of its character as Community law and without the legal basis of the Community itself being called into question.

Therefore EU law is to be supreme over subsequent national law.

In *Simmenthal* (106/77), the Court of Justice ruled that national courts, which are called upon to apply provisions of Community (now EU) law, are under a duty to give full effect to those provisions and if necessary to set aside any conflicting provisions of national legislation, even if adopted subsequently. It held that directly effective provisions of Community (now EU) law preclude the valid adoption of new legislative measures to the extent that they would be incompatible with Community (now Union) provisions. Any inconsistent national legislation recognised by national legislatures as having legal effect would deny the effectiveness of the obligations undertaken by the Member State. Therefore, to give effect to subsequent national law over and above the Community (now Union) legal system which Member States have accepted would be inconsistent and imperil the existence of the Community (now Union).

In the *Factortame* case (C-213/89), the Court of Justice, building on the principle laid down in *Simmenthal*, ie that a provision of EC (now EU) law must be implemented as effectively as possible, held that a national court must suspend national legislation that may be incompatible with EC (now EU) law until a final determination on its compatibility has been made. In the case of doubt national law should be suspended.

Next, it is necessary to consider whether the legal position established in the Union upsets traditional international law theories and practices.

Traditional international law implementation conforms to one of two theories of incorporation, either that of monism or dualism. The views of the ECJ contrast with both of these. Monism basically assumes that international law and national law form part of a single world system or hierarchy of laws. This means in relation to the acceptance of international law there would have to be no formal incorporation of international law into the national legal system by legislative transformation. The international law would be self-executing within the nations who adopt the monist position, ie it would be directly applicable within the state. All that is required by such a state to achieve this is a simple assent to, or ratification of, an international treaty.

Dualism, on the other hand, regards international law and national law as belonging to fundamentally different systems of law which exist alongside each other but are distinctly separated, as in watertight compartments. In order to overcome the barrier existing between the two systems, legislation is required to transform rules of international law into the national legal system before it can have any binding effect within the state.

If a Member State conformed to monism, international law joins the national hierarchy of law but enjoys no special status and it can be overruled by later national law. However, there is a presumption that, in the case of inconsistency, there was no intention by the national parliament to be inconsistent unless this was express.

If a Member State continued to adhere to dualism in respect of EU law and there was no transformation, the EU law would remain outside the legal order. However, when transformed it would merely take on the status of national law and would be subject to the usual rules including the view that later laws overrule earlier laws.

The EU legal order, as a new legal order, does not conform to this strict division. For example, Treaty Articles and certain forms of Union legislation, eg Regulations are not transformed in the national legal orders to have validity but are directly applicable, see Art 288 TFEU (ex 249 EC). Member States which previously had conformed to the dualist approach did not in fact transform these types of legislation into the national legal orders but instead simply acceded to the

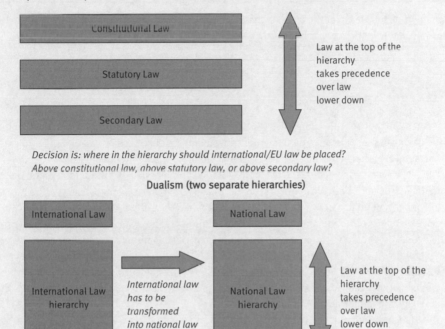

Monism (single hierarchy)

Example of one way in which international/EU law could be interwoven with national law

Constitutional Law

Statutory Law

Secondary Law

Law at the top of the hierarchy takes precedence over law lower down

Decision is: where in the hierarchy should international/EU law be placed?
Above constitutional law, above statutory law, or above secondary law?

Dualism (two separate hierarchies)

International Law

National Law

International Law hierarchy

International law has to be transformed into national law by a national Act

National Law hierarchy

Law at the top of the hierarchy takes precedence over law lower down

Community (now Union) and adopted Treaty Articles and Regulations automatically; see, for example, the UK and Germany. In addition to this, other forms of EU law, whilst not directly applicable, can also have affects in the Member States without transformation in certain circumstances. See the Court of Justice development of the doctrine of direct effects in the cases of *Van Gend en Loos* (26/62), *Van Duyn* (41/74) and *Grad* (9/70).

The traditional view that the later law will prevail was not just limited to an express overrule or inconsistency but also to the implied overruling in cases of inconsistency, whether intentional or not. Implied repeal of earlier law was recognised in both common law and civil law jurisdictions. The case law of *Van Gend en Loos* (26/62), *Costa* v *ENEL* (6/64) and *Simmenthal* (106/77), noted above, contradicts this form of repeal in the EU legal order and which must now be adopted in the Member States, although it has taken some time for this to be accepted in some of the Member States, eg the UK, Germany and France. When in conflict, EU law is supreme regardless of whether it is later or earlier than the national law. Therefore, the principle that later laws overrule earlier laws may still be valid domestically but it is now possible for an earlier EU law to overrule a later national law; see, for example, the case of *Marleasing* (C-106/89) in this respect.

Question 3

Comment on the view that the biggest obstacle to accepting the supremacy of EU law in the UK was and is the doctrine of parliamentary sovereignty.

Commentary

This question concerns the supremacy of EU law and how this was catered for when faced with the difficult constitutional issue of parliamentary sovereignty in the UK.

The subject matter of this question is clear and can be divided into three parts.

First, it is necessary to outline the reasoning for the supremacy of EU law from the Union point of view, largely achieved by considering the leading cases from the Court of Justice.

Secondly, a definition and the consequences of the doctrine of parliamentary sovereignty must be given. Both these parts are reasonably straightforward and would thus be fairly descriptive passages. You should try to be more concise in your description of the meaning and scope of parliamentary sovereignty than for courses in constitutional law but could certainly employ much of the work done for this topic in that subject. Certainly you should consider the limitations which have been acknowledged and point out the doctrine of parliamentary sovereignty itself is subject to criticism and qualification.

The third part requires more thought, especially in structuring your answer. Set out the issues to be tackled and explain that at first sight these two doctrines appear to be incompatible. You should then consider the European Communities Act 1972 and whether this has reconciled the two doctrines. Finally, consider how the UK courts have considered this relationship. The latest cases should now be overriding the dicta of older cases, eg the judgment of Lord Bridge in *Factortame* (C-213/89) is of more use than the judgments of Lord Denning in *McCarthys* (129/79) and Lord Diplock in *Garland* (12/81), and the more recent case of *R Jackson* v *AG* ([2006] AC 262) is now instructive.

Answer plan

- Summarise Union position on supremacy of EU law
- Outline UK doctrine of parliamentary sovereignty
- The European Communities Act 1972
- UK cases: *McCarthys, Garland, Factortame* and *Jackson*

Suggested answer

The EU Treaties do not contain a specific legal base or express declaration for the supremacy of EU law but some articles logically imply supremacy. If the Constitutional Treaty had come into force, supremacy of EU law would have been expressly stated, and the replacement, 2007 Lisbon Treaty only indirectly acknowledges this supremacy in Declaration No 17. Those presently implying supremacy are: Art 4(3) TEU, the fidelity clause; Art 18 TFEU prohibiting discrimination on the grounds of nationality; Art 288 TFEU providing for the direct applicability of Regulations; and Art 344 TFEU ensuring Union dispute resolution autonomy. The Court of Justice has developed the reasons and logic for the supremacy of EU law.

The *Van Gend en Loos (26/62)* case affirmed the Court's exclusive jurisdiction in interpreting EU legal provisions to ensure uniform interpretation in the Member States. In the *Costa v ENEL (6/64)* case, its autonomous nature was emphasised. The case questioned whether a national court should refer to the ECJ if it considers Community (now EU) law may be applicable or in the view of the Italian Government, simply apply the subsequent national law. According to the ECJ the voluntary limitation of sovereignty and the need for an effective and uniform Community (now EU) law requires its supremacy. To give effect to subsequent national law over and above the EU legal system would be inconsistent.

To summarise the Union view on supremacy according to the Court of Justice is that EU law, because of its unique nature, denies the Member States the right to resolve conflicts of law by reference to their own rules or constitutional provisions. EU law obtains its supremacy because of the transfer of state power and sovereignty to the Union by the Member States in those areas agreed. Furthermore, the Member States have provided the Union with legislative powers to enable it to perform its tasks. There would be no point in such a transfer of power if the Member States could annul or suspend the effect of EU law by later national law or provisions of the constitutions. If that were allowed to be the case, the existence of the EU legal order and the Union itself would be called into question.

A precondition of the existence and functioning of the Union is the uniform and consistent application of EU law and the EU legal order in all the Member States. It can only achieve such an effect if it takes precedence over national law. Therefore, the legal and logical consequences of this are that any provision of national law which conflicts with EU law must be invalid.

The meaning of parliamentary sovereignty must now be considered.

Basically, in the terms of Dicey, the doctrine of parliamentary sovereignty means that there are no legal limitations of Parliament and it has the right to make or unmake any law whatsoever. Further, no person or body is recognised as having a right to override or set aside the legislation of Parliament. The doctrine also implies that it is impossible to bind future Parliaments. Any subsequent Act expressly or impliedly overrides a prior Act and even international treaties can be expressly overridden by municipal law. See generally the cases of *Vauxhall Estates* ([1932] 1 KB 733), *Ellen Street Estates* ([1934] 1 KB 590) and *Mortesen v Peters* ([1906] 8 F(J) 93) to support these contentions. There is no constitutional role for UK courts: they cannot review the validity of Acts passed by Parliament.

They must enforce and apply Acts of Parliament equally. See the cases of *Burmah Oil Co.* v *Lord Advocate* ([1965] AC 85) and *British Railways Board* v *Pickin* ([1974] AC 765) to support these views.

There are, however, limitations to parliamentary sovereignty, most notably those devolving power externally and concerned with a change of state. Dicey admitted that there were political limits to the sovereign power of Parliament. Parliament could abdicate or divest itself of power to another body. This may be irreversible and although it would be possible to pass an amending Act it would be politically impossible to regain power once surrendered, unless by the acceptance of the entity to whom power had been surrendered. Dicey was referring not only to complete abdication but also to partial abdication or transfer of powers.

The arguments of abdication of political sovereignty must also apply in favour of the European Communities and now Union. The issue thus focuses on how the UK tried to resolve the clash of parliamentary sovereignty and Community (now EU) law supremacy. The European Communities Act 1972 (ECA 1972) was passed in an attempt to overcome this.

In contrast to the earlier practice of incorporation, the ECA 1972 did not reproduce the whole of the Treaties or subsequent secondary legislation as Acts of Parliament. If this was so, the words of any future Act could override the prior Treaty. The Community Treaties were adopted by a simple assent. The Act therefore impliedly recognises the unique new legal system and is regarded as a very special, even constitutional, form of UK legislation by its attempt to bind future Parliaments. It had still, however, to ensure that Community (now EU) law was supreme, not only as against prior UK legislation but also future UK legislation.

Section 2(1) recognises the legal validity and direct applicability of Community and now Union Treaties and Regulations already existing and provides that all such future Community and now EU legal provisions shall also be recognised. The subsection recognises the doctrine of direct effects and allows for future developments by the Court of Justice. This is termed in the Act as 'enforceable Community right . . . and similar expressions'.

Section 2(4) is the subsection which recognises the supremacy of Community and now EU law and therefore concerns sovereignty. Any such provision and any enactment passed or to be passed (that refers to any Act of Parliament past or future) shall be construed and have effect subject to the foregoing provisions of this section. That is a reference back to the entire section and in particular s 2(1) and means any future Act of Parliament must be construed in such a way as to give effect to the enforceable Community (Union) rights. This is achieved by denying effectiveness to any national legislation passed later which is in conflict with Community (EU) law.

Section 3(1) instructs the courts to refer questions on the interpretation and hence the supremacy of Community (EU) law to the Court of Justice if the UK courts cannot solve the problem themselves by reference to previous Court of

Justice rulings. This follows the *Costa v ENEL* (6/64) ruling and is backed up by s 3(2), which requires the courts to judicially follow decisions of the Court of Justice on any question of Community (EU) law. This would include direct effects and supremacy although it does not expressly say so.

Therefore, it can be argued, the combination of ss 2(1) and 2(4) with the control of ss 3(1) and 3(2) achieve the essential requirements of the recognition of direct effects and the supremacy of EU law for past and future UK legislation.

It is contended that the 1972 Act purports to bind future Parliaments and negates the doctrine of parliamentary sovereignty. However, the effect of a cleverly drafted piece of legislation may be negated by the judicial reception it receives in the courts. The acid test of any piece of legislation is the interpretation given to it in the courts and in order to assess its worth we must consider the case law of the UK courts.

As yet the courts have made no express statement on how these two seemingly conflicting doctrines can be resolved. Whilst a number of cases have provided views, expressed as *obiter dicta*, on what they might do in the case of an intention on the part of Parliament to legislate in conflict with the Community, it has not yet arisen in reality (see the judgments of Lord Denning in *McCarthys* ([1979] ICR 785) and Lord Diplock in *Garland* ([1983] 2 AC 751). A clear statement on this topic is contained in the case of *Factortame (No 2)* ([1991] 1 AC 603 at 645). In this case Lord Bridge commented on the view that the earlier decisions in favour of Community (EU) law were an attack on parliamentary sovereignty. He considered that if the supremacy of Community (EU) law over the national law of Member States was not always inherent in the EEC Treaty, it was certainly well established in the jurisprudence of the Court of Justice long before the UK joined the Community. He thus considered that Parliament accepted the limitation of its sovereignty when it enacted the ECA 1972 was entirely voluntary. He concluded that, under the terms of the 1972 Act, it has always been clear that it was the duty of a UK court to override any rule of national law found to be in conflict with any directly enforceable rule of Community (EU) law. According supremacy to Community (EU) law in those areas to which they apply was therefore nothing new. National courts must not be inhibited by rules of national law from granting interim relief in appropriate cases because it is no more than a logical recognition of supremacy. In *R v Secretary of State for Employment, ex parte EOC* ([1995] 1 CMLR 395), the House of Lords confirmed the conclusion reached in *Factortame* and held that in judicial review proceedings the UK courts could declare an Act of Parliament to be incompatible with EC (EU) law, although this does not extend to being able to annul the UK Act of Parliament, nor indeed command a government to repeal the act or compel or command a minister to change the law. However, in the Metric Martyrs case (*Thoburn v Sunderland City Council* [2002] 1 CMLR 50), the High Court expressed the view that the ECA 1972 had acquired a constitutional quality which prevented implied repeal.

Finally, in a 2005 case, *Jackson*, Lord Steyn acknowledged that the supremacy of Parliament remained a general principle of the EU constitution, but that it was a common law principle established by the judges in a different era. This suggests that it is viewed as a doctrine which might need qualification by the courts in future. In respect of the ECA 1972, in the same case Lord Hope, suggested that even an intentional or express repudiation of EU law might not be followed by the new Supreme Court and expressed the view that whilst Parliament did not actually say that it could not enact legislation which was in conflict with Community law, in practice his opinion was that was the effect of s 2(1) when read with s 2(4) of the ECA 1972.

The conclusions are that it is true that the ECA 1972 has transferred sovereignty in certain areas as agreed for an indefinite period, but whether it has completely overruled the doctrine cannot be stated. The real problem in trying to reconcile these doctrines is that legal reasoning isn't fully reconcilable with the practical realities of Union membership. Whilst it may be *legally* possible to repeal the 1972 Act and leave the Union, that is *practically* and *politically* untenable. Thus, as far as membership of the Union is concerned, the doctrine of parliamentary sovereignty is, at least, in abeyance, if not completely undermined. As such, the UK seems to have gone further than some of the other Member States. Areas of law still the exclusive jurisdiction of the UK are still subject to the full weight of the doctrine. Despite the many views expressed about the UK's future in the EU, it is incredibly improbable that any political party in the UK capable of forming a working government, would even contemplate repealing the ECA 1972 and withdrawing from the EU.

Question 4

How does the European Communities Act 1972 ensure that EU law which is directly effective or directly applicable has that status in the United Kingdom and prevails over conflicting UK law? What problems, if any, have been experienced in practice in attaining the aims of the Act?

 ## Commentary

This is a question which concentrates on the practical clash of EU and national legislation and puts the theories of the last question to the test. It requires you to consider the legal argument of how membership was accommodated in the UK legal system and the reception of Community (now EU) law in the UK courts.

First, you should look in detail at the Act and how it sets out to achieve its aims. Then you need to see how it works in practice, ie to look at how the UK courts have interpreted and applied it.

Whilst there are a number of earlier cases which discuss the perceived relationship and the effect of the **European Communities Act 1972 (ECA 1972)**, it would be better to concentrate on the latest cases which provide a truer reflection of the present situation. However, a brief review of earlier case law would still be acceptable.

Answer plan

- UK incorporation of Community (EU) law
- The ECA 1972, ss 2 and 3
- UK case law: *McCarthys*, *Garland*, *Marshall*, *Duke*, *Pickstone* and *Litster*
- The *Factortame* litigation and *Jackson* case

Suggested answer

EU law implementation in the UK is primarily concerned with how the 1972 Act observes and takes account of such well-established EU law concepts or doctrines of direct effects and supremacy of EU law and the difficulties in respect of sovereignty.

In contrast to the earlier practice of incorporation of international law treaties which followed the dualist approach to international law, the ECA 1972 did not reproduce the whole of the Community Treaties or subsequent secondary Community and now EU legislation as Acts of Parliament. If this was so, the words of any future UK Act could impliedly override and thus repeal the inconsistent part or parts of the Treaty as it would simply have the status of any other UK Act of Parliament.

All prior Community (EU) legislation was adopted by a simple Act of Accession, except for those Directives which required national law implementation. The Act therefore impliedly recognised the unique new legal system and is now regarded as a very special form of UK legislation by its attempt to bind future Parliaments.

The most important provisions of the Act, which concern the acceptance of Community and now EU law, are as follows. Section 2(1) recognises the direct applicability and thus validity of Community (EU) law Treaty provisions and Regulations and arguably the doctrine of direct effects. This is termed in the Act as 'enforceable Community right and similar expressions'. Thus those rights or duties which are, as a matter of Community (EU) law, directly applicable or effective are to be given legal effect in the UK. It also provides that all such future Community (EU) legal provisions shall also be given legal effect and enforced and followed in the UK.

Section 2(2) allows for the implementation of Community (EU) obligations such as Directives or Decisions, which are not automatically applicable in the

UK, via Orders in Council or Statutory Instruments. The Executive has power to make secondary legislation to give effect to Community (EU) obligations and any arising developments.

Section 2(4) recognises the supremacy of Community (EU) law and therefore concerns sovereignty. It states that any such provision and any enactment passed or to be passed (that refers to any Act of Parliament past or future) shall be construed and have effect subject to the foregoing provisions of this section. That is a reference back to the entire section, in particular s 2(1), and means any future Act of Parliament must be construed in such a way as to give effect to the enforceable Community (EU) rights in existence. This is achieved by denying effectiveness to any national legislation passed later which is in conflict. This is further controlled by the directions to the UK courts. Section 3(1) instructs the courts to refer questions on the interpretation and hence the supremacy of Community (EU) Law to the Court of Justice if the UK courts cannot solve the problem themselves by reference to previous Court of Justice rulings. This follows the *Costa* v *ENEL* (6/64) ruling and is backed up by s 3(2) which requires the courts to follow decisions of the Court of Justice on any question of Community (EU) law. Therefore, it can be argued the combination of ss 2(1) and 2(4) with the control of ss 3(1) and (2) achieve the essential requirements of the recognition of direct effects and the supremacy of EU law for past and future UK legislation.

The views of the courts in decided case law is thus now paramount here because the application of EU law is dependent on the national judiciary.

The most important of the earlier cases is *McCarthys Ltd* v *Smith* ([1979] ICR 785) in which Lord Denning MR expressed the view that it was the court's bounden duty to give priority to Community law under ss 2(1) and (4) of the ECA 1972 in cases of deficient or inconsistent national law, ie unintentional inconsistency. Lord Denning (in comments made *obiter*) thought that with regard to an express or intentional repudiation of the Treaty or expressly acting inconsistently, the courts would be bound to follow the express and clear intent of Parliament to repudiate the Treaty or a section of it by the subsequent Act. Following a reference made to the ECJ (case 129/79), the Court of Appeal ([1981] QB 180 at 199) later confirmed Community (EU) law is now part of UK law and whenever there is any inconsistency Community (EU) law has priority.

In *Garland* v *BREL* ([1983] 2 AC 751), UK and Community (EU) law were regarded by the House of Lords as clearly inconsistent. A reference was made to the Court of Justice (12/81), which ruled that Community law covered the situation in the case. The House of Lords considered themselves bound in view of the Court of Justice ruling and ECA 1972 to interpret the national law in such a way as not to be inconsistent with the UK obligations under Community law. They concluded (*obiter*) that UK courts should interpret UK law consistently, no matter how wide a departure from the words of the UK Act the interpretation needed to be.

In a case brought at roughly the same time as the *Marshall* (152/84) case, *Duke v GEC Reliance* ([1988] AC 618), also dealing with equal retirement ages but involving a private employer, the House of Lords rightly concluded that the Directive itself could not be enforced by Mrs Duke, against individuals, ie it had no horizontal direct effects. However, when seeking an alternative solution via the ECA, the House of Lords held ss 2(4) and (1) only refer to directly effective or directly applicable Community law so that Mrs Duke's claim was defeated. At the time this judgment was considered to be a very backward step by a UK court and seems to uphold the supremacy of the UK Parliament over Community (EU) law.

In the case of *Pickstone v Freemans plc* ([1988] AC 66) the House of Lords followed the advice of the Court of Justice in the *von Colson* (14/83) case to interpret and apply national legislation adopted for implementation of a Directive in conformity with the requirements of Community law, but suggested this could only be done under s 2(4) of the ECA 1972 where the actual words are reasonably capable of being interpreted to read in conformity with EC law.

In the case of *Litster v Forth Dry Dock & Engineering Co Ltd* ([1990] 1 AC 546) the UK secondary legislation which purported to implement the obligations contained in the EEC Council Directive 187/77 was considered to be ambiguous. The Directive did not give rise to direct effects because a private employer was involved. The House of Lords could not achieve a satisfactory result in keeping with the European Directive and the case law of the Court of Justice, by a literal attempt, and concluded that under s 2(4) it must use the Community legislation to interpret the later UK legislation and imply additional provisions to achieve consistency. In *CR Smith Glaziers (Dunfermline) Limited v Commissioners of Customs and Excise*, the House of Lords held that 'It was the duty of a UK court to construe a statute, so far as possible, in conformity with European law.' The case considered the construction of provisions adopted by the Commissioners which did not conform with the terms of the Sixth VAT Directive (77/388). Accordingly, the ECJ held that it was necessary to adopt an alternative interpretation which did conform to it.

Two cases known as *R v Secretary of State for Transport, ex parte Factortame Ltd* (C-213/89 and C-221/89) are particularly important cases in respect of the supremacy of Community (EU) law. A party seeking to rely on Community (EU) law sought an interim injunction against the crown not to apply a disputed national regulation issued under a UK Act whilst the merits of the case were being referred to the Court of Justice. This was something not previously acceptable as courts could not set aside UK law. The House of Lords considered that if Community law rights are to be found to be directly enforceable in favour of the appellants those rights will prevail over the inconsistent national legislation, even if it has been passed later. It was said (*obiter*) that:

This [s 2(4)] has precisely the same effect as if a section were incorporated into [the national statute] which in terms enacted that the provisions [of an Act] were to be without prejudice to the directly enforceable Community rights of nationals of any Member State of the EEC.

Upon the return of the procedural aspect from the Court of Justice, the House of Lords held that, if a national rule precludes a court from granting an interim relief, in order to determine whether there is a conflict between national law and Community (EU) law, the court must set aside that rule: in effect to ignore national law. Lord Bridge considered that if the supremacy of Community law over the national law of Member States was not always inherent in the EEC Treaty, it was certainly well established in the jurisprudence of the Court of Justice long before the UK joined the Community. He concluded that under the terms of the 1972 Act it has always been clear that it was the duty of a UK court to override any rule of national law found to be in conflict with any directly enforceable rule of Community law. Therefore, national courts must not be inhibited by rules of national law from granting interim relief in appropriate cases because it is no more than a logical recognition of supremacy. In *R v Secretary of State for Employment, ex parte EOC* ([1995] 1 CMLR 395), the House of Lords confirmed the conclusion reached in *Factortame* and held that in judicial review proceedings the UK courts could declare an Act of Parliament to be incompatible with EC (EU) law, although this does not extend to being able to annul the UK Act of Parliament nor indeed command a government to repeal the Act or compel or command a minister to change the law.

In a 2005 case, *Jackson*, Lord Hope suggested that even an intentional or express repudiation of EU law might not be followed by the new Supreme Court and expressed the view that whilst Parliament did not actually say that it could not enact legislation which was in conflict with Community law, in practice his opinion was that was the effect of s 2(1) when read with s 2(4) of the ECA 1972.

The view now of s 2(4) ECA 1972 is that it is a direct rule to give priority, rather than a rule of construction which requires there to be national law to construe or even to limit the function of the court to a reasonable construction. As far as the House of Lords is now concerned entry to the Communities (EU) and s 2(4) of the ECA 1972 has led to the modification of the doctrine of parliamentary sovereignty because implied repeal of previous Acts of Parliament, as far as EU law obligations are concerned, would not be heeded by the courts. Indeed, in the Metric Martyrs case (*Thoburn v Sunderland City Council* [2002] 1 CMLR 50), the High Court expressed the view that the ECA 1972 had acquired a constitutional quality which prevented implied repeal. Whether this overrides the *dictum* in *McCarthys Ltd v Smith* ([1979] ICR 785) is open to question. It remains open for Parliament to expressly repeal the Act. In such a case the courts would of course have to observe this faithfully.

Question 5

How have the courts of Member States other than the UK reacted to the Court of Justice's view on the supremacy of EU law?

Commentary

To be capable of answering this question, you must have at least taken account of the position in other Member States in your course on EU law. This is not always the case or the depth of treatment may vary considerably. The states which may have been concentrated on are those whose courts may have been reluctant to accept EU law supremacy in all cases or whose legal orders presented seemingly intractable barriers. As a contrast with these states it may be worthwhile making a brief contrast with a state which found no difficulty in accepting the supremacy of EU law. Your choice of states to consider will then very much depend on those considered in your particular course.

Answer plan

- States easily accepting EU law supremacy: Benelux countries
- Reception and judicial acceptance in Germany
- Reception and judicial acceptance in Italy
- Reception and judicial acceptance in France

Suggested answer

A number of states have not experienced any problems so far; see, for example, Luxembourg, Netherlands and Belgium. The latter state provides a good example of an unproblematic acceptance of the supremacy of EU law.

In Belgium, the constitution was amended to allow for the transfer of powers to institutions governed by international law (Art 25a). However, Belgium was a dualist country whereby later laws would prevail over earlier laws including international treaties if simply converted into national law. The courts in Belgium have no role in respect of judging the validity of international agreements but accepted Community (EU) law supremacy as if it were a monist country and not by dependence on a Belgium statute (see *Minister for Economic Affairs* v *SA Fromagerie 'Le Ski'* [1972] CMLR 330). It was held that in the case of conflict between national law and the directly effective law of an international treaty, the latter would prevail, even if earlier in time.

In Germany, in contrast, some difficulties were experienced, especially in respect of the provision of fundamental rights in the German constitution (*Grundgesetz*) and in the Community (EU) legal order.

Article 24 of the German constitution allows for a transfer of powers and membership of international organisations and was used to establish membership of the European Communities. Article 25 declares general rules of public international law to be an integral part of federal law and to take precedence over national law but it is silent as to the effect of international law on the German constitution.

Previously, German courts had been divided as to the effect of Community (EU) primary law and secondary law and at times courts had refused to make a reference in cases of doubt or not accept Community (EU) law supremacy, thus denying the parties to the case the chance to see whether Community (EU) law would have affected the outcome of the case. However, the view of the Federal Constitutional Court is paramount because of its constitutional position in the German state.

In the *Internationale Handelsgesellschaft* case ([1974] 2 CMLR 540), the Constitutional Court held that as long as the recognition of human rights in the Community had not progressed as far as those provided for by the *Grundgesetz*, German courts had the right to refer questions on the constitutionality of secondary Community law to the Federal Constitutional Court with the possible result that Community law may be ignored if it did not have sufficient regard for basic rights. This position changed in the *Wunsche Handelsgesellschaft* decision ([1987] 3 CMLR 225). The Federal Constitutional Court has accepted that Community recognition and safeguards of fundamental rights through the case law of the Court of Justice are now sufficient and of a comparable nature to those provided for by the *Grundgesetz*. Thus, as long as EU law ensures the effective provision of fundamental rights the Federal Constitutional Court will not review EU law in the light of the rights provisions of the constitution. It also stated that it would not be prepared to accept constitutional complaints from lower courts on this basis. The basis for the decision is not, however, the inherent supremacy of EU law but the fact that Art 24 of the *Grundgesetz* allowed a transfer of powers to the Union and the subsequent accession act obliges the German courts to accept the supremacy of EU law.

Following these cases there would seem to be no procedural difficulty in getting Union rights at least considered in the proper forum in Germany. Any court which refuses either to follow a previous ruling of the Court of Justice or make an Art 267 TFEU (ex 234 EC) ruling may be subject to the review of the Federal Constitutional Court for an arbitrary breach of Art 101(1) of the *Grundgesetz*.

The Federal Constitutional Court held in the *Brunner* case ([1994] 1 CMLR 57) that, the German Accession Statute to the Treaty on European Union was compatible with the German constitution and thus rejected claims that it was unconstitutional, although again there was a statement to the effect that a review function of the Constitutional court would still be maintained to ensure Community (EU) law complied with the provision of fundamental rights. This was confirmed in the Lisbon Judgment (2008) by the same court.

The German courts are still able to provide conflicting evidence in respect of their recognition of the supremacy of EU law. In 1996, in one of a series of cases arising from the German courts challenging the Community (EU) banana regime preference of ACP states and not the traditional South American countries supplying Germany (*Federal Tax* case of 9/1/1996, 7 EuZW 126 (1996)), the Federal Tax Court upheld German law on the basis of basic rights over the Community (EU) rules. In contrast is the German Supreme Court ruling (*Bundesgerichtshof*) in the *Brasserie du Pécheur* v *Federal Republic of Germany* (C-46/93) case, which accepted the principle of state liability on the part of the German state for a legislative breach. In this case, however, the Court held that the breach had not been sufficiently serious to impose liability.

In Italy the position both constitutionally and judicially was and is very similar to Germany, whereby both had new constitutions set up after the Second World War with strong provisions for fundamental rights. Both allowed a transfer of power to international organisations but were silent as to the effect on constitutional law (see Art 11 of the Italian Constitution).

As in Germany, the focus in Italy is on the Constitutional Court. Given that two of the leading cases on supremacy, *Costa* v *ENEL* (6/64) and *Simmenthal* (92/78), arose from Italy, it should certainly have been clear to the Italian Constitutional Court what was expected of it. Again there has been a mixed reaction, also along the lines of the German Constitutional Court.

In *Granital SpA* v *Administrazione delle Finanze* (see (1984) 21 CML Rev 756–72) the supremacy of Community (EU) law was accepted on the basis of an interpretation of Art 11 of the Italian constitution allowing for the limitation of sovereignty in favour of international organisations, and by reason of the case law of the Court of Justice. The case did, however, make the reservation that Italian law should only be cast aside where directly applicable Community (EU) law exists, similar in effect to the judgment of the House of Lords in the *Duke* case ([1988] AC 618).

A later decision in *Fragd SpA* v *Amministrazione delle Finanze* (see (1990) 27 CML Rev 93–5) suggests the Italian Constitutional Court is still prepared to review Community (EU) law in the light of the fundamental rights provision in the Italian Constitution.

The French courts are divided into two hierarchies with their own appeal courts and final appeal. They have had, however, significantly different attitudes to EU law, despite the fact both are subject to Art 55 of the French Constitution which is monist and gives international law a rank above municipal law, but is silent as to the effect on the Constitution. This is the point that has led to discrepancies between hierarchies.

The courts of ordinary jurisdiction have felt no hesitation in making Art 234 EC (now 267 TFEU) references to the Court of Justice and giving supremacy to Community law on the basis of Art 55 of the Constitution. The French Supreme Court of Ordinary Jurisdiction, the *Cour de Cassation*, has in fact gone further and found for the supremacy of Community (EU) law without direct reference to Art 55 of the Constitution and more on the basis of the inherent supremacy and direct effects of Community (EU) law itself. See the *Café Vabre* case ([1975] 2 CMLR 336) in which Art 95 EEC (now 90 EC) was held to prevail over a subsequent national statute. These rulings have been consistently followed by the lower courts and reference to either Art 55 of the Constitution or even the above decisions is rarely made (see, for example, *Garage Dehus Sarl* v *Bouche Distribution* ([1984] 3 CMLR 452)).

French administrative courts deal with complaints by citizens against any acts of the state administration. The Supreme Administrative Court, the *Conseil d'État*, has from time to time completely denied the supremacy of Community (EU) law or the need to make reference to the Court of Justice, relying heavily on the French principle of law, known as the *acte clair* (see, for example, *Minister of the Interior* v *Cohn-Bendit* ([1980] 1 CMLR 543)). The French court held individuals could not directly rely on Directives to challenge an administrative act. The court declined to follow previous Court of Justice rulings or make a reference itself.

More recently, however, cases have demonstrated a much more cooperative attitude on the part of the French administrative courts. In *Nicolo* ([1990] 1 CMLR 173), the *Conseil d'État* reviewed the supremacy of international law including EEC Treaty Articles and held the latter to take precedence over subsequent national law, largely on the basis of Art 55 of the Constitution. In *Boisdet* ([1991] 1 CMLR 3), incompatible national law was declared invalid in the face of a Community (EU) Regulation. In doing so the *Conseil d'État* followed the case law of the Court of Justice. The *Rothmans* case ([1993] CMLR 253) confirms the supremacy of Community (EU) Directives over subsequent national law and that public authorities cannot enforce the incompatible national law.

In *Dangeville* (see [1993] PL 535), the Paris Administrative Court of Appeal upheld the ruling of the ECJ in *Francovich* (C-6 and 9/90) and imposed a liability to pay damages for the failure to implement a Community (EU) Directive.

The Treaty on European Union has been declared compatible with the constitution after amendment to the constitution and has been ratified and thus takes priority over French national law (Art 88). As a result of that change the French Constitutional Court has declared that it will no longer review Community (EU) law in the light of the Constitution, save in relation to express elements which his taken to mean those protecting fundamental rights in a way similar to the German Constitutional Court (Decision 2004/496 of 10 June 2004).

Whilst it can be seen that there have been some problems in other Member States and there may continue to be problems, by and large the supremacy of EU law is increasingly recognised and applied in other Member States and the EU legal order continues to make its mark on the national legal orders.

Further reading

Allen, T, 'The Limits of Parliamentary Sovereignty' [1986] Public Law 614.

Craig, P, 'Sovereignty of the United Kingdom Parliament and Factortame' (1991) 9 YEL 221.

Craig, P, 'Britain in the European Union', in Jowell, J, and Oliver, D (eds), *The Changing Constitution*, 6th edn (Oxford: Oxford University Press, 2007).

Dashwood, A, 'The Relationship between the Member States and the European Union/ European Community' (2004) 41 CML Rev 355–381.

Foster, N, 'The Effect of the European Communities Act 1972 s. 2(4)' (1988) 51 MLR 775.

Foster, N, 'The German Constitution and EC Membership' [1994] Public Law 392.

Gaja, G, 'New Developments in a Continuing Story; The Relationship between EC Law and Italian Law' (1990) 27 CML Rev 83.

Hoffmeister, F, 'German *Bundesverfassungsgericht*: *Alcan* Decision of 17 February 2000; Constitutional Review of EC Regulation on Bananas, Decision of 7 June 2000' (2001) 38 CML Rev 791.

Maher, I, 'Community Law in the National Legal Order: A Systems Analysis' (1998) 36 JCMS 237.

Manin, P, 'The *Nicolo* Case of the *Conseil d' État*: French Constitutional Law and the Supreme Administrative Court's Acceptance of the Primacy of Community Law over Subsequent National Statute Law' (1991) 28 CML Rev 499.

Millns, S, 'The Treaty of Amsterdam and the Constitutional Revision in France' (1999) 5 EPL 61.

Mitchell, JDB, 'What Happened to the Constitution on 1st January 1973?' (1980) 11 Cambrian Law Review 69.

Oliver, P, 'The French Constitution and the Treaty of Maastricht' (1994) 43 ICLQ 1.

Schmid, C, 'All Bark and No Bite: Notes on the Federal Constitutional Court's "Banana Decision"' (2001) 7 ELJ 95.

Wade, HWR, 'Sovereignty and the European Communities' (1972) 88 LQR 1.

Wade, HWR, 'What has Happened to the Sovereignty of Parliament?' (1991) 107 LQR 1.

5

The Jurisdiction of the Court of Justice

Introduction

This chapter deals with questions on the range of actions or types of procedure provided for under the TFEU (ex EC Treaty). These are the actions under Arts 258–260, 263, 265, 267, 268, 277 and 340 TFEU (ex 226–228, 230, 232, 234, 235, 241 and 288 EC). Whereas a division is often made in textbooks between the actions which are considered directly by the Court of Justice and those which are only heard indirectly by the Court of Justice in the course of litigation before a national court, such a division seemed rather artificial in a book on questions and answers. The reason for taking this view is that many questions ask for alternative actions or procedures to be considered in the event that the most obvious or first action proves to be too difficult or unsuccessful for the applicant. Another reason is that not all textbooks make the same division and whilst there is some consistency maintained between direct and indirect actions, some make further distinctions between actions seeking to enforce EU law in the Member State and other actions which are classified as administrative actions concerning challenges of the legality of EU law or actions of the institutions.

Grouping them all together in one chapter avoids having to split the subject matter, which concerns essentially one topic, ie the jurisdiction of the Court of Justice, into two, three or even four separate and smaller chapters. Thus, all questions concerned with the procedural jurisdiction of the Court of Justice are dealt with in this chapter with the exception of some mixed topic questions in the final chapter.

The range of questions is quite considerable under this broad heading. Questions can range from a straightforward consideration on the procedure of each action to the difficulties for applicants in these actions; the setting of difficult problem questions on the procedural aspects to questions requiring a consideration of more than one action. Mixed questions which concern both procedural law and the substantive law of the EU have, however, been reserved to the last chapter of the book which also includes a general question on the overall range and effectiveness of remedies for individuals in the EU legal order.

This chapter includes a mixture of essay and problem-type questions.

Question 1

Discuss the effectiveness of the Art 258 TFEU procedure in ensuring compliance of EU law on the part of Member States.

 ## Commentary

The question is concerned with the authority which has been provided by the Treaty under Art 258 TFEU (ex 226 EC) to the Commission to prosecute Member States for a failure to comply with their obligations under EU law. It allows the Commission to police the application and implementation of EU law by the Member States. It requires, first of all, a description of the procedure for the actions under Art 258 TFEU. In so describing the procedure you could, if these were featured in your course, give an idea of how many cases reach the Court of Justice under these actions.

Having provided a description, you are required to consider whether this procedure is effective in ensuring Member States' compliance with EU law. Whilst not an express requirement of this part of the answer, it may nevertheless be useful to suggest other ways in which compliance may be required or encouraged.

 ## Answer plan

- Article 258 TFEU
- Stages of the enforcement procedure
- Status and effectiveness of the initial ECJ judgment
- Secondary action for a breach of Art 260 TFEU
- Sanctions and interim measures
- Alternative actions: direct effects and state liability

Suggested answer

The Art 258 TFEU procedure is provided to allow the Commission to pursue its task of policing the application and compliance with the Treaties and secondary EU law obligations. In order for a procedure to commence, a breach of an obligation by a Member State must be suspected by, or brought to the attention of, the Commission. A breach or failure to act is most often observed in the forms that a Member State has failed to implement EU legislation, mainly Directives, or that the implementation was incomplete or dilatory or the Member State has failed to remove national legislation which is now in conflict or inconsistent with EU legislation or obligations. This includes decisions of the Court of Justice. A breach may also be the action of a Member State in enacting or maintaining legislation or national regulations incompatible with the Treaty or secondary EU law. The failure can be attributed to all organs of the state, not just the government.

If the Commission thinks a breach is probable, Art 258 TFEU requires certain administrative procedural steps to be taken before a court action can result. The first part of Art 258 TFEU states: 'If the Commission considers that a Member State has failed to fulfil an obligation under the Treaties, it shall deliver a reasoned opinion on the matter'. This means the Commission must have reached a conclusion that the Member State is in breach of an obligation before it can commence an action before the Court. The matter can be brought to its attention by its own investigations and supervision of implementation by Member States, by the Member States, by the EP or by individual citizens or companies.

Having decided a state has breached its obligations the Commission will inform the state and give the state the opportunity to answer the allegation or correct its action or inaction before the formal procedure of Art 258 TFEU begins.

Not every suspicion of infringement by the Commission will even result in the initial letter being sent to the Member State. The initial letter has been held to be essential for the commencement of proceedings before the Court (*Commission v Italy* (274/83)). In 2006, the Commission sent out 1,536 formal notice letters stating its point of view. Following the reply from the Member State or after a reasonable time where no reply is received the Commission will then deliver a reasoned opinion which records the reasons for the failure of the Member State. This is delivered to the Member State and is registered by the Court of Justice. Many of the original complaints will have been settled informally by this stage and the resulting number of reasoned opinions in 2006 was 680.

If the state should then fail to comply with the reasoned opinion of the Commission within a reasonable time, the Commission then has the discretionary right to bring the matter before the Court of Justice. 189 cases were brought in 2006. These figures are produced each year in a Report on monitoring the application of Community law. In 2002 there were 995 formal notices, 487 reasoned opinions and 180 referrals to the ECJ.

The final stage of the procedure is action before the Court of Justice and its judgment which is merely declaratory. It is possible, however, for the Court to order interim measures, as it did, for example, in case C-213/89 *Factortame*. After the judgment the state is required to take the necessary measures to comply with the judgment. The Court of Justice delivered 62 judgments in 2002 and 90 judgments in 2006.

Having considered the actual procedure, its effectiveness in securing compliance must now be considered. Other international tribunals are unable to enforce their judgments against miscreant Member States, for example, the International Court of Justice at the Hague or the European Court of Human Rights in Strasbourg, and the best that can really be achieved is the issue and discussion of a report on the failure or breach and the hope that the ensuing political pressure will encourage compliance.

Whilst the initial judgment of the Court of Justice is only declaratory and carries no specific sanctions, Member States are placed under a further obligation under Art 260 TFEU to comply with the judgment by taking the necessary measures. If they do not do this a further action may lie against them by the Commission under Art 258 TFEU for a breach of Art 260 TFEU. This has taken place a number of times and increasingly so; in 1989 eg it was used on 26 occasions and in 1998 the Commission commenced 39 actions for a breach of Art 228 EC (now 260 TFEU). The leading instance of this is *Commission v Italy* (second Art Treasures case) (48/71). The Commission discerned that because Italy had not complied with the Court's judgment in the first Art Treasures case (7/68), judgment should be given that Italy had also failed in its obligation under Art 228 (now 260 TFEU). Despite the fact that Italy complied with the original decision prior to judgment, the Court held that Italy had also failed to comply with Art 228 (now 260 TFEU).

Prior to the Treaty on European Union, the judgment was, however, only declaratory but other methods to secure the eventual compliance of the Member States were possible in the Community legal order. However, even prior to the TEU coming into force it was rarely necessary to rely on other methods of enforcement. Despite the lack of direct sanctions the Art 260 TFEU procedure can be regarded as effective, in that in most actions the Member States complied with the judgment in good time.

Articles 260–261 TFEU provide that sanctions can be requested by the Commission in an action to establish that the Member States have failed to comply with a previous judgment of the Court of Justice. This has already occurred in a number of requests by the Commission for penalty payments to be imposed on 14 occasions to 1999 against France, Germany, Greece, Italy and Luxembourg. Eight of these referrals by the Commission were withdrawn after the infringement was corrected and six were awaiting judgment with the prospect of daily fines of hundreds of thousands of ECUs. After three more cases were settled in 2000, only one resulted in judgment. This was *Commission v Greece* (C-387/97) in which a penalty of 20,000 per day was imposed by the ECJ from the date of judgment (4/7/2000). Since then, a fine has been levied against Spain in case C-278/01 for not complying fully with the Bathing Water Directive (76/160). This time the fine was set at 624,000 per year for each per cent of beaches not meeting the standards set. At the time of judgment 15% of beaches had not met the standard. *Commission v France* (C-304/02) is a very instructive case both in terms of what the court can do in fining Member States and for the comments made in the case. The case highlights the unique nature of this fining possibility which does not exist in the national or indeed international legal systems against states. It also established that the Court of Justice could impose both a lump sum and periodic payment to encourage compliance.

The conclusion is that with fines, the revised Art 260 TFEU is having an effect in securing compliance. The Lisbon Treaty has amended Art 260 to provide for a one-step process where Member States fail to notify measures transposing a directive. Instead of taking an action under Art 258 TFEU first, the Commission can use Art 260 TFEU and request a fine at the same time. The considerable saving of time this would achieve should further encourage compliance on the part of the Member States.

There are also interim measures under Art 279 TFEU (ex 243 EC) which are an additional tool to encourage compliance and which have been used to prevent the continued breach of Community law by the Member States (see eg *Commission v UK* (Pig Producers) case 53/77 and the Special Road Tax for Lorries in Germany (C-195/90R)). The Commission successfully applied for interim measures in both cases to suspend the application of the national measures alleged to breach EU law whilst the substantive question in each case was being considered by the Court of Justice.

Alternatively, actions by individuals in the national courts to defend or establish their individual rights based on EU law, which are referred to the Court of Justice under Art 267, also serve to bring to the attention of the Commission and the Court of Justice a failure by the Member State. In most circumstances the Member States amend their laws to comply with their Community obligations without the need for an Art 258 TFEU action by the Commission. Many examples could be cited here but leading cases are *Van Gend en Loos* (26/62), *Marshall* (152/84) or any similar case where direct effects have upheld individuals' rights under EU law, in the face of conflicting national law.

Whilst straying from the direct question, it would nevertheless be acceptable to say that a recent development which may spur on Member States to comply far more than any of the above actions is the prospect of having to compensate in each case where an individual has suffered damage as a result of the failure of the Member State to comply with a Community obligation. In the case which decided this, ie *Francovich* (C-6 and 9/90), the provision of law was a Directive. There are three conditions to such an action:

The Directive must provide an individual right.

It must be determined by the provisions of the Directive alone.

There must be a link between the breach and the damage caused.

There are an ever growing number of cases in this area which have clarified the circumstances under which the Member State will be held liable. The Court of Justice held in *Hedley Lomas* (C-5/94) that a breach of Community (now EU) law will be sufficiently serious to establish liability where a state violated an established principle of Community law (Art 34 EC (now 35 TFEU) on exports), especially where the Member State had legislated in direct contravention of a Treaty obligation. It was not necessary for a state to already have been held in breach of Community law in a previous Art 258 TFEU (ex 226 EC) action by the Commission. In fact, failure to take any measures to transpose the Directive within the time limit set will suffice to establish a sufficiently serious breach of EU law (*Dillenkofer* (C-178, 179, 189 & 190/94)). A Member State will not have sufficiently seriously breached EU law where it can be shown that the Directive in question is open to several interpretations (see *British Telecommunications* (C-392/93)).

Hence then, if Art 258 TFEU itself is not sufficient to secure compliance, first at the administrative stage, with the threat of fines looming or at the judicial stage with the imposition of fines, then an action by individuals to impose liability on the state for failure to comply with EU law almost certainly will be. The vast majority of Commission actions (c 95%) are though settled and secure compliance well before the judicial stage, yet alone relying entirely on individuals to secure compliance. Overall, it may be argued, the system does work reasonably effectively.

Question 2

In 2008 the Council of Ministers issued a fictitious Directive on washing machine specifications which was to be implemented by all Member States by 1 January 2010. The controversial nature of the Directive, which would have opened the ailing British washing machine industry up to competition from other Union Member States, and the pressure on parliamentary time meant that the UK Government did not alter its own regulations on the specifications which must be met by washing machines marketed in the UK. However, the UK Government did issue a circular in June 2010 to all customs officers, advising them of the existence of the Directive and informing them that all washing machines which met the specifications in the Directive were to be granted access to the UK market, even if they did not meet the stricter requirements of the UK regulations.

In February 2010, Danny, an importer of washing machines, had a consignment of French washing machines held up at customs at Dover because, although they met the requirements of the Directive, they did not meet the specifications contained in the UK regulation. The washing machines were not released until mid-June when the customs received the government circular.

In March 2010, the Commission instituted proceedings under Art 258 TFEU and, following the issue of a reasoned opinion in September 2010, the UK Government introduced a regulation to implement the directive.

The UK Government, in response to the reasoned opinion, observes:

(a) that it was unable to comply with the Directive because of the lack of parliamentary time;

(b) that the circular issued in June was sufficient to comply with the requirements of the Directive;

(c) that, in any event, the Directive had now been implemented by the new regulation, and the proceedings under Art 258 TFEU no longer served any useful purpose;

(d) that France had also failed to implement the Directive within the time limit.

1. Advise the EC Commission as to the validity of these arguments by the UK Government.

2. Briefly outline if there are any other parties who could take action against the UK.

 ## Commentary

This question concentrates on the ability of Member States to resist a conclusion under Art 258 TFEU that they have breached Community law obligations and the alternative actions which may be taken against Member States to either encourage compliance or obtain a remedy in the case of a breach of EU law. Whilst the question does involve the free movement of goods, it is not a question on the free movement of goods and should not therefore be answered as one. This would miss the focus or point of this question.

It requires you initially to consider defences which have been raised by a Member State in an attempt to avoid being found in breach of EU law obligations. Various specific grounds are mentioned and you should therefore only address these in turn. To complete this part it would be helpful to provide a conclusion as to whether you would regard the UK to be in breach according to the case law of the ECJ.

You are further asked then to discuss whether any other parties could take action against the UK. This part of the question is more open than the first part in that there are a number of possible alternatives to consider. These include action by the importers to challenge the right of the UK to prevent imports taking place and requesting a reference under Art 267 TFEU, or action by the importers to claim damages if suffered as a result of the UK action or an action by another Member State.

 ## Answer plan

- Art 258 TFEU and a consideration of the defences
- The establishment of a breach of EU law
- An action by another Member State under Art 259 TFEU
- A preliminary ruling request from a national court under Art 267 TFEU
- Action for damages by individuals against the Member State (*Francovich*)

Suggested answer

1   In the EU legal order, Art 258 TFEU provides an enforcement action whereby ultimately the Commission can take a Member State before the Court of Justice to establish a breach of a EU law obligation. Member States, though, have raised various defences to justify their non-compliance with obligations, which may be acceptable in international law, but without success in the EU legal order under Art 258 TFEU.

(a) The first reason given by the UK is similar to the argument of *force majeure* or overriding necessity raised in the case of *Commission v Belgium* (Re: Duty on Timber (77/69)). Belgium failed to implement a Community (EU) Directive and was taken before the ECJ by the Commission. The Belgian Government pleaded that it should not be held responsible to the negligence of the Belgium Parliament in not completing the implementation. This was rejected by the ECJ. Similarly, the argument raised that the delay in implementing Community (EU) measures were the consequence of political difficulties by Italy in the Art Treasures case (7/68), that the delay in implementing Community (EU) measures was the consequence of political difficulties, was rejected by the ECJ.

(b) The suggestion that the circular, which only advised the appropriate authorities but did not actually bring UK law into compliance, would be an adequate defence is also likely to be held to be insufficient. See the case of *Commission v France* (Re: the French Maritime Code) (167/73) in which the formal rules were not amended but a change in practice was advised to the French authorities. The ECJ held that this was not sufficient to comply with Community (EU) law obligations.

(c) The defence that no legal interest remained was raised in *Commission v Italy* (the Italian Pigmeat case (7/61)). However, it was held that, as long as the Commission has an interest, it can bring a case before the Court of Justice and therefore the interest can continue even when the infringement no longer exists. Furthermore, in the case of *Commission v Italy* (Slaughtered Cows case (39/72)) the ECJ held that where a legal issue remains unsettled an interest remains.

(d) An argument based on reciprocity, ie that another Member State's or EU institution's own failure to act justifies a defendant Member State's failure to comply with an obligation, is an acceptable defence was put forward in *Commission v Belgium and Luxembourg* (90–91/63). The states involved claimed they were merely taking reciprocal action in disregarding Community (EU) Directives because the Council had delayed in passing legislation. The ECJ held that the Community (EU) was a new legal order whose structure involves the prohibition of Member States taking justice into their own hands. Similarly, where other Member States have not complied with their obligations the ECJ has held (*Commission v France* (232/78)) that this does not entitle non-compliance on behalf of the defendant Member State, even where the Member State's constitution specifically allows for this (French Constitution, Art 88).

It is likely therefore that all of these defences raised will be rejected by the ECJ and the UK will be found in breach of its (EU) law obligation.

2 In addition to the action under Art 258 TFEU by the Commission, individuals affected either by a refusal to allow imports or suffering damages resulting from delays may consider attempting the following actions.

Additionally, the French Government might be interested in assisting the French manufacturers of washing machines whose products have been denied access for so long. It may consider taking an action under Art 259 TFEU to establish a breach by the UK. Such actions are, however, extremely rare (only five so far and of those only three resulted in a judgment by the ECJ) and it is likely that they would leave it up to the Commission to take an Art 258 TFEU action.

An individual who is affected by the action of the UK may point to the breach of a EU obligation or duty by a Member State as a defence to prosecution by that Member State or where they seek to challenge national rules which operate against their interest. It was early in the life of the Communities that the Art 234 EC (now 267 TFEU) preliminary ruling procedure was seen to short circuit or, alternatively viewed, to complement the use of Arts 226 and 227 EC (now 258–259 TFEU). This was objected to by the Dutch Government in the *Van Gend en Loos* case (26/62), which thought that it was up to the Commission only and not individuals to take action or claim rights against Member States. This claim was firmly rejected by the Court and, by the establishment of the doctrine of direct effects, was able additionally to place the policing of Community (EU) law in the hands of private individuals, who often have more reason to bring actions. Danny might therefore consider an action before the national courts to get his machines released without too much delay.

Individuals may benefit by as well as helping to bring about the compliance with Art 258 TFEU actions, as shown in *Commission v France* (Advertising of Alcoholic Beverages) (152/78). It was held that a French ban on advertising foreign spirits was discriminatory and contrary to Community (EU) law. France failed to remove its legislation and prosecuted an importer for advertising. Waterkeyn, the advertiser, referred to the previous judgment as a defence. In *Procurieur de la République v Waterkeyn* (314 316/81) it was held that individuals could rely on such past judgments as a defence to protect their rights.

Alternatively, an individual may attempt to obtain damages from the Member States where the breach by the Member State is claimed to have caused damage to individuals who then make a claim against the Member State to recover. This form of action at the moment is now well established and proving to be extremely effective in encouraging Member States to comply with EU law obligations if they find themselves having to pay out significant damages in an increasing number of cases.

It was tried in the case of the French turkey producers who, following the Commission Art 169 (now 226) action against the UK in the *Poultry Meat* case (40/82) which held a British ban was contrary to Community (EU) law, sought an action for damages against the Ministry of Agriculture who applied the ban. The claim was dismissed as showing no good cause of action unless it could be shown that the Ministry acted in bad faith, in which case the proper action is that for judicial review and not a tort action for damages. However, in *Bourgoin SA* v *Ministry of Agriculture* [1986] 1 CMLR 267 and [1987] 1 CMLR 169, the case was settled out of court and the Government paid £3.5 million compensation to the French farmers.

The case of *Francovich* (C-6 and 9/90) had the result that the Italian Government were obliged to pay the claimants as a result of failure to implement Community (EU) legislation. There are three conditions to such an action:

The Directive must provide an individual right.

It must be determined by the provisions of the Directive alone.

There must be a link between the breach and the damage caused.

It is not necessary to show that the Member State has already been held in breach of its Community obligations in an Art 258 TFEU action by the Commission (*Hedley Lomas* (C-5/94)). In fact, it was held in *Dillenkofer* (C-178, 179, 188–190/94) that a failure by a state to take any measure to transpose a Directive in the prescribed time constitutes a sufficiently serious breach of Community (EU) law in order to found liability, as long as the other two conditions are also met.

In *Brasserie du Pécheur* v *Germany*; *Factortame* v *UK* (C-46 and 48/93), the ECJ extended the principle of state liability to all violations whatever organ of the state causes the infringement. The Court equated the criteria of *Francovich* liability to those which are applied in the case of liability of the EU institutions to pay damages for their wrongful legislative acts under Arts 235 and 288(2) (now 268 and 340). These are:

(a) there must have been a serious breach by the Community (EU) law-making institution of a superior rule of law for the protection of the individual;

(b) the law-making institution has manifestly and gravely disregarded the limits of its powers; and

(c) there must be a causal link between the breach and the damage suffered.

In considering this, the ECJ would take into account:

(i) whether the scope of the EU provision was clear and precise;

(ii) the extent of the margin of appreciation left to the Member States;

(iii) the intentional or voluntary character of the infringement;

(iv) whether the error of law was excusable or inexcusable;

(v) whether the attitude of the EU institutions had contributed to the breach.

In the *Factortame* case the Court considered that the UK Government was well aware of the Commission's attitude to the Merchant Shipping Act, as well as the views of national courts that these rules infringed Community (EU) law. Moreover, the UK Government had failed to implement the judgment of the ECJ of 10 October 1989.

Given the facts of the case to hand, it is likely there would be a similar result and the UK would be liable for any damage suffered by Danny as a result of the breach by the UK.

Question 3

Natural and legal persons face substantial obstacles in challenging the validity of EU secondary law under Art 263 TFEU. Outline the requirements which must be met by an individual seeking to challenge:

(a) a Decision addressed to him;

(b) a Decision addressed to another person or to a Member State;

(c) a Regulation.

Do you consider the requirements of Art 263 TFEU to be unduly restrictive to individuals?

 ## Commentary

This question concentrates on the admissibility element or otherwise known as the '*locus standi*' requirements of an Art 263 TFEU action and the particular difficulties encountered by the so-called non-privileged applicants. In order to put your answer in context you must briefly outline the purpose and procedure of an Art 263 TFEU action. You are then required to address the requirements which must be met by an individual seeking to challenge acts in the given circumstances in the question, giving examples from the case law of the Court of Justice where you consider appropriate. Finally, you are asked to consider whether the requirements as outlined are unnecessarily restrictive for individuals. This requires you to engage in a more general discussion of the purposes of such an action and will be possible if you have undertaken wider reading than just from textbooks on the topic.

Note now that applications by legal and natural persons under Art 263 TFEU will be heard by the General Court (previously named the CFI) rather than the ECJ itself, although there are limited grounds of appeal to the ECJ. Also note now, that case law by the CFI (now General Court) and opinions of AGs in the ECJ have not been supported by the ECJ itself, which has maintained its previous position on individual access. For the moment, the question still needs to be answered based on the mass of previous case law but with the new cases and possible trends noted. You could note at the end, that the Member States did make a significant but unclear change to Art 230 (now Art 263 TFEU) in the 2007 Lisbon Treaty, which I have briefly noted in the suggested answer.

Answer plan

- Outline Art 263 TFEU
- Restrictive individual *locus standi* under Art 263 TFEU
- ECJ case law on individual access, especially *Plaumann* v *Commission*
- Latest position, especially in respect of the amendment to Art 263 TFEU
- Discussion of reasons for restrictiveness

Suggested answer

Article 263 TFEU provides for the action brought before the Court of Justice to review the validity of acts of the institutions of the Union. If those acts are found to be invalid, the Court of Justice including the General Court has the sole right to declare acts void. There are two elements in respect of the action: admissibility and the merits or substance of the action. The first presents the greatest barrier to the non-privileged legal or natural individual applicants in practice.

The article names the Member States, the Council, the European Parliament and the Commission as privileged applicants, who have the right to attack any act. It further names the Court of Auditors, the European Central Bank and the Committee of the Regions as institutions who may invoke Art 263 TFEU as a matter of course but only to protect their own prerogative powers. All other persons are termed non-privileged applicants. Article 263 TFEU as amended by the Lisbon Treaty states that any natural or legal person may institute proceedings against an act addressed to that person or which is of direct and individual concern to them, and against a regulatory act which is of direct concern to them and does not entail implementing measures. The exact consequences of the changes introduced are though unclear until further clarification is provided by the Court of Justice.

(a) To challenge an act addressed specifically to the applicant automatically gives standing according to Art 263 TFEU and is confirmed in numerous cases; for example, any case concerned with a challenge by an individual to a Decision issued by the Commission under its powers granted under competition policy in Arts 101 and 102 TFEU and Regulation 1/2003.

(b) In order to challenge an act not addressed to them, ie to someone else or a Member State, it must be shown to be of direct and individual concern to the applicant.

(c) In the case of challenging regulatory acts, they must be also of direct concern and not entail implementing measures.

The new version appears to have increased the possibility of challenges which can be brought by individuals with full *locus standi* to all acts addressed to them and not just Decisions, although in practice individuals will be addressed with Decisions only and not other forms of legislative or administrative act. Acts not addressed to them, can be challenged, if of direct and individual concern. This change also appears to be an expansion of rights in that there is no need now to show a Regulation is a Decision or a bundle of Decisions providing it is of direct and individual concern. However, as will be outlined below when dealing with the case law, if an Act in the form of a Regulation can be shown to be of direct and individual concern, then it has already been demonstrated that for that applicant, at least, the Act was not a Regulation but Decision. As such then the change introduced by the Lisbon Treaty appears to reflect previous case law.

A further uncertainty remains that the term 'regulatory act' is not defined in the amended Treaties, and whilst it is probable it should be read as referring to the administrative acts of the Commission and other EU bodies, this will require confirmation first, which can only come from the Court of Justice. For the moment then, we simply know that the challenge against regulatory acts will require only direct and not individual concern. Many of these aspects will be considered in further detail in the light of the previous case law developed below. The new elements, however, have not yet been confronted in the courts to see what exactly the changes will mean and whether what appears to be an easing of the *locus standi* requirements by the Member States is recognised by the Court of Justice and the General Court.

In order to consider what precisely an individual must do in order to determine whether they are able to gain *locus standi*, a number of considerations must be taken into account before an action can proceed to the merits of the challenge and until new case law emerges this can only be along the lines of the previous case law.

Whilst the jurisdiction of the Court is limited to the legally binding acts of the Council and the Commission, and acts of the EP and European Council intended to have legal effects, it was held in the *Noordwijks Cement Accord* case (8–11/66) that other acts may be subject to review. The test to apply to a particular act is whether it has binding legal effects or changes the legal position of the applicant. Further, in *Commission* v *Council* (ERTA) (22/70) it was held that Art 249 EC (now 288 TFEU) is not exhaustive and special acts such as the minuted discussions of the Council, for the European Road Transport Agreement, could also be challenged. Thus the true nature of the measure is the determining factor.

If the act is addressed to the plaintiff, then the plaintiff has *locus standi*. If the act is addressed to someone else, the question is then, is the act of direct and individual concern to the applicant? If yes, the applicant has *locus standi*. If no, there is no *locus standi*.

According to the previous case law, many applicants fail to gain admissibility, trying to show either that a Regulation was really a Decision or that it was of direct or individual concern to them. One of the difficulties in looking at problems in this area and trying to apply the available case law is that the Court of Justice has not always taken the same route In answering these questions. Sometimes it can be shown that if something is of individual concern, it follows logically that if it is a Regulation which is challenged, this Regulation must be, in substance, a Decision for the applicant, and now post Lisbon, an act that can be challenged by an individual, although not necessarily for others. Therefore, establishing *locus standi* can sometimes be done by considering direct and individual concern first, and the changes to Art 263 are presumed to reflect this. For example, in the CAM case (100/74), the Regulation was able to be challenged because of its direct and individual concern. Additionally, in the UNICME case (123/77), it was held that if the act is of direct and individual concern, there is no need to consider whether the measure is a Decision or a Regulation. However, in *Codorniu v Commission* (C-309/89), despite the ECJ confirming that the Regulation was a legislative measure applying to traders in general, it could still be of individual concern to one of them. Codorniu had distinguished themselves by the ownership of a trademark for the term Crement from the year 1924, which term the Community (EU) had tried to reserve for French and Luxembourg producers.

In looking at direct and individual concern, which is still clearly relevant post Lisbon, the Court of Justice often defines 'individual' first. Individual concern has been very hard to demonstrate. In *Plaumann v Commission* (25/62), a Decision was addressed to the German Government refusing permission to reduce duties on clementines. The test was whether the decision affects the applicant by virtue of the fact that he is a member of the abstractly defined class addressed by the rule; for example, because he is an importer of clementines, or does it affect him because of attributes peculiar to him which differentiate him from all other persons. Plaumann was held to be one of a class of importers and not therefore individually concerned. See also the *Codorniu* case (C-309/89) where the company had clearly distinguished itself as individually concerned. The CFI (now General Court) held in the *Jégo-Quéré v Commission* case (T-177/01) a strict application of individual concern should no longer apply and that individual concern should be established:

> if the measure in question affects his legal position, in a manner which is both definite and immediate, by restricting his rights or by imposing obligations on him. The number and position of other persons who are likewise affected by the measure, or who may be so, are of no relevance in that regard.

However, this adverse impact test was clearly rejected by the ECJ in case C-50/00P, *Unión de Pequeños Agricultores v Council* which means the position on individual access is as it was. Indeed, the ECJ confirmed this in the Commission appeal

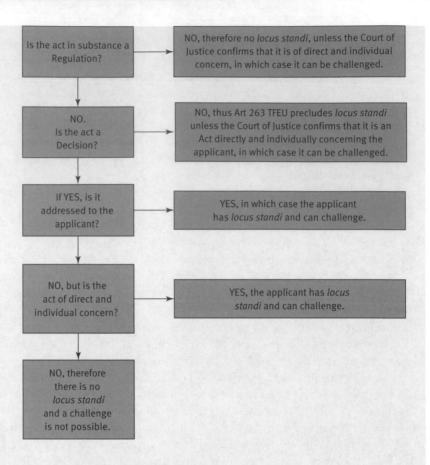

case of *Jégo-Quéré* (C-263/02) such that the test remains of individual concern—which the company in the case did not prove, hence the application for annulment was denied and the previous judgment of the CFI was overturned.

'Direct' has been held to mean the effect of the decision on the interests of the applicant must not depend on the discretion of another person (see the *Alcan* case (69/69) and the *Zuckerfabrik Schöppenstedt* case (5/71)).

After the requirements of *locus standi* have been proved, the merits or substantive grounds of the action must be proved and these are provided in Art 263 TFEU.

The second part of this answer addresses the issue of whether the requirements are restrictive. They certainly have been restrictive but too restrictive? The national courts also impose a requirement to show an interest in seeking to challenge administrative and legislative acts, eg there are *locus standi* requirements in seeking judicial review in the UK.

The reasons for the difficulties in demonstrating *locus standi* have been subject to much debate as to whether it is the policy of the Court of Justice concerned with 'floodgates' arguments whereby some sort of filter system is necessary or desires to promote the Court more as a supreme Court of the Member States and not one directly accessible as a first instance court for individuals. To some extent this has been answered by the establishment of the Court of First Instance (now General Court) to handle these cases which elevates the Court of Justice into the role of an appeal case in relation to these categories of cases.

Those cases held to be admissible often arise from the application of retroactive legislation. The applicants thus belonged to a fixed and identifiable group which could not be added to. Other arguments revolve around discussions about balancing the interests of the Union and individuals in the Union. The decision-making procedure in the EU is a much more complex procedure and often the result of compromise which makes legislation more difficult to enact. The inevitable economic choices of the Union are likely to affect individuals and must be allowed to be made otherwise the ability of the Union and within it the Commission and Council to operate would be undermined. Individuals' actions should not hinder the institutions' ability to operate. Comparisons with the Member States may be made that such challenges are also subject to equally tight *locus standi* requirements. In those areas, by contrast, individuals find it easier to achieve standing such as competition law, state aids and anti-dumping measures; it may be argued that the very often closer involvement of particular individuals makes the difference. The applicants are likely to be the ones involved in the process by informing the Commission of certain situations or can be seen clearly to be affected by the measures complained about. This then sets them apart from the many other challenges arising most frequently against legislative decisions made under the Common Agricultural Policy. However, the overall picture remains that of a restrictive *locus standi* for applicants unless the recent developments become the norm.

Arguments which justify the strict requirements are that the role of the Court of Justice, apart from competition law and anti-dumping cases, is not really a court for individuals. It is an EU court for the institutions and the Member States. There should be no direct individual access. Furthermore, there is the provision of the indirect action via Art 267 TFEU or an action for damages under Art 340 TFEU as an alternative, which may also lead to EU law being challenged. This appears to be favoured by the Court and the Treaty by the provision of Art 267 TFEU. Consequently, it may therefore be argued, the requirements are not too restrictive. It is to be noted though that the Member States have amended the wording of Art 230 (now 263 TFEU) when the Constitutional Treaty was drafted which was carried forward to the 2007 Lisbon Treaty. The new Art 263 TFEU, as noted above, provides that individual can challenge regulatory acts which are of direct concern (and not having to be of individual concern) but which do not entail implementing measures. It would appear at this stage then, in the light of the new Art 290 TFEU definitions, that Regulations and Decisions would remain as they are and that the new rights would apply to the delegated powers exercised by the Commission, excepting those requiring implementing measures, it remains though unclear as to whether this will make an action any less restrictive for individuals.

Question 4

Following a widespread conversion to produce animal feed, there was a considerable over-production and consequent surplus of sweet lupins in the EU in 2010. As a result, fictitious Council Regulation (1/2011) was enacted on 10 January 2011 which provided that exporters of sweet lupins during 2011 were entitled under the Regulation to incentives of €100 per tonne of sweet lupins exported. On 11 January 2011, R Hood Ltd applied for a licence to export 1,000 tonnes of sweet lupins. The company was granted the licence on the payment of a deposit of €5,000 which would be forfeited if the company did not comply with the requirements of the licence.

In February 2011, there was a sudden serious disruption in the sweet lupin crop which resulted in a considerable shortage of sweet lupins in the EU and on 2nd February 2011, the Commission enacted fictitious Regulation 4/2011 which eliminated without prior notice the refund subsidies of sweet lupins, making exporters liable instead for a levy of €5 per tonne exported. In enacting the Regulation, the Commission was specifically required to include in its considerations those who had already obtained licences to export sweet lupins in the 2011 marketing year but did not provide reasons for that.

R Hood Ltd exported 400 tonnes of its quota before 2 February 2011 and is presented with a levy of €2,000. It must export the remaining quantity of its quota (600 tonnes) or lose the deposit of €5,000. Exporting the 600 tonnes will however make it liable to a further levy of €3,000.

Advise R Hood Ltd on whether, and on what grounds, if any, it can successfully challenge the second Regulation.

Commentary

The question specifically requests you to advise the company as to whether they can challenge the second Regulation enacted by the Commission. Hence you are immediately taken to a consideration of an action under Art 263 TFEU and you will need to consider both the admissibility of an action and the merits, if found to be admissible. The biggest task in answering problems on Art 263 TFEU is trying to resolve the often conflicting case law of the Court of Justice in considering the challenges to EU Regulations because of the restrictive *locus standi* requirements for the individual, non-privileged applicants. Although not always previously dealt with in this way by the ECJ, and possibly not in the future following the changes introduced by the Lisbon Treaty, it is now advised to go straight to the issue of whether it is direct and individual to the applicant. Having considered the admissibility and if you have found it to be proved, you can then consider the merits or grounds of the action to determine whether R Hood Ltd will be successful in its challenge.

Whilst not specifically required by the question, you may consider whether there are other grounds by which the Regulation could be challenged, particularly if the challenge using Art 263 TFEU proves unsuccessful.

Answer plan

- Outline pertinent facts
- Outline the applicable law, especially **Art 263 TFEU**
- Consider admissibility for individuals and relevant case law
- Consider the merits of the application
- Suggest alternative possibilities to challenge the Regulation

Suggested answer

On the facts given, if the second Regulation goes unchallenged R Hood Ltd face the situation where they either export the remaining 600 tons and become subject to a further levy of €3,000, or do not export and lose the deposit of €5,000 for failing to comply with the earlier Regulation. Neither of these alternatives would be welcome. R Hood are therefore interested that the second Regulation should not apply to them and that they can rely solely on the first Regulation.

Challenges to EU legislation can be undertaken under Art 263 TFEU action to annul Acts of the institutions but only if specific requirements are met, particularly in terms of individuals who seek to challenge EU acts. For these so-called non-privileged applicants, admissibility has been the most difficult part of the action because of strict *locus standi* rules. There is, however, more than just one issue to consider in respect of admissibility:

> The institution challenged must be one envisaged by the Treaty – here it is the Commission, clearly named in Art 263 TFEU.

> The Act challenged must also be one within the scope of Art 263 TFEU. In the present case it is a Regulation, which is one of the legislative Acts of the EU institutions and authorised under Art 288 TFEU.

However, because a Regulation is a normative act applicable generally, it has in the past carried greater requirements on the part of legal and natural applicants to challenge it. Article 263 TFEU provides that the applicant must show the act is of direct and individual concern to them.

The final consideration in respect of applicability which is of vital importance is the time limit. Article 263 TFEU states that the challenge must be made within two months of the publication of the measure challenged. In the present problem, given that no further date or information is provided, it is assumed that the challenge is made within the required two-month period. If it is outside of this then the application is inadmissible.

Therefore, admissibility is dependent on the ability to challenge the Regulation. It has been held that Regulations are normative acts of general concern as provided by Art 288 TFEU and therefore cannot individually concern applicants. As a result the ECJ has held that true Regulations cannot be challenged; see *KSH* v *Council and Commission* (101/76), as they apply to categories or persons and not to individuals, although in the case of *Codurniu SA* v *Commission* (C-309/89) it would seem that the Court confirmed the true status of a Regulation for all others but nevertheless allowed a challenge from an individual applicant. In *Fruit and Vegetable Confederation* v *Commission* (17/62) it was held that it is the nature and content of a provision that is the determining factor and not the form or label it is given. In *International Fruit Company* v *Commission* (41–44/70), a group of fruit importers were held entitled to challenge a Regulation where the identity of the natural or legal persons affected was already known and thus fixed and identifiable. The Regulation was thus the equivalent of a bundle of Decisions addressed to each applicant. Therefore, if you can demonstrate that the Regulation has in mind or indeed has named, either in the Regulation or in the annexe, a number of individuals to whom it applies, it will be considered by the ECJ to be a bundle of Decisions rather than a Regulation (see the case of *Roquette Frères and Maizena* v *Council* (138 and 139/79)). In the particular area of anti-dumping measures, the Court of Justice has held that despite being a measure of general application, certain individuals may challenge Regulations as if Decisions, especially when one of the articles of the Regulation specifically referred to the applicant companies (see the *Japanese Ball-Bearings* cases (113, 118–121/77)). In the present case, the Regulation under challenge was required specifically to take account of those who have already exported in 2011; thus it is arguable that the Regulation was really a bundle of Decisions, although it is not stated if they were individually named, so this could thus be argued either way. Post Lisbon reforms, there will be less focus on this aspect and more on 'individual' although both contribute to the determination of whether the Act concerns individuals.

The applicant is required to satisfy the test of direct and individual concern. In order for the application to be admissible, the act must be of direct and individual concern to the applicant. In this answer, 'direct' will be considered first. Direct will be demonstrated if there is no intervening action by the Member State agencies or any other discretion. In this problem there is not; therefore, it is of direct concern (see the *Alcan* case (69/69)).

Individual concern, on the other hand, has been very hard to demonstrate and has often been tested by the Court of Justice first or at the same time as direct concern to decide admissibility as in *Plaumann* v *Commission* (25/62). A Decision was addressed to the German Government refusing permission to reduce duties on clementines. The test was whether the decision affects the applicant by virtue of the fact that he is a member of the abstractly defined class addressed by the rule, for example, because he is an importer of clementines, or does it affect him because of attributes peculiar to him which differentiate him from all other persons? Plaumann was held to be one of a class of importers and not therefore individually concerned. The ECJ confirmed in the Commission appeal case of *Jégo-Quéré* (C-263/02) that the test remains of individual concern. It therefore remains a question of an open or closed and fixed class. A much more likely exception to the rule that individuals cannot challenge Regulations and also fitting within the closed group, is because of the retroactive effect of the Regulation which imposes an export levy on exports, which at the time of export attracted a subsidy. The cases of *Bock* (62/70) and *Töpfer* (106 and 107/63) would be applicable here.

As a result of the fact that specifically included in the Regulation are those who have already exported and that the legal rules have changed with retroactive effect, Hood is directly and individually concerned. The company is in the group of those which have already exported sweet lupins in 2011 and the new Regulation also applies retroactively to exports already made.

Therefore, if this is admissible, the merits or substance of the action can now be considered. The grounds of challenge are exhaustively but widely listed in Art 263 TFEU. Two which appear applicable in this case are an infringement of an essential procedural requirement or an infringement of the Treaty or of any rule of law relating to its application.

In response to the first one, specific requirements are laid down by Art 296 TFEU that all Community secondary law must give reasons and refer to any proposals and opinions made in respect of the provisions. The Court of Justice has held that insufficient or vague or inconsistent reasoning would constitute a breach of this ground. It was held in *Germany v Commission* (Wine Tariff Quotas) (24/62) that reasons must contain sufficient details of the facts and figures on which they are based. Although Art 296 TFEU requires the reasons for legislation and the opinions on which they are based to be stated, there is no express requirement to state the legal base. However, it was held in *France v Commission* (C-325/91) that there is a requirement to state the Treaty base, without which the measure is void.

In the present case there are no reasons stated, hence it will be held to be in breach of the essential procedural requirement of Art 263 TFEU. Whilst this is a clear breach, it may be worthwhile suggesting that other, less certain grounds might be raised in respect of fundamental rights breaches amounting to a breach of a rule of law relating to the application of Community law, also considered by Art 263 TFEU.

The grounds then might include general principles of legitimate expectation to be able to export all of the sweet lupins without penalty and that there should be no retroactive law or double jeopardy of sanction. In addition, the removal of subsidies without prior notice can be argued to breach the same ground. The case of *Töpfer* (112/77) would be good authority for those latter points.

The conclusion is that R Hood Ltd will be successful in the challenge to the second Regulation.

Other challenges, which may be possible but not necessary in view of the above conclusion, may include a damages action under Art 340 TFEU against the EU institutions, which is likely to be considered on the same substantive grounds. Furthermore, national proceedings including an Art 267 TFEU reference to ask the ECJ to rule on the validity of the EU act would be a possibility, providing there is a national element to the case, eg if the firm concerned were being fined or prosecuted by the national authorities in the national courts, the legality of their basis in EU law may be challenged, a point recently reconfirmed by the ECJ in case C-167/02 *Rothley and Others* v *EP*.

Question 5

'The circumstances in which an individual can recover damages for loss suffered as a result of a legislative act of the Union institutions are unduly restrictive.'
 Discuss.

 ## Commentary

The above question requires a discussion of the action for damages under **Art 340 TFEU (ex 288 EC)** which comes under the jurisdiction of the ECJ by virtue of **Art 268 TFEU (ex 235 EC)**. In order to answer the question, the main aspects of the procedure should first of all be outlined with particular emphasis on the requirements demanded by the Court of Justice in actions involving the legislative acts of the EU. Then you should consider whether an action for damages is unduly restrictive to individuals. This is best done by reference to case law for examples. The **Art 340 TFEU** action can also be contrasted to the actions under **Arts 263 and 265 TFEU** to demonstrate whether or not it is any more restrictive.

 ## Answer plan

- Outline the principal aspects of **Arts 268 and 340 TFEU**
- Outline admissibility and explain the Schöppenstedt Formula
- Subsequent case law of the ECJ further expounding *Schöppenstedt*
- Consider whether the different rules for administrative errors have now been changed
- Outline how damage is established
- Provide conclusions on whether the action is restrictive

Suggested answer

It may be stated that generally, in contrast to the challenge to EU acts under Art 263 TFEU and the action to establish an omission to act under Art 265 TFEU, there are less restrictive *locus standi* requirements imposed by Art 340(2) TFEU. Instead, it would appear that any attempt to restrict the number of cases is made at the stage of the consideration of the merits or grounds of the case by the ECJ and not at the stage of admissibility.

An action under Art 340(2) TFEU consists of the following requirements which have been identified as necessary to establish liability:

there must be a wrongful act or omission on the part of the EU which has breached a duty;

the applicant must have suffered damage; and

there must be a causal link between the act or omission and the damage.

With Art 340 TFEU actions, admissibility is not really a problem. First of all there is a much more generous time limit than with Arts 263 or 265 TFEU. Article 340 TFEU has a five-year limitation period on actions which commences from the occurrence of the event causing the damage, as held in the *Schöppenstedt* case (5/71). Furthermore, in contrast to Arts 263 and 265 TFEU, there is not a restrictive *locus standi* imposed by either Arts 268 or 340(2) TFEU and essentially, if an applicant can show that they have been damaged in some tangible and provable way, then *locus standi* is established.

Initially it was considered to be a dependent action following a successful action under either Art 263 or 265 TFEU. If this position would have been maintained it would have even more severely restricted its use. However, in the *Lütticke* case (4/69), the Court of Justice rejected this argument and declared that 'the action for damages provided by Arts 235 and 288(2) [now 268 and 340 TFEU] was established by the Treaty as an independent form of action and whose object was to compensate a party for damage sustained and not to secure the annulment of an illegal measure'. This ruling was confirmed in the *Schöppenstedt* case (5/71). Therefore, little difficulty faces applicants in respect of admissibility, the problem lies in proving an act of the EU caused damage.

The act or omission of the EU must be shown to be wrongful. In respect of actions claiming damage resulting from the wrongful adoption of legislative acts, stricter requirements are imposed on the breach of the duty. This is because the Court has decided that in challenging such acts, which involve the EU in making choices in economic policies, far more stringent requirements are necessary, otherwise the functioning of the EU would be hindered and the EU could not operate as it needs to. Thus, the Court of Justice has laid down a strict test in *Zuckerfabrik Schöppenstedt v Council* (5/71), which has been repeated often. Essentially this test provides that the EU does not incur liability on account of a legislative measure which involves choices of economic policy unless a sufficiently flagrant violation (or also sometimes termed; serious breach) of a superior rule of law for the protection of the individual has occurred. Note, however, that since case C-352/98P *Bergaderm*, the Court of Justice has provided that a single test should apply to both administrative and legislative acts, which bases liability on the degree and complexity in the process leading to the act.

It has proved extremely difficult to determine exactly how severe a breach or violation must be and how serious the resulting damage must be as can be observed from a review of the case law of the Court of Justice. It may be argued that the reasoning for this is very similar to the strict requirements for *locus standi* for Art 263 TFEU, in that the high degree of discretion that the institutions need to carry out the economic tasks necessarily affect many persons. Therefore, it is not just unlawful conduct that will attract liability, but it is the degree of unlawfulness of the conduct which is important under the formula developed by the Court of Justice.

This formula can then be divided into two parts although it is also suggested it can be divided into three parts. The first element is that the rule of law must be one for the protection of the individual. This should be taken together and not separate as 'a superior rule of law' which is 'for the protection of the individual'. The later *Bergaderm* case (C-352/98 P) requires that there has to be a sufficiently serious breach of a rule of law intended to confer rights on individuals. The rules of law which are accepted as coming within the formulation include general principles of law. The principles of equality, non-discrimination and legitimate expectation seem most often to be raised.

The protection of the individual has been interpreted to include the protection of classes of persons as with the importers in the *Kampfmeyer* case (5, 7, 13–24/66).

Thus, in the *CNTA* case (74/74), the Commission was held liable to pay compensation for losses incurred as a result of a Regulation which abolished with immediate effect and without warning the application of compensatory amounts. It was held to be a serious breach of the principle of legitimate expectation. In the *Gritz* and *Quellmehl (Dumortier Frères)* cases (64 et al/76), the ending of a subsidy was held to be a breach because it was retained on starch which was in direct competition, and hence discriminatory.

Secondly, the breach must be sufficiently serious. In *HNL v Council and Commission* (83/76) this was required to be 'manifest and grave'. This was interpreted later in *KSH v Council and Commission* (143/77) as conduct verging on the arbitrary. Factors which influence the Court of Justice in its determination of whether the breach is sufficiently serious are the effect of the measure and the nature of the breach.

The effect of measure relates to its scope, the number of people affected and the damage caused. For example, in *HNL* (83/76) there was little damage and did not, in the view of the Court, exceed the bounds of economic risk, thus the action was not successful. The damage must be over and above the risks of loss or damage normally inherent in business but, in the *Amylum and Tunnel Refineries* and *KSH Isoglucose* cases (116 & 124/77 and 143/77), even though the damage was severe and in the latter case, so extensive to have caused insolvency of the company, the actions were not successful. See the *Dumortier Frères v Council* (*Gritz and Quellmehl* cases) (64 and 113/76), and *Sofrimport* (C-152/88) in respect of the decision that the Court requires that only a small defined and closed group of applicants is affected. However, in the case of *Mulder* (C-104/89 and 37/90) the presence of a large group of claimants did not defeat a claim although a serious breach still had to be demonstrated and that there was no higher public interest of the Community (EU) involved.

The nature of the breach relates to its seriousness. In the *Isoglucose* case (143/77) the damage was extensive, causing the insolvency of one company but the action was not successful because the breach of the law was not verging on the arbitrary, although in the later case of *Stahlwerke Peine-Salzgitter v Commission* (C-220/91P) the ECJ held that it was no longer necessary to show that the conduct was verging on the arbitrary. The applicants in the *Sofrimport* case were successful because of the complete failure of the Commission to take into account the interests of the applicants, despite prior knowledge.

Other actions, which do not challenge the legislative acts themselves but only seek to show the wrongful act was a failure of the administration in the implementation of law, do not need to satisfy the formula under *Schöppenstedt* (5/71), hence a higher standard is imposed when individuals seek to obtain damages as a result of loss suffered from legislative acts of the EU.

Having established the existence of an act or omission attributable to the EU, damage to the applicant must be proved. Case T-376/04 *Polyelectrolyte Producers Group v Council and Commission* was rejected as inadmissible by the CFI (now General Court) as the allegations of loss made were unsupported by any evidence of loss. Damage can be purely economic as in the *Kampfmeyer* case (5, 7 and 13–24/66) involving a cancellation fee and loss of profits but this must be specified and not speculative, or it can be moral damage and anxiety (*Willame v Commission* (110/63)).

Finally, it must be shown that the act of the EU caused the damage. There must be a sufficiently direct connection between the act and the injury. The damages must be ascertainable, *Kampfmeyer* case (5, 7 and 13–24/66). It cannot, however, be too remote, as held in the *Lütticke* case (4/69). In *Dumortier Frères v Council* (*Gritz and Quellmehl*) (64 and 113/76) it was held that there was no need to make good every harmful consequence especially where remote. Damage must be a sufficiently direct consequence of the unlawful conduct of the institution concerned. In *Compagnie Continentale France* (169/73) it was held that the causal link was only established if, in the case, the misleading information given would have caused an error in the mind of a reasonable person.

The conclusion is that, whilst Art 340 TFEU does allow wider access to commence action, the actions seeking damages as the result of the adoption of a wrongful legislative act impose equally severe restrictions in proving the merits of the case, the result of which is that applicants rarely succeed.

In summary the requirements are:

time limit;

a wrongful act or omission by an institution of the EU ;

if the act is legislative, it must be sufficiently serious and the act must be a rule of law conferring individual rights;

there must be damage caused by the EU.

Question 6

A Welsh company, Welsh Foods, has invented a substance known as 'Isolactic', which can be used as a substitute for milk in the manufacture of butter, cheese and ice cream. Isolactic is also significantly cheaper than milk. A few months after Welsh Foods has begun commercial production of Isolactic, with encouraging results, the Council and EP, alarmed at the probable adverse consequences of Isolactic for EU milk producers, adopts a fictitious Regulation imposing a production levy on Isolactic producers. The effect of the levy, which is to be collected by the national authorities of the Member States on behalf of the Commission, is to make Isolactic significantly more expensive than milk.

Welsh Foods, which is one of only three firms in the EU making Isolactic, feels that the Regulation is discriminatory and that its effect will be to make production of Isolactic uneconomic, thus causing Welsh Foods to cease Isolactic production, without having recovered its research and development costs. Their losses are such that the company expects to be forced into liquidation within six months unless something is done.

Advise Welsh Foods whether it could recover damages from the EU for any losses it may suffer.

 Commentary

This is a problem-type question which deals with the application of much of the discussion which arose in the answer to the last question.

The action under Art 340 TFEU which might be contemplated for Welsh Foods concerns the adoption by the EU of a legislative act which is allegedly wrongful. Apart from admissibility, the problem raises the difficulty of demonstrating that the alleged breach is serious enough to be successful.

The material facts and issues arising in this problem can be identified easily. Welsh Foods consider the Regulation which imposes a levy on their production to be extremely damaging to them and that it was unlawfully enacted on the grounds that it is discriminatory. As a consequence, they seek damages. Hence under EU law, they would turn to the action under Art 340(2) TFEU.

It would be useful to set out the main considerations for an Art 340 TFEU action in an introductory paragraph. The question also involves a choice of Court issue which should be considered.

Answer plan

- Outline relevant facts in the problem
- Outline the Art 340 TFEU action for damages and admissibility issues
- Briefly consider the choice of court element involved
- Application of the *Schöppenstedt* formula and *Bergaderm* case to the facts
- Consider the substantive merits of the action
- Conclusions as to likelihood of success

Suggested answer

An action under Art 340(2) TFEU should be undertaken by Welsh Foods to recover losses already incurred.

First of all, it may be stated that for Art 340(2) TFEU, the *locus standi* requirements are much more relaxed and success is not so dependent on admissibility, as with Arts 263 and 265. There is a much more generous five-year time limit in which to make an application.

From case law it has been established that for a successful claim under Art 340(2) TFEU, an applicant must demonstrate:

a duty;

a breach of that duty by an action or inaction; and

damage which is caused as a result of the act or omission.

Before the action may commence, a further issue arises in this case regarding the choice of court. It is stated the levy is collected by national authorities. Hence, if there is an intervention by national authorities, the action should take place in the national courts with a reference to the Court of Justice if necessary (see *Haegemann* (181/73) and *Kampfmeyer* (5, 7, 13–24/66) cases). However, it also depends on the discretion given to the Member States. If none is given and they merely act as agents for the EU then the action can also commence in the Court of Justice. In case of doubt, it would be advisable to go to the national courts and ask for a reference rather than have the case dismissed by the Court of Justice.

In this case the applicants are seeking to challenge a legislative Act of the EU. It has been held in the *Schöppenstedt* case (5/71) that where actions concern legislative measures involving a choice of economic policy it is necessary to demonstrate in respect of the breach that it is a sufficiently serious breach of a superior rule of law for the protection of individuals. This then enhances the requirements to show both a breach of a duty and the level of damage suffered and that the breach must be a sufficiently serious one. According to the *Bergaderm* case (C-352/98P), the emphasis for the court is that the legislative act involved must confer an individual right rather than demonstrating a superior rule of law designed for the protection of individuals. Whilst the new formulation has been followed up in a number of cases the more complex approach in *Schöppenstedt* has not necessarily been abandoned. Hence then, the consideration of the possible breach can be divided into two parts, ie the breach of the rule of law for the protection of the individual and whether it was sufficiently serious.

The breach of a rule includes breach of general principles (*CNTA* case (74/74)). Equality and non-discrimination have been held to be recognised general principles. Non-discrimination is one covered specifically by Art 40(2) TFEU (ex 34(2) EC) and thus more likely to be regarded as a superior rule of law. There are many cases in which the Court of Justice has recognised general principles as superior rules of law (see the *HNL* (83/76), *Isoglucose* (103 and 145/77) and *Sofrimport* (C-152/88) cases).

In the *Gritz and Quellmehl Dumortier Frères* cases (64 and 113/76), the ending of the subsidy was held to be a breach of the principle of non-discrimination because it was retained on starch which was its direct competition.

Turning to the requirement that the breach be sufficiently serious, this has been further defined as 'manifest and grave' in the *HNL* case, and as 'verging on the arbitrary' in the *Isoglucose* cases although the later case of *Stahlwerke Peine-Salzgitter v Commission* (C-220/91P) suggests this latter requirement is not necessary. A breach of the rule on its own is not enough. In order to determine whether the breach was sufficiently serious a number of criteria must be considered and the nature and the effect of the breach must be examined. In the *Gritz* and *Quellmehl* cases the Court of Justice looked at the numbers affected, the extent of the loss suffered and the seriousness of the damage caused, ie is it far beyond the risks normally associated with business?

In the *HNL* case, which concerned the requirement to buy milk products rather than soya products, the increase in production costs was limited. The Court of Justice considered whether the company could pass on the increases with little loss of profit. If the company could not pass on the increases, then this suggests that the breach was serious, but if the company could pass on the increase then it is not sufficiently serious to succeed.

The damage must go beyond the risks normally associated with business. In the *Isoglucose* case (143/77), however, the damage was beyond normal, including causing the liquidation of some of the companies involved, but the breach was not flagrant and therefore not verging on the arbitrary.

The Court of Justice will look at the number of people affected, the degree of loss and most importantly whether there is a EU interest involved. The *Sofrimport* case (C-152/88) involved the import of Chilean apples which were on the high seas when the Regulation took effect. It was held that this involved a closed group because no other could be similarly affected after the date of the Regulation. However, in the more recent case of *Mulder* (C-104/89 and 37/90) the presence of a large group of claimants did not defeat a claim although a serious breach still had to be demonstrated and also that there was no higher public interest of the EU involved.

In applying this to the above problem it must first be determined whether there is an act which caused damage. The damage would be the losses incurred caused by the Regulation imposing the levy. However, since a Regulation involves a choice of economic policy, the action is subject to the *Schöppenstedt* (5/71) formula and it must be considered whether the superior rule of law has been breached, subject to the comments made about the *Bergaderm* case above.

The superior rule of law alleged to have been breached in the case of Welsh Foods is that of non-discrimination which is both contained in Art 40(2) TFEU and has been clearly acknowledged in previous case law. This can be answered by showing that equal or similar products have not been similarly affected. Factors in this consideration are whether they are substitutable products. In the *Isoglucose* (143/77) and *Gritz* and *Quellmehl* cases (64 and 113/76) the alternative products of sugar and starch were held to be in competition or substitutable and therefore the rule was breached. However, in the *Walter Rau* case (261/81), where equality of treatment was pleaded for margarine and butter, it was held the products were not substitutable and so there was no breach of the superior rule.

On balance in the case of Welsh Foods there is a likely breach as the product is in direct competition and can be used as a substitute for milk.

The attention then turns to whether the breach was sufficiently serious. As noted, a number of criteria can be considered, including the nature and the effect of the breach, the numbers affected and whether it was a closed group of three, and the seriousness of the damage. On the basis of the *Isoglucose* case, where companies were driven out of business, it would not be sufficiently serious but on the basis of the *Gritz* and *Quellmehl* cases (64 and 113/76) and the *Sofrimport* case (C-152/88), it was considered that the risk went beyond that normally inherent in business and in view of the small numbers involved, then it would be sufficiently serious. It is not, however, predictable with certainty. Whilst the group is not entirely fixed it is unlikely that others would join at this stage and the losses are enough to drive them out of business. Thus according to the information given in this case, it is likely but not certain that Welsh Foods will succeed with its action; however, the Council of Ministers does have a legitimate aim in preventing the re-establishment of the milk lakes and this may well weigh heavily in the decision of the ECJ.

Question 7

Define the circumstances in which the ECJ would refuse to accept a reference under the Art 267 TFEU preliminary ruling procedure, and outline the guidelines for courts of last instance and other national courts in determining whether a reference should be made to the ECJ on:

(a) the interpretation of EU law;

(b) the validity of EU laws.

 ## Commentary

This is a two-part question, clearly concentrating on the preliminary ruling procedure introduced under Art 234 of the EC Treaty. First, you should state the basic purpose of Art 234 and outline the procedure involved in national courts making references.

Secondly, you should discuss the right or ability of the Court of Justice to refuse to accept a reference, referring to established case law to assist your answer and then outline the guidelines for the national courts in making references.

 ## Answer plan

- Outline purpose of Art 267 TFEU
- Outline the roles of the ECJ and national courts
- Consider the ability of the ECJ to reject cases, giving case examples
- Note courts of last instance and the obligation of Art 267(3) TFEU
- Discuss the *Costa* v *ENEL* and *CILFIT* cases
- Consider Art 267(2) TFEU and the discretion to refer by other courts

Suggested answer

The purpose of Art 267 TFEU is to act as a bridge or a link between the EU and national legal systems. It is to ensure the uniform interpretation of EU law throughout the Member States and thus provide consistency in EU law. It provides the national courts with assistance in cases concerning EU law by obtaining rulings on the interpretation and validity of EU law.

It should be pointed out that Art 267 TFEU is a judicial device and not part of an appeal system, nor is it a remedy of the individual, therefore the decision to refer remains that of the Member State Court.

Article 267 TFEU basically provides that where a question of interpretation of the Treaty or a question of the validity and interpretation of Acts of the institutions arise, any court or tribunal in a Member State may request the Court of Justice to give a ruling on it. The national court should determine the facts of cases and decide whether a question of EU law arises which it considers must be resolved in order to decide a case before it. When the ruling of the Court of Justice is received the national court must faithfully apply that ruling to the case. Generally, references should not be made until the facts have been determined.

Initially, the Court of Justice stated that it was up to the Member States to decide whether a reference was necessary (see the case of *Da Costa* (28–30/62)). As the number of cases before the Court of Justice increased and a considerable backlog developed, the Court of Justice may well have been prompted to start considering whether all the references were entirely necessary. The Court has considered the validity of some of the references and has on occasion refused references which in its opinion are an abuse of the system. There may be genuine circumstances, particularly where EU law proves not to be relevant, where the Court of Justice is right to refuse the reference. Thus, in a limited number of cases the Court of Justice has decided that there are reasons not to accept and has refused a reference. It has decided that cases which do not involve a real dispute and that concern only a theoretical consideration, which will not give an answer to a case before a court or tribunal, will not be accepted. In *SPUC v Grogan* (C-159/90), the case had been terminated at the national level, therefore the Court of Justice held there was no question left to be resolved. In *Mattheus v Doego* (93/78) a contract's continuation was determinable by the entry of Spain, Portugal and Greece into the Community (now EU). The Court of Justice held it had no jurisdiction as this was a matter to be determined by the Member States and the potential new states and refused jurisdiction.

The case of *Foglia v Novello* (104/79) is of special importance. It concerned a contract for wine between a French buyer, Novello, and Italian supplier, Foglia. Clauses stipulated that the buyer and the carrier (Danzas) should not be responsible for French import duties which were contrary to Community (EU) Law. These were charged on the French border and reimbursed by Foglia. Foglia sought to recover from Novello who denied responsibility to pay them on the basis that they were illegally charged by the French authorities. The Italian judge made a reference to the Court of Justice asking whether the French tax was compatible with the Treaty.

The Court of Justice rejected the reference on the grounds that there was no genuine dispute between the parties and that the action had simply been concocted to challenge French legislation. The Court of Justice considered this to be an abuse of the Art 177 (now 267 TFEU) procedure. Not satisfied by this, the Italian judge made a further reference, *Foglia* v *Novello* (No 2) (244/80), in which he specifically pointed out that the previous case marked a radical change in the attitude of the Court of Justice to a national court's decision to refer. He requested the Court of Justice to give guidelines on the respective powers and functions of the referring court. The Court of Justice held its role was not to give abstract or advisory opinions under Art 177 (now 267 TFEU) but to contribute to actual decisions and that although discretion is given to the national courts, the limits of that discretion are determinable only by reference to Community (EU) law.

The Court of Justice has also held that facts and issues must be sufficiently clearly defined in case C-320/90 *Telemarsicabruzzo SpA*. A further case in which the Court has refused jurisdiction is *Meilicke* v *ADV/ORGA* (C-83/91). The Court of Justice held that the questions raised in the reference concerned could not be answered by reference to the limited information provided in the file, the Court would be exceeding its jurisdiction in answering what was really a hypothetical question. A refusal of jurisdiction also occurred in *TWD Textilwerke* (C-188/92) in which a Commission decision addressed to Germany was not challenged within the two-month time limit under Art 230 (now 263 TFEU) but instead via the national court and Art 234 (now 267). The ECJ held this to be an abuse of the procedure for not acting within the time limit, although the previous case of *Walter Rau* (133/85) and subsequent case of *Eurotunnel SA* (C-408/95) seem to suggest that this is an acceptable way to proceed. The fact that the case involved a Directive addressed to the Member States, which was most probably beyond the challenge of individuals via Art 263 TFEU, is likely to have influenced the ECJ in its decision.

However, if the Court of Justice goes too far, it may be infringing the discretion of the Member States. It has been argued that the case of *Foglia* v *Novello* may have gone too far in that direction. The Court of Justice may understandably have not wished to become involved in a dispute which challenged the law of another Member State and which arguably should have been pursued by either the offended Member State under Art 259 TFEU or by the Commission under Art 258 TFEU. It should, however, be stressed that the Court of Justice has refused jurisdiction in only a small minority of cases referred to it. It is not therefore a major problem. The Court has, however, issued guidelines in 1996, updated to 2009, to the national courts to help them to decide whether a reference should be made. These summarise the previous case law and will be considered further at the end of this answer.

Turning to the second part of the question, guidelines for national courts are contained both in the Art 267 TFEU itself and in the pronouncements of the Court of Justice.

The obligation for courts of last instance to refer on points of interpretation are covered by Art 267(3). As they are courts from whom there is no further judicial remedy they are obliged to refer, subject to the view of the Court of Justice in *Da Costa* (28–30/62), *Costa v ENEL* (6/64) and *CILFIT* (283/81) cases which essentially require there to be a materially identical question to be resolved before a national court of last instance can be relieved of the obligation to refer. The guidelines which the Court of Justice laid down in *CILFIT*, which would relieve the national court of the obligation to make a reference, suggest that national courts have a great deal more discretion than that given by Art 267 TFEU. The French principle of law *acte clair* is often quoted in this respect, so that national courts need not make a reference where the application of EU law is so clear that the outcome of the case is not in doubt. Although this point is now confirmed in the 2009 Guidelines (OJ 2009 C297/01), the Court of Justice also provided in *CILFIT* that before the obligation to refer was relieved, the national court should be sure that the outcome would be equally obvious to the courts in other Member States; something which in practice would be close to if not impossible to achieve. Hence the view that only materially identical cases would not require a reference to be made.

Courts of last instance which require a ruling on validity are also governed by Art 267(3) and the Court of Justice has confirmed that a declaration of validity must be referred, but if a decision on validity has already been made on the same provision, this has a general effect, which all courts may follow (see the *ICC* case (66/80)). The more recent cases of *Köbler* (C-224/01) and *Traghetti* (C-173/03) have re-emphasised the obligation of last instant courts to refer rather than rely on *acte clair*.

Lower national courts requiring interpretation have a discretion to refer but would also be able to apply previous judgments of the Court of Justice. Whilst it is not expressly stated, the application of the *Da Costa* principle would clearly be logical.

Finally, lower courts with questions of validity also have the discretion to refer or to allow an appeal to a higher court to decide the matter. They may not themselves rule on validity, and it was held in *Foto-Frost* (314/85) that they have an express obligation to refer where an answer to a question on validity is considered necessary to decide the case at hand. The 2009 Guidelines and the *Zuckerfabrik* case (C-143/88 and C-92/89), however, provided an exception where an urgent matter required interim measures suspending the application of an EU measure whilst a preliminary ruling was sought. The guidelines, which are not binding, also provide that the national courts should accompany questions with a clear statement of facts, reasons and national law where relevant. Changes have been introduced to the Court's Rules of procedure whereby a reference dealing with a question already considered by the ECJ will be subject to a simplified procedure and certain subject Art 267 references may also be heard by the General Court (previously CFI) (Art 256 TFEU). If, however, the General Court considers that a question raises a point on EU law consistency, the case may be referred to the

ECJ or exceptionally the ECJ may review a General Court decision but on more restrictive grounds than other appeals from the General Court to the ECJ. Basically, the unity of EU law must be at risk.

Question 8

The EC Commission addressed a (fictitious) Directive to the Italian Government requiring it to ensure that paid holiday schemes and sickness schemes are equalised for male and female workers. The Italian Dentists Association, a professional body to which 90% of Italian dentists belong, has, with the approval of the Government, constituted its own professional arbitration tribunal to settle disputes relating to pay and conditions of work. Decisions of the tribunal are legally binding and there is no appeal. Angelo, a trainee dentist, claims to have received unfair treatment by comparison with female trainees and brings a case before the tribunal.

The tribunal dismisses his claim to protection by the Directive on the grounds that he is not a worker but a trainee, despite the fact that the ECJ had held that the term 'worker' included trainees.

The tribunal panel do not want to make a reference under Art 267 TFEU, whereas Angelo insists that it must do so.

Consider whether there is a duty, ability or right for this tribunal for Angelo to have a question referred to the Court of Justice.

Commentary

The basic question is whether this tribunal can make a reference to the ECJ under Art 267, but first of all you have to consider whether this is a court or tribunal for the purposes of Art 267 and thus entitled to make references to the Court of Justice, because not all bodies have been so recognised. You should also consider the relevance of the fact that the question arising in the case has already been decided on by the Court of Justice and whether Angelo can insist a reference be made.

Answer plan

- Outline Art 267 TFEU
- Definition of what is a Court or Tribunal for the purposes of Art 267 TFEU
- Case law and guidelines of ECJ on 'Court or Tribunal'
- Outline obligation of courts of last instance to refer under Art 267(3) TFEU
- Consider the *Da Costa* and *CILFIT* cases and the need to refer

Suggested answer

The ability of a national court or tribunal to make a reference to the ECJ depends on whether it is a court or tribunal recognised by the ECJ for the purposes of Art 267 TFEU. If it is, it has a right to refer a question. A duty to refer arises when it is a court or tribunal of last instance and the obligation to refer has not been relieved under the criteria outlined by the Court of Justice in case law and guidelines.

The Court of Justice has accepted references from a varied number of bodies including administrative tribunals, arbitration panels and insurance officers. The determination of what is an acceptable court or tribunal is a question for the Court of Justice and is not dependent on national concepts. Certain criteria have, however, now been established by which it may reasonably be determined whether a particular body may refer to the Court of Justice for guidance under Art 267 TFEU. For example, it was clear from *Van Gend en Loos* (26/62) that administrative tribunals were acceptable for the purposes of Art 234 (now 267 TFEU). Whilst the majority of bodies which decide legal matters in the Member States pose no problem, it is the bodies which lie either partially or entirely outside the state legal system which raise the question of whether it is suitable for the Court of Justice to accept a reference from them. A few examples will highlight some of the considerations taken into account by the Court of Justice.

The *Vaassen* case (61/65) concerned a reference from the arbitration tribunal of a private mine employees' social security fund. The Court of Justice held that the panel qualified as a court or tribunal in the eyes of Community (EU) law because of the following criteria: It possessed its own power to nominate members, to approve rule changes, a power also in the hands of a government minister and the panel was a permanent body operating under national law and rules of procedure.

Broekmeulen v HRC (246/80) concerned a reference made by the appeal committee of the Dutch medical profession's organisation. This was held by the Court of Justice to be acceptable because it was approved and had the assistance and considerable involvement of the Dutch public authorities, its decisions were arrived at after full legal procedure, the decisions affected the right to work under Community (EU) law, they were final and there was no appeal to Dutch Courts, despite the fact that a legal remedy was in private hands.

In the next two cases jurisdiction was refused. In the case of *Borker* (138/80), a reference from the Paris Bar Association Council on the right of a French lawyer to appear as of right before German courts was refused on the ground that there was no lawsuit in progress and the Council was not therefore acting as a Court or Tribunal called upon to give judgment in proceedings intended to lead to a decision of a judicial nature. In *Nordsee* v *Nordstern* (102/81) there was no involvement by national authorities in the case. Despite the fact there was a legally binding decision and there was no appeal, the Court of Justice held because there was no involvement of national authorities in the process, there was not a sufficiently close link to a national organisation of legal remedies and thus the arbitrator could not come under Art 234 (now 267 TFEU).

Thus, it is not an essential factor whether the body is private or public or that there is no appeal from its decision. A strong indicator is the level of involvement by national authorities. However, the lack of an appeal may lead to instances where the national body itself has to interpret EU law without guidance if the Court of Justice is unwilling to accept jurisdiction, something which must be less desirable from a Union point of view. In *Dorsch* (case C-54/96), the ECJ provided guideline questions for national courts to pose. These are: whether the body is established by law, whether it is permanent, whether its procedure is *inter partes*, whether it applies rules of law and whether it is independent. The ECJ also issued a guideline statement in 1996, updated to 2009.

It must therefore be decided on a balance of factors whether the arbitration tribunal in the above problem is one which is acceptable for the purposes of Art 267 TFEU. The factors in the present case are:

the governmental approval;

the fact that 90% of all potential members are included; and

the legally binding decisions with no appeal.

The membership figure could be used as evidence to decide either way in that it would suggest that this is not the only way in which dentists can have disputes resolved. The other 10% must presumably be able to avail themselves of the ordinary national courts. On the other hand, since this body clearly is involved with EU legislation, it would defeat the uniformity of EU law if it cannot refer and must decide matters of EU law itself. Individuals, such as Angelo, may thus be deprived of their true rights. This, in the end, may be the most important consideration and is certainly one the Court of Justice would consider.

Thus, it is probable that it is a tribunal for the purposes of Art 267 TFEU.

The next question is whether it is obliged to refer or whether it has a discretion to refer. It can be stated immediately that whatever the answer to that question, it is clear that Angelo has no right under Art 267 TFEU to a reference and that this matter comes within the discretion of the tribunal where they have a discretion. As a tribunal against which there is not a judicial remedy under Art 267(3) TFEU, the tribunal is obliged to make a reference. This obligation will only be relieved if the question has already been decided and the case thus comes within the guidelines of the *Da Costa* (28–30/62) or the *CILFIT* (283/81) cases, although the cases of *Köbler* (C-224/01) and *Traghetti* (C-173/03) have re-emphasised the obligation of last instant courts to refer.

The tribunal is not obliged to refer where the provision in question has already been interpreted by the Court of Justice or the correct application is so obvious as to leave no scope for any reasonable doubt and therefore no question to be decided arises. The *Da Costa* case raised the same question as had previously been asked in the *Van Gend en Loos* case (26/62). The Court of Justice referred to its previous judgment in *Van Gend en Loos* as the basis for deciding the issue and advised that such a situation might, if the national court wished, excuse the obligation to refer.

The *CILFIT* (283/81) judgment expanded the decision of *Da Costa* (28–30/62). In *CILFIT* the Italian Supreme Court asked the Court of Justice directly in what circumstances it need not refer. The Court of Justice replied that in addition to the reason given in *Da Costa* a court might not refer if the correct application, but not interpretation, may be so obvious as to leave no scope for any reasonable doubt that the question raised will be solved. However, the Court of Justice qualified this by stating that the national court must be convinced that the matter is equally obvious to courts of other Member States, that it is sure language differences will not result in inconsistent decision in Member States, and EU law will be applied in light of the application of it as a whole with regard to the objectives of the Union. These criteria would be extremely difficult to fulfil if properly followed and the more recent cases of *Köbler* (C-224/01) and *Traghetti* (C-173/03) have re-emphasised the obligation of last instant courts to refer rather than rely on *acte clair*.

In the case of Angelo, the identical question has already been resolved by the Court of Justice who has given a ruling on the interpretation of the relevant provision, that a trainee is considered a worker under EU law and is thus subject to EU rules in respect of non-discrimination. Therefore, there would be no need to refer and the tribunal could simply apply the previous ruling of the Court of Justice. However, the national court retains its discretion to refer if it so wishes.

After the Treaty of Nice entered into force, new Rules of Procedure for the court provide a new simplified procedure under Art 104(3) for references identical to previous questions decided by the ECJ to be referred back to the national court.

The only problem left is that caused if the tribunal, despite its obligation to apply EU law, still followed its own decision in considering a trainee not to be a worker and not making a reference. In such circumstances it could not be prevented by the Court of Justice, although following case law such as *Francovich* (C-6 and 9/90), *Factortame III* (C-46 and 48/93) and *Köbler* (C-224/01), the state may be held liable for damages providing the criteria for such a claim are satisfied.

Question 9

Has Art 265 TFEU proved to be of any benefit to those capable of invoking it?

Commentary

This question concerns actions against the Council, the EP, the Commission, the European Council or the ECB for a failure to act. It is the remedy where the unlawfulness of the institution in question is the wrongful failure to act in violation of the Treaty. It can be divided into a discussion of those who are capable of invoking it and whether it has helped those who have got past the stage of admissibility. A description of the process itself should be given at the start. The 2007 Lisbon Treaty made only minor changes to this Article.

Answer plan

- Outline Art 265 TFEU
- Consider institutions which may be challenged and *locus standi* of applicants
- Types of measure which may be requested and case law of ECJ
- Procedural aspects of the action; definition of position
- The *Transport Policy* case and conclusions on usefulness

Suggested answer

Article 265 TFEU concerns actions against the Council, the EP, the Commission, the European Council or the ECB for a failure to act. It is the remedy where the unlawfulness of the institution in question is the wrongful failure to act in violation of the Treaty. This presupposes that there was a clear duty imposed on the institution to act in the first place. It complements an Art 263 TFEU action and can be pleaded in the same action. In *Chevalley v Commission* (15/70) the Court of Justice held it was not necessary to state which action was the subject of the application. Article 265 TFEU is designed to cover illegal inaction. Both provisions, however, have as their objective the ending of a situation of illegality. Both actions are also similar in respect of the institutions which may be challenged, originally only the Commission and the Council, but Art 265 TFEU has been extended under the Treaty on European Union to include the European Parliament and the ECB within its field of competence and by the Lisbon Treaty to include the European Council.

Those who are capable of invoking it are defined initially by Art 265 TFEU. Case law has then subsequently had the effect of excluding individuals in certain circumstances from having an application admitted.

The EU institutions and Member States have, under Art 265(1) TFEU, a privileged right of action which is not subject to restrictions on admissibility. Although not originally expressly stated that the EP is a privileged applicant, this was confirmed by the *Transport Policy* case (13/83). The privileged applicants can request general legislative acts as well as decisions without having to show any special interest (the *Transport Policy* case). The ECB was given the right to take action by the TEU in areas falling within its field of competence and all of the main institutions as defined by Art 13 TEU are now confirmed after the Lisbon Treaty changes to Art 265 TFEU.

Individuals, on the other hand, have a restricted right of *locus standi* under Art 265(3) TFEU, similar to Art 263 TFEU, because although there is no formal equivalent of the requirement of 'direct and individual concern' under Art 263 TFEU, case law has effectively established this position. Article 265 TFEU provides:

> Any natural or legal person may, under the conditions laid down in the preceding paragraphs, complain to the Court that an institution, body, office or agency of the Union has failed to address that person any act other than a recommendation or an opinion.

It was established by case law that to challenge under Art 265 TFEU, an individual must have been entitled legally to claim as a potential addressee. (See *Lord Bethell* v *EC Commission* (246/81), involving a complaint of a failure to act on price fixing by the airlines. Any potential act would be addressed to the airlines and not Lord Bethell.) This strict view on the *locus standi* requirements has been tempered by the ECJ in subsequent cases and now it can be observed that the requirements are analogous to the direct and individual concern of Art 263 TFEU (see the cases of *T Port* v *Bundesanstalt für Landeswirtschaft und Ernährung* (C-68/95) and *Gestevisión Telecinco SA* v *Commission* (T-95/96)).

The Court has in many cases rejected applications by individuals requesting measures of general legislative content (see *Chevalley* v *Commission* (15/70) and *Nordgetreide* v *Commission* (42/71)), in which it was held that applications are restricted to Decisions to be addressed to individuals. Regulations cannot be requested because by their very nature they are not capable of being addressed to specific individuals.

Furthermore, Art 265 TFEU cannot be used to get around the restrictive time limits of an action to annul under Art 263 TFEU; see the case of *Eridania* v *Commission* (10 and 18/68).

The action consists of a preliminary procedural step which must be taken before court action can ensue. Article 265(2) TFEU provides 'The action shall be admissible only if the institution concerned has first been called upon to act.' The applicant must request the institution to take a specific action as legally required and advise that the failure to do so will result in a court action under Art 265 TFEU. The invitation to act need not follow any precise form to qualify for the purposes of Art 265 TFEU. Only if the institution fails to define its position within the two-month period can the matter be brought before the Court. The application to the Court of Justice must be made within a further two-month period from the end of the initial two-month period.

If the institution complies with the request to act as in *EP v Council* (13/83), the Court of Justice will not allow the action to proceed.

The definition of position has also been seen to defeat actions because where the institution has explained its refusal to act, the action is inadmissible. In *Lütticke v Commission* (48/65) the applicants had requested the Commission to take action against the German Federal Republic regarding a breach of Community (EU) law. The Commission was of the opinion that there had been no breach so therefore refused to take action but also notified the applicant of this. The Court of Justice declared the application inadmissible on the grounds that the notification of the refusal was a definition of position. Thus a refusal to act is not actionable.

In the *Deutscher Komponistenverband v Commission* (8/71), a complaint that a decision taken by the Commission was wrong does not allow an applicant to proceed under Art 232 (now 265 TFEU) on the basis that the right decision was not taken by the Commission, ie it had failed to act in the right way.

In the *GEMA v Commission* case (125/78), a complaint was made to the Commission under Regulation 17 about Radio Luxembourg. When the Commission failed to take any action GEMA attempted an Art 232 (now 265 TFEU) action against the Commission. It was held that the letter from the Commission to GEMA stating its decision not to take action was a sufficient definition of position to defeat GEMA's action.

Until the *Transport Policy* case (13/83) a declaration by an institution of its unwillingness to act was regarded by some as constituting a sufficient definition of position for the purposes of the Court of Justice. However, the Court in the *Transport Policy* case stated that:

> In the absence of taking a formal act, the institution called upon to define its position must do more than reply stating its current position which in effect neither denies or admits the alleged failure nor reveals the attitude of the defendant institution to the demanded measures.

If it can be invoked successfully, and the case is proved, the institution is required under Art 266(1) TFEU to take the necessary measures to comply with the judgment of the Court of Justice, within a reasonable time. A continued failure to act would of course be actionable under Art 265 TFEU.

In the *Transport Policy* case the European Parliament had complained that the Council had failed in its Treaty obligations under old Arts 3, 61, 74, 75 and 84 to introduce a common policy for transport, lay down a framework for this policy and act on 16 specific proposals of the Commission.

The Court held with regard to the first claim that because the Treaty requirements were so vague there could not be said to exist sufficiently specific obligations as to amount to a failure to act despite the fact that even as such the obligations should have been completed long ago. The Court held that the obligation of old Art 61 of the EEC Treaty could be identified with sufficient preciseness as to constitute a failure on the part of the Council to lay down a framework.

The second claim of failure to act on 16 proposals of the Commission was only successful in respect of the proposals and freedom to provide services. The other measures were within the greater margin of discretion left to Council by the Treaty.

Apart from the *Transport Policy* case (13/83), admissible cases and those succeeding are extremely rare and despite the theoretical possibility that both privileged and non-privileged applicants may invoke, it has proved to be of very limited benefit to non-privileged applicants because of the other grounds on which its use has been restricted by the Court of Justice. It would seem that limited success is more likely in the areas of competition law and specifically anti-dumping and state-aid cases as a way of encouraging the Commission to investigate infringements (see the cases of *Gestevisión Telecinco SA v Commission* (T-95/96) and *Automec v Commission* (T-24/90)).

Question 10

In what circumstances will the 'plea of illegality' under Art 277 TFEU be available to litigants seeking to obtain benefit from it?

Commentary

Whilst it would be rare for a question to concentrate entirely on this less familiar article of the Treaty and certainly less employed article of the Treaty, it might nevertheless be the subject of a question. It is more likely you will have to consider an action using Art 277 within the answer to another question as can be seen already in some of the questions above, which have asked you to consider the possible alternative actions which an individual challenging EU law might consider, and in further questions on the jurisdiction of the Court of Justice in Chapter 10, on mixed questions. However, it will do no harm to concentrate on this action so as to become familiar with it. It might even be the case that your particular course has not considered this action at all, given the constraints on time whereby topics have to be considered according to priority, and not all of them make it into the course.

To provide therefore an answer to this question, a full explanation of the action and its availability to litigants needs to be given. The answer is thus straightforward and your only likely problem, given that the Article itself is not the subject of extensive treatment in textbooks, is finding enough to say about it. Hence the reason it is less likely to appear as a complete question in its own right. The 2007 Lisbon Treaty expanded the number of institutions whose acts can be challenged as inapplicable.

Answer plan

- Outline **Art 277 TFEU**
- *Locus standi* requirements and nature of the action
- Relationship with **Art 263 TFEU** and case law of the ECJ
- Substantive grounds of challenge
- Consequences of a successful action

Suggested answer

The action under Art 277 TFEU provides an alternative right to plead the illegality of an EU Regulation but it is not a right to plead this directly before the Court of Justice as in the action under Art 263 TFEU. It is not an action which can be used as an independent action nor one that can be used before the national courts. Article 277 TFEU reads:

> Notwithstanding the expiry of the period laid down in Article 263, sixth paragraph, any party may, in proceedings in which an act of general application adopted by an institution, body, office or agency of the Union is at issue, plead the grounds specified in Article 263, second paragraph, in order to invoke before the Court of Justice of the European Union the inapplicability of that act.

The action appears, at least at first sight, to be more easily available to litigants because it is not subject to the very restrictive *locus standi* requirements of Art 263 TFEU and is available to any party including Member States, the institutions and individuals. It is more likely to benefit individuals who are unable to scale the *locus standi* requirements of Art 263 TFEU.

It is to be stressed that Art 277 TFEU is not an independent or direct cause of action to the Court of Justice, ie it cannot be the sole basis for an action before the Court of Justice. In *Wöhrmann v Commission* (31 and 33/62), the Court of Justice held that Art 241 (now 277 TFEU) was only available in proceedings brought before the Court of Justice under some other action and only as an incidental or indirect action. This means that some other action must be taking place in which the validity of a EU general act is questioned and which may have a bearing on the outcome of the case (see *Italy v Council* (32/65)). There must be a connection with the plea of illegality and the main action, it cannot be self-standing.

The circumstances in which these criteria are likely to be met so that the illegality of a general act could be challenged would be where a challenge to some other form of EU law which is based on a general act is being made. Whilst Art 277 TFEU refers to general acts, which are effectively just Regulations, it has been held by the Court of Justice that other measures can be challenged. In

Simmenthal v *Commission* (92/78), a Decision was challenged which was based on prior Regulations and Notices. The Regulations themselves could not be challenged under Art 263 TFEU because of the time limits, but could be indirectly challenged via the Decision based on it under Art 277 TFEU. The Court of Justice held that it was not the form of the act which is important but the substance, therefore other acts which were normative in effect should be regarded as general measures that produced similar effects to a Regulation for the purposes of Art 241 EC (now 277 TFEU) and could therefore be challenged under Art 241 EC (now 277 TFEU), thus applying to Notices and Decisions.

However, Art 277 TFEU is not designed nor intended to provide a back door for those who had failed to commence an action under Art 263 TFEU, particularly after the two-month time limit has expired, but who could have done. For example, in *Commission* v *Belgium* (156/77) a Community (EU) Decision was challenged directly before the Court of Justice. The Court of Justice refused the Belgium state the ability to plead under Art 241 EC (now 277 TFEU) because it had allowed its right under Art 230 EC (now 263 TFEU) to expire. It is argued that this is a denial of Member State *locus standi*, but the real basis for the Court of Justice not admitting the case was that to allow it would make a nonsense of Art 263 TFEU time limits. See also, in this respect, *TWD Deggendorf* (C-188/92) in which a company was not allowed to indirectly challenge a Decision which it was specifically informed it could have done in time under Art 230 EC (now 263 TFEU). Instead, it provides relief for those who are unable to get standing to bring an action under Art 263 TFEU but who are nevertheless affected by a Decision based on an allegedly unlawful Regulation as in *Simmenthal*.

So, whilst a challenge merely to try to circumvent the time limits for a direct challenge under Art 263 TFEU will fail, Art 277 TFEU nevertheless allows a challenge to be made providing it is incidental to some other form of action before the Court of Justice. These would include actions under Arts 263, 265 or 340(2) TFEU.

The substantive grounds of the action are precisely the same as those listed for Art 263 TFEU. The *Simmenthal* case (92/78), for example, succeeded on the grounds that the general measure had been used for purposes other than those for which it was intended.

The result of such an action is that the Regulation, or other general measure, is declared inapplicable in that case and that case alone and not generally void (*Meroni* v *High Authority* (9/56)). Any acts based on a voidable Regulation, however, will also be void and will be withdrawn. However, in practice the consequences will be that the Regulation will not be applied in subsequent cases, as in the case of Art 267 TFEU references which result in a declaration of invalidity being made in the case by the Court of Justice, for example the *ICC* case (66/80).

Further reading

Albors-Llorens, A, 'The Standing of Private Parties to Challenge Community Measures: Has the European Court Missed the Boat?' (2003) 62(1) Cambridge LJ 72.

Arnull, A, 'Private Applicants and the Action for Annulment since *Codorniu*' (2001) 38(1) CML Rev 7.

Cortes Martin, JM, 'Ubi ius, ibi remedium? – Locus Standi of Private Applicants under Article 230(4) EC at a European Constitutional Crossroads' (2004) 11 Maastricht, Journal of European and Comparative Law 233–261.

Craig, P, 'Standing, Rights and the Structure of Legal Argument' (2003) 9 EPL 493.

Granger, MP, 'Towards a Liberalisation of Standing Conditions for Individuals Seeking Judicial Review of Community Acts: *Jégo-Quéré et Cie SA* v *Commission* and *Union de Pequenos Agricultores* v *Council*' (2003) 66(1) MLR 124.

Harlow, C and Rawlings, R, 'Accountability and Law Enforcement: The Centralized EU Infringement Procedure' (2006) 31 EL Rev 447.

Hilson, C, 'The Roles of Discretion in EC Law on Non-Contractual Liability' (2005) 42 CML Rev 677.

Rawlings, R, 'Engaged Elites Citizen and Institutional Attitudes in Commission Enforcement' (2000) 6(1) ELR 4.

Tridimas, T, 'Knocking on Heaven's Door: Fragmentation and Defiance in the Preliminary Reference Procedure' (2003) 40(1) CML Rev 9.

Usher, J, 'Direct and Individual Concern – an Effective Remedy or a Conventional Solution' (2003) 29 EL Rev 300.

Vogt, M, 'Indirect Judicial Protection in EC Law: The Case of the Plea of Illegality' (2006) 31 EL Rev 364.

Wenneras, P, 'A New Dawn for the Commission Under Articles 226 and 228 EC: General and Persistent (GAP) Infringements, Lump Sums and Penalty Payments' (2006) 45 CML Rev 31.

6

The Free Movement of Goods

Introduction

This substantive area of EU law is likely to be included in most courses on EU law. The area of law is regulated in the TFEU under Part Three, Title 1, Arts 26–36 TFEU (ex 23–31 EC). Whilst this title includes the Common Customs Tariff in Arts 31–32 TFEU (ex 26–27 EC), questions are more likely to be concentrated on the elimination of customs duties and measures having equivalent effect, Art 30 TFEU (ex 25 EC), and the elimination of quantitative restriction and measures having equivalent effect under Arts 34–36 TFEU (ex 28–30 EC). Whilst there was a change of position of the legal regime flowing from the 2007 Lisbon Treaty, the basic provisions governing the free movement of goods remained unchanged.

As with other substantive areas of EU law, questions can be posed both in the form of essay-type questions and problem-type questions. One particular topic of difficulty in this area, on which questions of either type are very likely, is concerned with the Court of Justice decisions and statements in the case of *Cassis de Dijon* (120/78) and the subsequent case of *Keck and Mithouard* (C-267 and 268/91). One of the two emergent rules from *Cassis*, the rule of reason, continues to cause difficulties. The questions in this chapter concentrate on charges and measures having equivalent effect, the restrictions allowed under Art 36 TFEU (ex 30 EC) and the principles of law which have emerged from the case of *Cassis de Dijon* and subsequent cases.

Although apt to cause difficulties in any part of the course, the renumbering of the EC Treaty by the Treaties of Amsterdam and now Lisbon is even more problematic in this area as very old Art 30 is old Art 28 and now Art 34 TFEU and very old Art 36 is old Art 30 but back again following Lisbon to Art 36 TFEU! Make sure you make it clear which Treaty you are referring to.

Question 1

'In spite of the aims of the EU Treaties, there is still not at the present time absolute freedom for a person in one Member State to import or export goods from or to another Member State.'

Discuss, explaining in particular the circumstances in which a Member State can lawfully restrict or prohibit the free movement of goods from another Member State.

Commentary

The first reference in this question is to the aims of the EU Treaties. You must therefore state the aims as contained in the preamble and Art 3 of the EU Treaty and generally introduce the provisions of the TFEU concerned with the free movement of goods, Arts 28–36 TFEU, the restrictions allowed the Member States in Art 36 TFEU and any tax on goods considerations arising from Art 110 TFEU. Outline, then, the rights provided by those Articles and the restrictions which are allowed the Member States by virtue of the TFEU. The further reasons whereby Member States can lawfully restrict the free movement of goods arising from the *Cassis de Dijon* case (120/78) should also be discussed, this latter part need only be covered briefly.

Answer plan

- Outline Art3 TEU and Arts 28–36 and 110 TFEU
- Consider the rights and restrictions contained in those Articles
- Directive 70/50 and *Dassonville* case
- Article 36 TFEU
- *Cassis de Dijon* and subsequent cases

Suggested answer

The internal market is defined in Art 26 TFEU (ex 14(2) EC) in the following terms:

> The internal market shall comprise an area without internal frontiers in which the free movement of goods, persons, services and capital is ensured in accordance with the provisions of the Treaties.

The aim is to achieve the circulation of goods without customs, duties, charges or other financial or other restrictions; to promote unlimited trade and to remove from the Member States the control over export and import matters. The Union is to be solely responsible for the latter.

The preamble of the old EC Treaty has previously proved instrumental in the Court's ruling in reaching a decision on cases involving the free movement of goods as have Arts 2 and 3 and the fidelity clause Art 10 and the prohibition of discrimination Art 12 EC. This will continue to be the case with the new Treaties, Arts 3 and 4 TEU and Art 18 TFEU.

There are four main groups of provisions in the TFEU connected with the free movement of goods:

customs duties and charges having equivalent effect, Arts 28–30 TFEU (ex 23–25EC);

the Common Customs Tariff, Arts 31–32 TFEU (ex 26–27 EC);

the use of national taxation systems to discriminate against goods imported from other Member States, Art 110 TFEU (ex 90 EC); and

quantitative restrictions or measures having an equivalent effect on imports and exports, Arts 34–36 TFEU (ex 28–30 EC).

Articles 28–30 TFEU are aimed at the abolition of customs duties and charges having equivalent effect and at prohibiting the introduction of any such measures.

Article 28 states that the Union shall be based on a customs union, with a common customs tariff, involving the prohibition of all customs duties on imports and charges having equivalent effect. This provision covers 'all trade in goods', goods being defined by the Court of Justice in *Commission v Italy* (Art Treasures case) (7/68) as 'products which can be valued in money and which are capable, as such, of forming the subject of commercial transactions'. The definition has been extended in *Commission v Ireland* (Dundalk Water Supply) (45/87) to include the provision of goods within a contract for the provision of services. Article 30 TFEU prohibits the introduction of new customs duties or charges having equivalent effect, and equally prohibits the increase of those which are already in existence. The prohibition applies both to imports and exports and was held to be directly effective in the leading case of *Van Gend en Loos* (26/62). The Treaty of Amsterdam has amended this by adding a second sentence to make it expressly clear that the prohibition also applies to customs duties of a fiscal nature.

Article 34 TFEU provides a general prohibition on quantitative restrictions and measures having equivalent effect. This article and Art 36 TFEU are those most closely concerned with the freedom to import and export goods and thus the answer to this question.

The concept of measures having equivalent effect has been defined by secondary legislation (Directive 70/50) and by the jurisprudence of the Court of Justice.

Directive 70/50, Art 2 defines 'measures having equivalent effect' to include those which 'make imports, or the disposal at any marketing stage of imported products, subject to a condition, other than a formality, which is required in respect of imported products only'. They also include any measures which subject imported products or their disposal to a condition which differs from that required for domestic products and which is more difficult to satisfy.

In *Procureur du Roi* v *Dassonville* (8/74) the term 'measures having equivalent effect' was held to include 'all trading rules enacted by a Member State which are capable of hindering, directly or indirectly, actually or potentially, intra-community trade'.

Basically, therefore, any measure which makes import or export unnecessarily difficult, and thus discriminates between the two, would clearly fall within the definition.

Thus, the basic regime promotes free movement but within the Treaty, Art 36 TFEU provides exceptions to the general prohibition of Art 34 TFEU. It states that Arts 34 and 35 shall not apply to prohibitions on imports, exports or goods in transit which are justified on any of the following four sets of grounds:

(a) public morality, public policy or public security;

(b) the protection of health and life of humans, animals or plants;

(c) the protection of national treasures possessing artistic, historic or archaeological value; or

(d) the protection of industrial and commercial property.

Therefore, Art 36 TFEU allows Member States to enact measures which can impede the free movement of goods, but this does not take account of the Court of Justice's restrictive interpretation or the fact that the application of these exceptions is subject to the limitation, set out in the second sentence of Art 36 TFEU, that they may not be used as a means of arbitrary discrimination, a disguised restriction on trade between Member States. The ECJ has refused many attempts to widen the scope of Art 36 TFEU or to allow the Member States to define the scope of it for themselves. Very few cases have thus survived the strict application of the second sentence of Art 36 TFEU to justify measures taken by Member States. Examples are, amongst others, *Commission* v *Ireland* (Metal Objects) (113/80), *Campus Oil* (72/83) and the *Prantl* case (16/83). In the *Prantl* case, the attempt by the Member State to classify any criminal restriction as coming within the scope of public policy under now Art 36 failed. The argument based on public security in the *Campus Oil* case (72/83) however succeeded, by which Irish laws insisting that 35% of petrol supplies be purchased from the State refinery were held to be acceptable. Another successful use of Art 36 TFEU was in the case of *R* v *Henn and Derby* (34/79) in which a ban on the import of pornographic

Derby

materials was upheld. It was, however, held to be necessary that similar domestic products were also prohibited.

The case of *Cassis de Dijon* (120/78) has added to the grounds on which Member States may restrict the free movement but only on an equal footing with domestic products. In the case, the Court of Justice stated that, in the absence of harmonising Community rules, obstacles to the free movement of goods, which are indistinctly applicable in that they apply or appear to apply to both domestic and imported goods, may be allowed only as far as these mandatory provisions are justified by an objective of public interest taking precedence over the free movement of goods. Mandatory requirements of the Member State could be imposed to relate in particular to:

the effectiveness of fiscal supervision;

the protection of public health; or

the fairness of commercial transactions; and

the defence of the consumer.

However, the measures are subjected to further requirements:

they must be justified and proportional, ie necessary to achieve the result;

there must be no Community system of rules; and

there must be neither an arbitrary discrimination nor a disguised restriction on trade.

The case of *Cassis de Dijon* had started to cause the ECJ problems because it was seized on both by Member States to justify restrictions and traders to attack virtually any nationally imposed restriction on trade practices or commercial freedom, particularly where rules were not just aimed directly at imports. The Court of Justice has therefore redefined its position in the *Keck* case (C-267 and 268/91). The Court considered that certain equally applicable non-discriminatory provisions restricting selling arrangements are not to be considered a hindrance on trade according to the *Dassonville* case (8/74) provided that they affect all traders and all domestic products and imports in the national territory, in the same manner and do not impose additional requirements (*Vereinigte Familiapress* C-368/95). In other words the national provisions impose an equal burden in law and in fact and therefore such rules fall outside Art 34 TFEU because they do not prevent imports.

Thus, if measures which are adopted by Member States satisfy either the provisions of Art 36 TFEU or the requirements laid down in the case of *Cassis de Dijon* for mandatory requirements, the Member State will be able, lawfully, to restrict the free movement of goods and thus there is not absolute freedom to import or export goods.

Question 2

'However wide the field of application of Article 34 TFEU may be, it nevertheless does not include obstacles to trade covered by other provisions of the Treaty. Thus, obstacles which are of a fiscal nature or have equivalent effect and are covered by Articles 28–30 and 110 TFEU do not fall within the prohibition of Article 34 TFEU.'
   Discuss.

Commentary

This quotation is taken from the Court of Justice judgment in the case of *Ianelli and Volpi* v *Meroni* (case 74/76), as amended to take account of the renumbering of the Treaty but it is not necessary to know that, or even that it is a quotation from the Court of Justice, to be able to discuss the meaning of the quotation. Instead, however, you will need to consider the scope of the application of Art 34 TFEU by considering the provision itself and by giving examples from the case law of the Court of Justice. The first sentence of the question suggests that the scope of application of Art 34 TFEU does not extend to prohibiting obstacles which are covered by other Treaty Articles. The question proceeds in the second sentence to spell out which other Treaty Articles serve to cover the obstacles that lie outside the scope of Art 34 TFEU. It suggests the Treaty Articles create mutually exclusive categories.

   Essentially, the question seeks to determine whether Arts 28–30 and 110 TFEU apply only to charges or measures with an equivalent effect or to fiscal measures and Art 34 TFEU applies only to physical measures and that there is no overlap.

Answer plan

- Outline Art 34 TFEU and illustrative case law
- Outline Directive 70/50 and relevant case law
- Outline Arts 28–30 TFEU and illustrative case law
- Outline Art 110 TFEU and illustrative case law
- Compare scope of three sets of articles

Suggested answer

Article 34 TFEU provides a general prohibition on quantitative restrictions and measures having equivalent effect. Its scope has been determined both by legislation and case law. In *Geddo* v *Ente Nationale Risi* (2/73), the Court of Justice held that a prohibition on quantitative restrictions covers measures which amount to a total or partial restraint of imports, exports or goods in transit. The most obvious examples of quantitative restrictions on imports and exports are complete bans or quotas restricting the import or export of a given product by amount or by value. These are clearly in contravention of Art 34 TFEU and prohibited. The cases of *Commission v France* (Import of Lamb) (232/78) and *Commission v UK* (Import of Potatoes) (231/78) are straightforward examples of unlawful import bans.

The concept of measures having equivalent effect was defined by Directive 70/50, Art 2, which provides 'measures having equivalent effect' to include those which 'make imports, or the disposal at any marketing stage of imported products, subject to a condition, other than a formality, which is required in respect of imported products only'. They also include any measures which subject imported products or their disposal to a condition which differs from that required for domestic products and which is more difficult to satisfy.

In *Procureur du Roi v Dassonville* (8/74) the term 'measures having equivalent effect' was held to include 'all trading rules enacted by a Member State which are capable of hindering, directly or indirectly, actually or potentially, intra-community trade'.

Basically, therefore, any measure which makes import or export unnecessarily difficult, and thus discriminates between the two, would clearly fall within the definition.

Article 34 TFEU has been held to apply widely to a number of indirect measures including:

- a government sponsored advertising campaign in *Commission v Ireland* (Buy Irish Campaign) (249/81);

- national marketing rules in the *Commission v Belgium* (Packaging of Margarine) (314/82 and 189/83);

- import bans on health grounds on food additives have been held to be in breach of Art 34 TFEU in two cases against Germany, *Commission v Germany* (Beer Purity) (178/84) and *Commission v Germany* (Sausage Purity) (274/87);

- in *R v Pharmaceutical Society of Great Britain* (267/87) the rule of the Pharmaceutical Society prohibiting dispensing pharmacists from substituting for the product named on a doctor's prescription, any other with identical therapeutic effect except under certain exceptional conditions, was also held to be capable of coming within the operation of Art 34 TFEU.

Moreover, the scope of Art 34 TFEU applies not just to measures which are directly discriminatory but also to measures affecting both imports and domestic goods termed equally or indistinctly applicable measures. Directive 70/50, Art 3 provides that measures which are equally applicable to domestic and imported goods will breach Art 34 TFEU where the restrictive effect on the free movement of goods exceeds the effects necessary for the trade rules, ie they would be disproportionate to the aim and would thus tend to protect domestic products at the expense of the imports. See, for example, cases concerned with health checks and spot checks, *Commission v UK* (UHT Milk) (124/81) and *Commission v France* (Italian Table Wines) (42/82).

Thus, the scope of Art 34 TFEU is extremely wide, covering physical trade barriers, government assistance and measures which are applicable to both imports and domestic products. The scope of Arts 28–30 and 110 TFEU will now be outlined to compare with Art 34 TFEU.

Articles 28–30 TFEU are aimed at the abolition of customs duties and charges having equivalent effect and at prohibiting the introduction of any such measures.

Article 28 TFEU states that the Union shall be based on a customs union, with a common customs tariff, involving the prohibition of all customs duties on imports and charges having equivalent effect.

Article 28 TFEU prohibits the introduction of new customs duties or charges having equivalent effect, and equally prohibits the increase of those which are already in existence. The prohibition applies both to imports and exports. A customs duty is usually clear to recognise but a charge having an equivalent effect is more difficult and has been the subject of a considerable body of case law. In *Commission v Luxembourg and Belgium* (Gingerbread) (2 and 3/62), the Court of Justice held that:

a duty, whatever it is called, and whatever its mode of application, may be considered a charge having equivalent effect to a customs duty, provided that it meets the following three criteria:

(a) it must be imposed unilaterally at the time of importation or subsequently;

(b) it must be imposed specifically upon a product imported from a Member State to the exclusion of a similar national product; and

(c) it must result in an alteration of price and thus have the same effect as a customs duty on the free movement of products.

Furthermore, charges which are argued to be fees for services rendered have also been classified as contrary to Art 30 TFEU unless they meet specific criteria including that they have been sanctioned under either EU or international law. The Treaty of Amsterdam amended what is now Art 30 TFEU by adding a second sentence to make it expressly clear that the prohibition also applies to customs duties of a fiscal nature which are applied when goods cross the border.

However, if a fee, imposed by a Member State on imported goods, is a measure of internal taxation, it cannot be a charge having equivalent effect, and cannot be caught by Arts 28–30 TFEU. It is instead governed by Art 110 TFEU on taxation but Art 110 TFEU is designed to prevent circumvention of the customs rules by the substitution of discriminatory internal taxes.

Article 110(1) TFEU prevents Member States from imposing on imports internal taxation of any kind in excess of that imposed directly or indirectly on similar domestic products. This prohibits discrimination in favour of the domestic products. Article 110(2) TFEU prohibits Member States from imposing on the products of other Member States any internal taxation of such a nature as to afford indirect protection to other products. This serves to cover products that may be different but are nevertheless in competition with the domestic products.

Taxation was defined in *Commission v France* (Re: Reprographic Machines) (90/79) as a general system of internal dues applied systematically to categories of product in accordance with objective criteria irrespective of the origin of the products. In *Molkerei-Zentrale* (28/67) the Court of Justice ruled that the words 'directly or indirectly' were to be construed broadly and embraced all taxation which was actually and specifically imposed on the domestic product at earlier stages of the manufacturing and marketing process.

Article 110 TFEU is therefore complementary to Arts 28–30 TFEU in that it is also concerned with outlawing fiscal measures which are discriminatory. Article 28 TFEU applies to charges which occur as goods pass a frontier and Art 110 TFEU should apply only internally within the importing state. Articles 28 and 110 TFEU were held to be mutually exclusive by the Court of Justice in the case of *Deutschmann v Germany* (10/65).

The final part of the answer must address the issue of whether Arts 28 and 110 TFEU overlap in any way with Art 34 TFEU. The area of fees charged for inspection has emerged as the situation where all of the articles under examination may come into play. The imposition of charges or alleged taxes may occur at the same time or following an inspection of goods. Thus a consideration of measures having equivalent effect may be undertaken, the result of which may be that the inspection proves to be a breach of Art 34 TFEU and not excused by Art 36 TFEU. If a fee is charged, it will still have to be considered either as a measure of taxation under Art 110 TFEU or under Arts 28–30 TFEU because it may not be acceptable as a tax, see *Dansk Denkavit* (29/87). However, if it is the case that a Member State claims that a charge made on import inspection is a tax and there is not a fee levied at a similar stage internally of a counterpart domestic product, it may be held to be a charge having equivalent effect, as in the cases of *Commission v Belgium* (314/82) and *Commission v Denmark* (C-47/88). The distinction, however, between the physical barrier of the inspection and the fee charged remains quite distinct. The Court of Justice has considered in the case of *Ianelli and Volpi v Meroni* (74/74) that Arts 28–30 and 110 TFEU do not overlap with Art 34 TFEU. It is possible that inspections may be lawful, but the fees for them may not; see, for example, the *Marimex* case (29/72). Note though, as a matter of law and logic that if an inspection was held to be unlawful, it must follow that the fee levied for it must also be unlawful. Therefore, the conclusions to be drawn from observing the scope of the articles are that there is no overlap of Arts 28–30 or 110 with Art 34 TFEU.

Question 3

Healthy-eat Ltd is a manufacturer of fruit-flavoured yoghurt and breakfast muesli. It has recently decided to try to export to the Continental market. In order to ensure the products are in good condition when they reach the shops in the Member States, certain measures are taken by Healthy-eat Ltd in the marketing of three special Continental product lines. The first is 'frozen yoghurt' containing only natural ingredients. The second is unfrozen yoghurt to which pre-servatives are added. The third is muesli in sealed cellophane bags. All the ingredients of the products are listed on the packaging.

Healthy-eat Ltd found that the products were particularly popular in Germany and for four months sales boomed until Germany imposed a ban, justified on 'public health grounds', on the importation of any dairy product containing preservatives. A new German consumer protection law forbids the application of the description yoghurt to all frozen yoghurts. Following this, consignments of yoghurt were turned back at the frontier.

Meanwhile, consignments of muesli were subject to long delays at the German ferry port whilst spot checks for health reasons are carried out. These involve opening three packets in every fifth case of muesli. Payment was required for the inspections and parking fees were imposed on the trucks whilst they were parked up waiting for the inspections to take place.

When Healthy-eat Ltd challenged the parking fees and charges for the health checks, they were told that they are the equivalent of an internal tax imposed on domestic food products to finance a system of factory inspection in the German food industry.

Advise Healthy-eat Ltd as to its rights under EU law.

Commentary

This problem is concerned with the free movement of goods including aspects of charges having equivalent effect, measures having equivalent effect and internal taxation measures. A brief introduction to the area of law and the attitude of the Court of Justice would help to set the scene before answering the specific points in the question.

The material facts to be considered are the yoghurts containing additives, frozen yoghurts and the checks and payments for the muesli. The issues thus arising are whether the bans breach **Art 34 TFEU** or whether the measures introduced by the German Government are justified under EU law by **Art 36 TFEU** or justified under the rule of reason from the case of *Cassis de Dijon* (120/78). Furthermore, it must be considered whether the charges are in fact non-discriminatory taxation or charges contrary to the Treaty. As there are a number of issues a good structure to your answer is vital.

Answer plan

- Introduce area of law and attitude of the ECJ to prohibitions and exceptions
- Set out facts and applicable Treaty provisions (**Arts 34, 36 and 110 TFEU**)

- Outline **Directive 70/50** and the *Dassonville* and ECJ case law
- Consider in turn the various bans against **Arts 34 and 36 TFEU** and *Cassis de Dijon*
- Address the spot checks and charges under **Arts 30, 34** and, if taxation, **Art 110 TFEU**
- With the aid of relevant cases, reach conclusions on all the issues

Suggested answer

The applicable legal regime is that of the free movement of goods contained in the EC Treaty under Arts 28–30 , 34–36 and 110 TFEU concerned with taxation. Free movement of goods is one of the fundamental freedoms guaranteed by the EU Treaties and is a cornerstone or one of the foundations of the Union. As a result, the Court of Justice has interpreted the legislative provisions widely and the exceptions allowed the Member States have been interpreted restrictively. Furthermore, Art 110 TFEU may be applicable, because a claim has been made that the charges are equivalent to a domestic tax.

The problems that have been identified are those concerned with the additives in yoghurts, the frozen yoghurts and the checks and payments for the muesli.

First of all, in relation to the yoghurt with preservatives, Art 34 TFEU prohibits all quantitative restrictions or measures having equivalent effect. Measures which are in breach of Art 34 TFEU are those which meet formulae provided by the provisions of Directive 70/50 or the Court of Justice in the *Dassonville* case (8/74) in that they impose measures to hinder imports. The imposed ban would appear to be the case here. However, Art 36 TFEU allows exceptions on public health grounds and this is what Germany pleads in respect of the ban on preservatives. There is considerable case law now dealing with bans on health grounds to the effect that any measure must be reasonable and proportional to the aim; see the *UHT Milk* case (124/81) and the German Beer Purity Law case, *Commission* v *Germany* (178/84). In the latter case it was not contested that the prohibition on the marketing of beers containing additives fell within the definition of a measure having equivalent effect to a quantitative restriction in present Art 34 TFEU but the German Government argued instead that it was justified, under present Art 36 TFEU, on public health grounds. The Court of Justice held that the use of a given additive permitted in another Member State where, having regard to the results of international scientific research, in particular the work of the World Health Organisation, amongst others, and to eating habits in the country of importation, does not constitute a danger to public health. Certain of the additives used in beers from other Member States were permitted in Germany in the manufacture of almost all drinks other than beer. Therefore, there must be a real danger to human health, the alleged harmful effects must be proved and the additives must be banned in all products. It is thus unlikely therefore that this ban will be acceptable, unless it meets those strict requirements laid down by the Court of Justice.

The second problem concerns the ban on the grounds that the term 'yoghurt' cannot be used to describe frozen yoghurt. If not excused or justified, this will also be a breach of Art 34 TFEU. This time, however, the justification for the prohibition is not made on the basis of Art 36 TFEU but based on the new consumer protection law. As the rules appear to apply to both imports and domestic products and consumer protection lies outside Art 36 TFEU the case law of the Court of Justice, notably the case of *Cassis de Dijon* (120/78), must be considered. The Court held that Member States are allowed to impose restrictive mandatory rules provided they apply to both imports and domestic products and providing certain criteria were met. This rule has become known as the rule of reason. The criteria are that the measure must not be covered by a EU system of rules, it must be proportionate and it must not be an arbitrary restriction or a disguised discrimination.

Thus, the question that must be asked is whether the measure applies to national and imported frozen products equally and whether a more appropriate measure could protect the consumer. The German Beer Purity Law case, *Commission v Germany* (178/84), and the Italian Pasta Purity Law case, *Drei Glocken GmnH v USL Centro-sud* (407/85), would be applicable here. It was held that protection would be equally, if not better, served by appropriate labelling together with an indication of the sell-by date, to guarantee consumer information. Hence, unless the measures meet the above, they will not be acceptable. In fact, there is a case concerned with deep frozen yoghurt in which the insistence of the French authorities that it be given a different description than yoghurt was held to be capable of infringing Art 34 TFEU; see *Smanor* (298/87).

The aspects concerned with the muesli involve a consideration of both measures and charges having equivalent effect. Are these 'spot checks' for health reasons prohibited under Art 34 TFEU or permitted under Art 36 TFEU? Provided they are only random spot checks and they take place with the same frequency as checks on the equivalent domestic product, they will be acceptable. They must not be an arbitrary discrimination or a disguised restriction on trade. They are also subject to the principle of proportionality; see *Commission v France* (Italian Table Wines) (42/82) and *Commission v UK* (UHT Milk) (124/81). The checks in this case appear disproportionate and discriminatory because they are systematic.

The charges for the checks are argued to be an equivalent tax and must first be considered whether they are. If not an acceptable tax, it then needs to be considered whether they are then an acceptable or unacceptable charge prohibited by Arts 28–30 TFEU .

Article 110 TFEU allows internal taxes to be imposed on imports as long as it is the equivalent of an internal tax and is not discriminatory in its application. In *Denkavit v France* (132/78), it was held that the tax to which an imported product is subject must be imposed at the same rate on the same product, be imposed at the same marketing stage and the chargeable event giving rise to the duty must be the same for both products. The chargeable event here is different because, if a tax, it would be on distribution whereas the domestic product would be taxed pre-production, and thus would not come within the provisions of Art 110 TFEU.

It must now be considered whether the fee imposed is an unlawful charge. The Statistical Levy case (*Commission v Italy*) (24/68) defined a charge having equivalent effect to include: 'any pecuniary charge, however small and whatever its designation and mode of application, which is imposed unilaterally on domestic or foreign goods by virtue of the fact that they cross a frontier', and which is not a customs duty in the strict sense. The Court held that 'such a charge is a charge having equivalent effect even if it is not imposed for the benefit of the Member State concerned, even if it is not discriminatory or protective in effect and even if the product on which it is imposed is not in competition with any domestic product'.

Under certain conditions charges may be acceptable. If they are health checks with a legal basis in EU law, they may be charged for; see *Commission v Germany* (Health Inspections) (18/87). They cannot be regarded as charges having effect equivalent to customs duties if the fees do not exceed the cost of the actual inspections in respect of which they are charged; the inspections in question are mandatory and uniform for all the products in question in the EU; the inspections are provided for by EU law in the interests of the EU; and the inspections promote the free movement of goods. It would seem unlikely that EU law would be the basis of these inspections, particularly as the inspections appear to be breaching Art 34 TFEU, and therefore the charges in this case do not meet the criteria and thus would appear to breach Art 28 TFEU.

The parking fees will also be held to be charges having equivalent effect to customs duties, prohibited by Art 28 TFEU; see two cases concerned with customs warehouses, *Commission v Belgium* (314/82) and the *Marimex* case (29/72).

In conclusion, none of the products could be restricted lawfully under EU law.

Question 4

The UK Government has banned the import from France of nitrate fertilisers on the grounds that excessive nitrates in the soil are a danger to animal and human health. There is no ban on the production of this type of fertiliser in the UK but there is a Government-issued code of practice advising that other types of fertiliser must be used.

The UK Government has also banned the import from Germany of all types of aerosol spray which contain CFC propellants on the grounds that CFCs constitute a danger to the environment. In the UK, a law which phases out the manufacturer of CFC aerosols, over the next two years, has come into effect on the same day as the ban. Other CFC products are not banned domestically.

The French and German Governments are considering asking the Commission to take action and need to know whether these bans are a breach of EU provisions on the free movement of goods. You are asked to advise them.

Commentary

You are asked to comment on the two bans on the import of goods coming under EU law provisions on the free movement of goods. As an introduction, you should briefly outline the free movement of goods as one of the fundamental areas of Union law and that the Court of Justice, if it considered these bans, would interpret the provisions with the aims of the Union in mind and any restrictions allowed the Member States, restrictively. The principal provisions to consider are **Art 34 TFEU** which prohibits quantitative restrictions on imports. **Article 36 TFEU**, however, allows the Member States to restrict imports for specific reasons and these include the protection on health grounds of humans and animals. You should therefore consider whether the bans come within **Art 34 TFEU**. Then you should determine whether the reasons given by the UK will be held to be justified under EU law. Not all the grounds stated by the UK Government are mentioned in **Art 36 TFEU**, only the health grounds in respect of the nitrate fertilisers are contained in that Article. The protection of the environment is not contained in **Art 36 TFEU** and the case of *Cassis de Dijon* (120/78) must therefore be considered.

Hence, you should identify the material facts, and outline the applicable law to discuss the issues that arise and the likely outcome of the case.

Answer plan

- Introduce area of law and attitude of the ECJ to prohibitions and exceptions
- Outline facts and law: **Arts 34, 36 TFEU, Directive 70/50** and the *Dassonville* case
- Consider issues against the case law of **Arts 34 and 36 TFEU** and *Cassis de Dijon*
- Consider the post-*Cassis* case law
- With the aid of relevant cases, reach conclusions on all the issues

Suggested answer

The free movement of goods has been declared to be one of the fundamental policies of the original Common Market and hence now the Union. As a result, the Court of Justice has adopted a liberal interpretation of the freedoms to allow goods to circulate freely in the Union and at the same time adopted a restrictive approach to measures enacted by the Member State which impinge on these freedoms. This problem question is concerned generally with the ban on import quotas and measures having equivalent effect under Art 34 TFEU and the grounds by which the measure may either be justified under Art 36 TFEU, which provides a number of grounds by which a Member State can lawfully restrict imports including the protection of life and health of humans and animals. Additionally, there is the prospect that the ban may be excused under reasons recognised by the Court of Justice in case law.

There are two issues to be decided in this answer. The first one concerns a ban on the import of fertilisers and the second one the ban on imports of CFC propellants.

The ban on the import of fertilisers is a clear prohibition on imports and thus comes within the terms of Art 34 TFEU, as confirmed both by Directive 70/50 and the case of *Dassonville* (8/74), in that it directly hinders the import of goods. The ban is therefore contrary to EU law. The only question remaining would be whether the ban can be justified by the grounds cited by the UK. The measures can be justified on the grounds that it is protecting the health and life of humans and animals included in Art 36 TFEU. However, the second sentence of Art 36 TFEU does not allow a health ban to be an arbitrary discrimination or a disguised restriction. In the case of the fertilisers, discrimination is still present because domestic products are not similarly banned and would therefore not justify the UK in preventing imports; see the *Commission v UK* (UHT Milk case) (124/81) or the *Commission v UK* (Turkey Imports case) (40/82). Yet, it may be argued by the UK that there is a government code of practice which acts as the equivalent of a ban on domestic products and therefore there is no discrimination. For such an argument, that non-legally enforceable means of preventing discrimination have not previously been accepted by the European Court of Justice; see the case of *Commission v France* (Merchant Seamen) (167/73). Additionally, it must be proved by those relying on the ban that a threat to life and health exists and that the fertilisers banned from import are banned domestically as well. This case is therefore similar to the bans on imports on health grounds in the purity cases; see *Commission v Germany* (Beer and Sausage Purity) (178/84 and 274/87). The ban appears not to conform with the second sentence of Art 36 TFEU and is thus a breach of Art 34 TFEU.

The second ban relating to the CFC aerosol products from Germany also applies in respect of domestic CFCs and is thus equally applicable, which is also termed indistinctly applicable. Directive 70/50, Art 3, provides that bans which apply both to imports and domestic products may also infringe Art 34 TFEU. Such measures can, however, also be justified under Art 36 TFEU, except that in this case the grounds given, environmental grounds, are not covered by Art 36 TFEU. However, although the measure may be in breach of Art 34 TFEU it may nevertheless be excused if it meets criteria established by the Court of Justice in case law. The case of *Cassis de Dijon* (120/78) and subsequent case law have added to the grounds by which the Member States may lawfully restrict the free movement of goods. The measure taken must, however, apply on an equal footing with domestic products. In the case of *Cassis de Dijon*, the Court of Justice stated that, in the absence of harmonising EU rules, obstacles to the free movement of goods may be allowed as far as these provisions are justified by an objective of public interest taking precedence over the free movement of goods. Mandatory requirements of the Member State could be imposed to relate in particular to:

the effectiveness of fiscal supervision;

the protection of public health; or

the fairness of commercial transactions; and

the defence of the consumer.

However, the measures are subjected to further requirements:

they must be justified and proportional, ie necessary to achieve results and not arbitrary;

there is no EU system of rules; and

there must be neither an arbitrary discrimination nor a disguised restriction on trade.

Thus, if measures which are adopted by a Member State satisfy either the provisions of Art 36 TFEU or the requirements laid down in the case of *Cassis de Dijon* for mandatory requirements, the Member State will be able, lawfully, to restrict the free movement of goods.

It must therefore be established that the interest cited by the Member State as the ground for preventing imports comes within the reasons acceptable to the Court of Justice. The ground stated of environmental protection was recognised by the Court of Justice in *Commission v Denmark* (Disposable Beer Cans) (302/86) as an interest which comes within the scope of the ruling in the *Cassis de Dijon* case (120/78) and the principle of the rule of reason.

It must then be established whether it satisfies the criteria established by the Court of Justice in the *Cassis de Dijon* case:

It must apply to both imports and domestic products.

There must not be in force an applicable EU system.

The measure must not be a disguised restriction on trade or an arbitrary discrimination.

It must meet the requirements of proportionality.

From the facts of the present case, it is not stated that there is a EU regime on the matter therefore it is to be concluded that this aspect is satisfied. However, the national rule will only apply to imports and domestic products after the expiry of the two-year phasing-in period and not all CFC products are covered by the ban, which they should be. At the present time it would seem to fail on the fact that it does not apply immediately to all domestic CFC products. The rule would more likely be justified if it applied to all CFCs and there was no delay in phasing in the requirements of the domestic ban. It is likely to be concluded that, whilst probably satisfying the requirement of proportionality, the ban is acting as a disguised restriction on imports and thus contrary to Art 34 TFEU.

The French and German Governments would be best advised to encourage the Commission to take action against the UK. It may also be possible for any individual exporters and/or importers who have suffered damage to take the UK Government before the UK courts for damages under the *Francovich* state liability principle.

Question 5

'The *Cassis de Dijon* case (120/78) has helped clarify the complicated mass of case law on Articles 34–36 TFEU and has done this in a sense notably favourable to the basic Union objective of creating a unified market.'
    Discuss.

Commentary

The answer to this question requires a discussion of the case law on Arts 35–36 TFEU and the ruling of the Court of Justice in the *Cassis de Dijon* case. It would be best dealing with the material by considering the Treaty Articles first, then the case law arising from Arts 34–36 TFEU and finally considering the *Cassis de Dijon* case and the follow-on cases. Whilst the law has moved on in free movement of goods and selling arrangements and subsequent case law needs also to be considered, it is still possible to be asked questions concentrating on what the case of *Cassis de Dijon* achieved. Selling arrangements and subsequent cases are considered in Question 6 below.

For this answer, provide a basic outline of Arts 24–36 TFEU and explain why you consider the emergent body of case law from these articles to be complicated, if this is your opinion. Then consider the *Cassis de Dijon* case itself. Finally, the particular issues to be answered are whether it is considered that the *Cassis de Dijon* ruling has clarified the complicated mass of case law and whether it has helped achieve the creation of a unified market. It is important for the answer to this question to be aware and to address the fact that the *Cassis de Dijon* case is important for two principles of law.

A further part of that answer would include considering the approach of the ECJ, ie that Art 36 TFEU is an exception to the general principle of the free movement of goods and is therefore to be construed narrowly and to consider any refinements of the *Cassis de Dijon* case which have taken place as a result of the misunderstandings as to the application of *Cassis* in some instances and the further attempts of the ECJ to clarify its scope, for example, notably in the *Keck* and *Mithouard* case (C-267 and 268/91) and subsequent cases.

Answer plan

- Outline Art 34 TFEU , Directive 70/50 and case law arising from these
- Consider then the exceptions provided by Art 36 TFEU and its case law

- Discuss *Cassis de Dijon* in detail and the difficulties which arose from it
- Address briefly the *Keck* and *Mithouard* cases and follow-up cases
- Come to a view on the statement made in the question

Suggested answer

The main provisions of Arts 34–36 TFEU will first be considered. Article 34 TFEU lays down a general prohibition on quantitative restrictions and measures having equivalent effect. In *Geddo* v *Ente Nationale Risi* (2/73), the Court of Justice held that a prohibition on quantitative restrictions covers measures which amount to a total or partial restraint of imports, exports or goods in transit. The concept of measures having equivalent effect has also been defined by secondary legislation (Directive 70/50) and by the jurisprudence of the Court of Justice. Directive 70/50, Art 2 defines 'measures having equivalent effect' to include those which 'make imports, or the disposal at any marketing stage of imported products, subject to a condition, other than a formality, which is required in respect of imported products only'. They also include any measures which subject imported products or their disposal to a condition which differs from that required for domestic products and which is more difficult to satisfy. Therefore, any measure which makes import or export unnecessarily difficult, and thus discriminates between the two, would clearly fall within the definition.

In *Procureur du Roi* v *Dassonville* (8/74) the term 'measures having equivalent effect' was held to include 'all trading rules enacted by a Member State which are capable of hindering, directly or indirectly, actually or potentially, intra-community trade'.

Article 36 TFEU provides exceptions to the general prohibition of Art 34 TFEU. It states that Arts 34 and 35 TFEU shall not apply to prohibitions on imports, exports or goods in transit which are justified on any of the following four sets of grounds:

(a) public morality, public policy or public security;

(b) the protection of health and life of humans, animals or plants;

(c) the protection of national treasures possessing artistic, historic or archaeological value;

(d) the protection of industrial and commercial property.

The application of these exceptions is subject to the limitation, set out in the second sentence of Art 36 TFEU, that they may not be used as a means of arbitrary discrimination or a disguised restriction on trade between Member States.

The cases arising from Arts 34–36 TFEU (ex 28–30 EC) are considered complex because of the difficulties which have arisen from cases in which there is no apparent discrimination. These are cases where the Member State has adopted measures restricting imports which apply equally to imports and domestic products. Whilst Directive 70/50, Art 3 provides that such measures are capable of infringing Art 34 TFEU, they could also be justified under the grounds given in Art 36 TFEU. For example, the protection of the health or life of humans or animals is a frequently argued ground for import restrictions and virtually every sort of good, especially foodstuffs, has been subjected to restrictions on health grounds and other rules applicable to both imports and domestic products. The Court of Justice has developed two main principles of law to deal with such situations. First, the principle of equivalence, often referred to also as the principle of mutual equivalence, which provides that if a product meets the equivalent standards of another Member State, these products should be regarded as meeting the standards of the state of import. Furthermore, all measures seeking to prevent or restrict the import of goods should be proportionate. Thus, if any less drastic method of protecting health existed, short of a ban, this should be employed. Hence, the systematic opening of sealed milk cartons for health checks amounted to import restriction in the UHT Milk case, *Commission v UK* (124/81) (confirmed in the *Cassis de Dijon* case (120/78)). The health of consumers would be adequately protected by the necessary controls being carried out in the country of production to meet all the reasonable requirements of the country of import.

A further complication has arisen because it was previously considered to be the case and confirmed by the Court of Justice that the grounds under Art 36 TFEU are exhaustive. However, Member States were looking and still look for grounds by which they may lawfully restrict the import of non-domestic goods. Many new grounds to justify a restriction on imports were claimed by the Member States. It was in the case of *Cassis de Dijon* that the Court of Justice stated that obstacles to the free movement of goods resulting from disparities in the national laws on the marketing of products must be accepted, as far as these provisions are necessary to satisfy mandatory requirements relating in particular to:

the effectiveness of fiscal supervision;

the protection of public health;

the fairness of commercial transactions; and

the defence of the consumer.

The rules which hinder trade may be acceptable if they are in pursuit of a special interest the Member State has the right to protect. However, the Court of Justice narrowed the scope of the possible exceptions by adding to this so-called 'rule of reason' the requirement that measures taken to satisfy such mandatory requirements must be applied to imported and domestic products (ie indistinctly applicable); there can be no applicable EU regime, they must be proportionate and must neither be an arbitrary discrimination nor a disguised restriction on trade.

The case of *Cassis de Dijon* had started to cause the ECJ problems because it was seized on both by Member States to justify restrictions and traders to attack virtually any nationally imposed restriction on trade practices or commercial freedom, particularly where rules were not just aimed directly at imports. Complex litigation has arisen from this area of law. The Sunday trading case law serves as a good example of the confusion that can arise as a result of the seemingly more relaxed regime introduced. A ban on Sunday trading is a restriction on trade so traders claimed it breached Art 34 TFEU. It was not overtly discriminatory but applied to imported goods and domestic goods. The grounds given to justify by the Member State were not contained in Art 36 TFEU. Earlier case law before the Court of Justice led to contradictory national decisions depending on whether the courts took into account the protection of workers, which would appear to justify a ban on Sunday trading, and the attempt to keep Sunday special which appeared not to justify a ban; see *Torfaen BC v B & Q plc* ([1990] 3 CMLR 455) and *B & Q Ltd v Shrewsbury* BC ([1990] 3 CMLR 535). However, the Court of Justice held in *Stoke City Council v B & Q plc* (C-169/91) that the UK's restrictions on Sunday trading do not conflict with Community law. It held such rules reflected 'choices relating to particular national or regional socio-cultural characteristics'. The Member States have the discretion to make such choices. Thus, there is no breach of the present Art 34 TFEU by Sunday trading rules. The Court of Justice redefined its position in the *Keck* case (C-267 and 268/91) and held that certain equally applicable provisions restricting selling arrangements are not to be considered a hindrance on trade according to the *Dassonville* case and thus conform to the present Art 34 TFEU, provided that they affect all traders and all domestic products and imports in the national territory, in the same manner. Or, looked at in another way, an impediment to trade is acceptable where the rule in question impedes both the trade in domestic products and imported products equally. It was an attempt to remove many national rules which were introduced for reasons other than those which were a restriction on imports. Thus, providing national rules do not impede access to markets but merely regulates them without discrimination, either direct or indirect and in law and in fact, they will be acceptable. Subsequent cases have accepted Dutch laws concerning the times and places at which petrol could be sold (*Tankstation't Heukske* (C-401 and 402/92)), Belgian laws prohibiting offering products for sale at a loss of profit (*Belgapom* (C-63/94)), but *Vereinigte Familiapress Zeitungsverlags v Bauer Verlag* (C-368/95) witnessed a return to pre-*Keck* considerations. An Austrian law prohibiting the offering of free gifts linked to the sale of goods was the basis for an Austrian publisher's suit against a German magazine containing a prize crossword puzzle. The ECJ repeated its position established since *Keck* that certain national rules would not breach Art 34 TFEU unless imposing additional requirements. Austrian rules would constitute a hindrance to free movement if the content of the magazine had to be altered for the Austrian market. However, maintaining the diversity of the press was the legitimate public interest objective given by the authorities and accepted by the ECJ. It remains up to the national judge to determine whether the ban is proportionate, or whether less restrictive aims to reach the objective are available. Thus, this case does not involve a rule falling outside of Art 34 TFEU but restriction which could nevertheless be justified under the *Cassis de Dijon* rule of reason. It is clear also from the *Heimdienst* case (C-254/98) that selling arrangements which either in law or in fact discriminate against non-national providers and thus impede or hinder movement will not escape Art 34 TFEU but might still be justified under *Cassis* considerations. This development was confirmed in *Gourmet International* (C-405/98) such that some equal burden selling arrangements would nevertheless infringe Art 34 TFEU where they had a greater discriminatory impact on imports.

In summary, the two principles of law arising from *Cassis de Dijon* (120/78) are the principle of equivalence and the rule of reason. Whilst the rule of reason appears to have widened the grounds by which Member States can justify import restrictions and complicated matters by providing an extra set of rules to consider, the national interests claimed must nevertheless comply with strict criteria. In combination with the principle of equivalence, which combats technical rules imposed by the Member States, the criteria make it more restrictive for the Member States to impose restrictions; see as examples the beer and sausage purity cases, *Commission v Germany* (178/84 and 274/87). Furthermore, with the refinement of the *Keck* cases, it can be concluded that the *Cassis de Dijon* line of case law is essentially favourable to the Union objective of the unified market by encouraging the free movement of other Member State products, which may not be available in the host market and thus subject to a ban which would not affect any of the host state's products. The principle of equivalence in *Cassis* is most important in this respect by allowing national rules to survive in the host state and thus provides more choice for the Union consumer and does not as a result encourage the same minimum or maximum Eurostandard to be established for every product and is therefore essentially helpful in creating a unified market. However, the case law following *Cassis de Dijon* have themselves added to the complicated mass of case law in Arts 24–36 TFEU.

Question 6

How, why and with what success did the ECJ 'clarify' the scope of application of Art 34 TFEU in cases 267 & 8/91 *Keck and Mithouard* and subsequent cases?

Commentary

This question invites a longer look at the case law development after *Cassis de Dijon* and in particular asks that you consider the judgment in *Keck and Mithouard* and subsequent cases. The *Keck* case was regarded as a correcting case to stop the abuses of **Art 34 TFEU (ex 28 EC)** which were taking place by traders seizing on any national rule and arguing that it prevented imports and was thus a breach of **Art 34 TFEU**. This is the why part of the question. How, simply relates to outlining the judgment in *Keck* itself and the final part is determining from the cases subsequent to *Keck*, whether the ECJ did in fact clarify the confused law in this area.

Start with an introduction to the free movement of goods and a definition of **Art 34 TFEU** though and a brief run through the development of the confusion over its scope and application.

Answer plan

- Define **Art 34 TFEU** and its expanding scope of application
- Outline the reasons why the *Keck* judgment was considered necessary
- Consider what *Keck* was supposed to achieve
- Consider subsequent cases to see if it had the desired effect
- Summarise the present state of the law after these developments

Suggested answer

This question concerns the case law development of one of the central elements of the free movement of goods regime provided by the TFEU. The free movement of goods has been declared to be one of the fundamental policies of the Common Market and hence the EU. As a result, the Court of Justice adopted a liberal interpretation of the freedoms to allow goods to circulate freely in the EU and at the same time adopted a restrictive approach to measures enacted by the Member State which impinge on these freedoms. Article 34 TFEU prohibits quantitative restrictions and all measures having the equivalent effect. This prohibition has been progressively interpreted by the Court of Justice, most notably through the case of *Procureur du Roi* v *Dassonville* (8/74) to include essentially any measure which makes import or export unnecessarily difficult and which discriminates between domestic products and imported products.

However, Art 34 TFEU prohibits not only national rules that overtly discriminate against imported products, subject to the possibility of justification under Art 36 TFEU, it may also be used to challenge national rules which on their face make no distinction between domestic and imported goods and are termed equally or indistinctly applicable.

The *Cassis de Dijon* case (120/78) took *Dassonville* further by showing that these indistinctly applicable rules could also breach Art 34 TFEU by their dual burden effect. This is where the imported product has to comply with two sets of product requirements in order to be marketed lawfully in the state of import – those operated by the state of origin and those of the state of importation, placing an additional burden on the import, eg the *Rau Margarine* case (261/81) requirement that margarine be marketed in a different shape in the host state from the home state such that a separate production line would have to be set up for the Belgium market.

The case of *Cassis de Dijon* had started to cause the ECJ problems because it was seized on both by Member States to justify restrictions and by traders to attack virtually any nationally imposed restriction on trade practices or commercial freedom, particularly to get round national laws which were not just aimed directly at imports and which actually were serving another genuine purpose not connected with trying to restrict free movement of goods. Hence Art 34 TFEU slowly extended through court action to cover so-called 'Equal Burden' measures which are neither directly nor indirectly discriminatory and where the same requirement applies to both without adding an additional burden on the imports.

See, as good examples of these, rules relating to Sunday trading in the UK: case 145/88 *Torfaen BC v B & Q plc* ([1989] ECR 3851, [1990] 3 CMLR 455) and *B & Q Ltd v Shrewsbury BC* ([1990] 3 CMLR 535) and protecting the film industry in France: cases 60–61/84 *Cinéthèque*.

The ECJ recognised that traders were using Community (now EU) law to challenge laws which were not aimed at restricting imports but in fact restricted the sales of all goods without regard to origin, eg the Sunday trading laws in the UK, many of which were enacted in Victorian times for then understandable reasons far from any consideration of the EU and free movement of goods.

When presented with a suitable occasion, the ECJ was able to reconsider the case development in this area. In cases C-267 & 268/91 *Keck and Mithouard*, the French prohibition of goods sold at a loss was argued to be a restriction of sales and thus imports and thus like the earlier Sunday trading and videos cases, contrary to Art 34 TFEU. The rule though affected all goods. Hence the ECJ singled out selling or marketing arrangements as not coming within the concept outlined in *Dassonville* or Art 34 TFEU and held that providing national rules do not impede access to markets but merely regulate them without discrimination, either direct or indirect, they will be acceptable, ie such rules therefore fall outside the scope of Article [34] of the Treaty. However, there were problems with the *Keck* judgment and instead of clarifying the law as was hoped, it raised more questions than provided answers including what was actually overruled and what are 'selling arrangements'?

Selling arrangements are broadly defined as rules relating to the market circumstances in which the goods are sold. They are measures dealing with where, when, how and by whom goods may be sold: eg cases C-401 and 402/92, *Tankstation't Heustke* accepting Dutch laws concerning the times and places at which petrol could be sold and there may be all sorts of good reasons behind this, safety paramount, ensuring petrol supplies in country or remote areas by restricting sales outlets – ie guaranteeing a wider catchment area and thus sales.

See also *Commission* v *Greece* (C-391/92) in which Greece prohibited the sale of any processed milk for babies other than in pharmacies.

But there appeared cases which showed that some selling arrangements hindered market access or acted in a manner which favours domestic (disadvantages imports) such as rules on marketing, advertising and sales promotion which can be problematic.

These difficulties have led slowly to the development of a test of market access discrimination.

Selling arrangements are not automatically outside, but a rebuttable presumption and the question posed is whether the national selling arrangement prevents access to the market or impedes access any more than it impedes the access of domestic products.

See cases C-34-36/95 *Konsumenten-ombudsmannen* v *De Agostini* in which TV advertising directed at children under 12 was prohibited, however, other ads were allowed. The measure was considered to be a selling arrangement which applied without discrimination, thus equal burden. However, it was held that would seem to have a greater impact on products from other Member States because of the difficulties faced in trying to get access to the market, advertising being the only effective form of promotion. If the national court found that the impact of the prohibition was different it would therefore breach Art 34 TFEU unless justified by Art 36 TFEU or the mandatory requirements under *Cassis*.

In the subsequent case C-405/98 *Gourmet International*, a ban on alcohol advertising was challenged under the same argument that it had a greater impact on imported products trying to gain access to the Swedish market because without advertising consumers would only be familiar with domestic products. Thus it was held that the measure would be caught by Art 28 EC Treaty (now 34 TFEU) if it prevents access to the market by products from another state, or impedes access any more than it impedes access of domestic products.

In the *Heimdienst* case (C-254/98), a non-discriminatory Austrian law which applied to all operators trading in the national territory (Austrian and other EU) required goods sold on the doorstep to come from a locally established premises. It was held to be a selling arrangement but one which impeded access to the market of the Member State of importation for products from other Member States more than it impeded access for domestic products.

This has been termed a test of differential impact, ie affecting imports more than domestic products. Thus cases involving situations which, although classified as certain selling arrangements, have a different burden on imported goods, albeit that some domestic goods might also be affected, breach Art 34 TFEU and to be saved, must be justified.

So, the first assumptions after *Keck* were that all selling arrangements fell outside Art 34 TFEU. There followed a correction to bring back into Art 34 TFEU any selling arrangements which were in fact discriminatory in either law or fact which, whilst not actually preventing imports, hindered or restricted them in some way and which would therefore be caught by Art 34 TFEU unless justified under *Cassis* such as the advertising cases. It means though that each case must be carefully assessed on its own facts of how, if at all, the market for the imported goods is disturbed by the national rule. Clarification is thus still sought.

Further reading

Barnard, C. *The Substantive Law of the EU: The Four Freedoms* 3rd edn (Oxford: Oxford University Press, 2010) chs 2–4.

Barnard, C, 'Fitting the Remaining Pieces into the Goods and Persons Jigsaw' (2001) 26 EL Rev 35.

Connor, T, 'Accentuating the Positive: the "Selling Arrangement", the first Decade, and Beyond' (2005) 54 ICLQ 127.

Davies, G, 'Can Selling Arrangements be Harmonised?' (2005) 30 EL Rev 371–385.

Kaczorowska, A, 'Gourmet Can Have His *Keck* and Eat It!' (2004) 10(4) ELJ 479.

Koutrakos, P, 'On Groceries, Alcohol and Olive Oil: More on Free Movement of Goods after Keck' (2001) 26 EL Rev 391.

Snell, J, 'Non-Discriminatory Tax Obstacles in Community Law' (2007) 56 ICLQ 339.

Weatherill, S, 'Recent Developments in the Law Governing the Free Movement of Goods in the EC's Internal Market' (2006) 2 ECRL 90.

Wilsher, D, 'Does Keck Discrimination Make Any Sense? An Assessment of the Non-discrimination Principle within the European Single Market' (2008) 33 EL Rev 3.

7

The Free Movement of Persons

Introduction

In this area of substantive EU law both essay-type questions and problem-type questions are possible, although it is my assumption that problem-type questions will be more frequent. The area of law straddles three main subdivisions, comprising the free movement of workers, involving most of the secondary legislation and case law, and then the freedom of establishment and the freedom to provide services. Additionally now, although dealt with within the Treaty very early on (Arts 20–25 TFEU (ex 17–22 EC)), Union citizenship is also considered a part of this topic because of the overlap or possible extension of workers' rights to general rights of citizenship. Hence, you are now likely to get questions which also concentrate on this new area and I have included questions containing citizenship aspects at the end of this chapter. Otherwise, questions can concentrate on any one of the topics or involve a combination of any two or all three. It may be that in your course only the free movement of workers is covered or that questions will only arise on the free movement of workers. Consultation of your course syllabus, past exams and current teaching staff will reveal whether you need to cover all three for the purposes of question answering or whether only one topic in this area of law will be examined.

An addition to this area of law is Directive 2004/38 on the right of citizens of the Union and their family members to move and reside freely within the territory of the Member States which has amended Regulation 1612/68 and repealed Directives 64/221, 68/360, 72/194, 73/148, 75/34, 75/35, 90/364, 90/365 and 93/96 and Regulation 1251/70. Whilst not changing the substance of the answers to any great degree, it will make modifications to the answers necessary and, of course, change the citation for the rights provided. The Directive can be found in the 21st and subsequent editions of *Blackstone's EU Treaties & Legislation* collection. Following this extensive addition, it is not surprising that the 2007 Lisbon Treaty had little further effect on Union law in this area, except renumbering the provisions of the EC Treaty in the new TFEU. It keeps citizenship in part two of the TFEU and further provides a right of free movement in the Charter of Fundamental Rights which is now attached to the Treaties by Declaration (No 1). Apart from changes in terminology, the rights themselves have not been changed in any significant way.

This chapter includes all types of question on the issues mentioned above: combination essay-type questions, combination problem-type questions, problem questions concerned only with the free movement of workers, an essay-type question concentrating on the free movement of professionals and questions which involve citizenship and wider free movement issues.

Question 1

The Court of Justice has interpreted the provisions of Arts 45–62 TFEU (ex 39–55 EC) and the secondary legislation in a more liberal manner than would be dictated by a purely functional view of the Treaty based on its economic motives.
   Discuss.

Commentary

This is a very wide question and covers the topics of the free movement of workers, the freedom of establishment and the freedom to provide services. You must therefore plan carefully to make sure you are covering relevant material.

Two statements are made in the question which must be discussed: the view that the Court of Justice has been liberal in its interpretation of the provisions and the fact that this leads to quite different consequences than the Court of Justice taking a purely functional view of the economic motives of the Treaty.

The answer could be structured in two ways. The first would be to consider the functional economic view and then give examples of the Court's liberal interpretations. In this way, a form of control or basic position is established first which can be used to compare with the later case law. Alternatively, and also valid, would be to give the examples first from case law of the liberal interpretations and compare these with how a purely functional view would look. Both achieve a correct end result.

The range of legislation noted in the question is very wide, covering a number of Treaty Articles and secondary legislation. It would be too time-consuming to go through every provision. The liberal interpretation could be demonstrated by an overview and then by explaining selective examples. The functional view, on the other hand, appears to be restricted to considering Treaty Articles and secondary provisions and it would seem best to take an overview of the Treaty objectives and then select examples from the provisions.

You might make a general mental note to help frame your mind in answering the question or indeed even incorporate into the answer the statement that the free movement of persons is one of the fundamental principles or foundations of the Union. But is this because (a) it assists the economic goals of the Union; or (b) it improves the opportunities and working conditions of the work force; or possibly (c) a combination of both of these?

Answer plan

- Provide a broad outline of the rights contained in Arts 45–62 TFEU
- Outline the consequences of liberal and functional approaches
- Provide examples of ECJ liberal interpretations of workers and Art 45 TFEU
- Case law on secondary law including *Diatta*, *Reed* and *Deak* cases
- Consider students and services and establishment case law
- Conclusion as to whether a more liberal than functional approach has persisted

Suggested answer

Articles 45–62 TFEU cover the areas of the free movement of workers, freedom of establishment and the freedom to provide services. The free movement of persons has been described as one of the fundamental foundations of the Union but the reason why it may be so described is not obvious. Two main grounds might be given. One, that it is fundamental because the area assists the economic goals of the Union in establishing an internal market in which all factors of production can freely circulate. Alternatively, the view might be taken that the aims for these areas of EU law are to improve the opportunities and working conditions of the individuals in the work forces of the Member States.

Essentially, the Treaty Articles provide that workers and the self-employed can take up employment opportunities in the other Member States without discrimination on the grounds of nationality. Furthermore they should enjoy the same rights and benefits granted in such circumstances to nationals but that certain restrictions may be made in respect of employment in the public service. These basic rights can be viewed, then, in two ways.

A purely functional view might be that the economic motives are paramount and therefore it is only the economies of the EU and the Member State that are important. The granting of individual rights are incidental and just a way of ensuring that the commodity of labour can be imported and exported to suit the demands of European capital and so that it can take advantage of the free market and can compete equally in attracting and securing labour. The personal rights given to workers are then secondary to the prime objectives in setting up the internal market and ensuring that business in the Member States is operating under the same rules. Under this view, it would be expected that the rights would be subject to the minimum interpretation possible to give effect to the rights granted.

For example, there would be no right to be in other Member States whilst unemployed and looking for work; the Member States would have complete freedom to discriminate in the public service or rights would not be extended to members of the family or to students.

The contrasting view is that of the liberal interpretation. The Court of Justice clearly interprets all parts of the Treaty in a distinct style using the so-called teleological approach. This means that specific measures are interpreted in the light of the objectives and goals of the Union and are not just subject to a literal interpretation of the words.

It is clear that in respect of the free movement of persons the Court of Justice has gone far beyond a literal or functional interpretation of the provisions and has, in its judgment, sought to give the widest possible scope to the rights provided. The following are examples and are not exhaustive.

Article 45 TFEU (ex 39 EC) and the secondary legislation have been held to provide the status of worker to those who are not employed in the host state and have entered for the express reason to search for work; see the *Antonnisson* (C-292/89) and *Lebon* (316/85) cases. The term 'worker' for the purposes of EU law also applies to those in part-time work and those who have worked only a few hours per week or were paid largely in kind. See, eg, the cases of *Kempf* v *Staatssecretaria van Justitie* (139/85), *Lawrie-Blum* v *Land Baden-Würtemberg* (66/85) and *Steymann* v *Staatssecretaris van Justitie* (196/87). More recently the cases of *Trojani* (C-456/02) and *Ninni-Orasche* (C-413/01) confirm the liberal view of the ECJ in respect of who can constitute a worker under the Treaty.

The general prohibition of discrimination contained in Art 45 (ex 48 EEC) was considered in the *Alluè and Coonan* v *University of Venice* case (33/88) concerning two non-national language teachers employed by the University of Venice. It was held that discrimination in circumstances where the rule was being applied to both nationals and other EU citizens would still be present but affected the non-nationals indirectly, ie indirect discrimination is covered by Art 45 TFEU.

The exception, allowed the Member States under the public service provision in Art 45(4) TFEU, has been restricted in two ways. First, once a worker is employed in the public service, there can be no discrimination in respect of the conditions of work and employment. Furthermore, entry is not restricted to levels of the public service which do not exercise power conferred by public law and safeguard the interests of the state. See the cases of *Sotgui* v *Deutsche Bundespost* (152/73) and *Commission* v *Belgium* (149/79). Such restrictions on the Member States' ability are not to be perceived from a functional view of the provision.

When we turn to the secondary legislation, even more surprising interpretations can be cited as examples. Whilst it may be possible to perceive that a non-EU national spouse has the right to stay in a Member State after separation from the EU worker, as in *Diatta* (267/83), it is unlikely that one would realise from the legislation that the rights to the same treatment in social matters would include the right to the companionship of a cohabitee; see *Netherlands* v *Reed* (59/85). The case law on Art 7(2) of Regulation 1612/68 has certainly demonstrated the very liberal interpretation that can be achieved by the Court of Justice. These include the right of members of the worker's family, regardless of nationality, to join the worker but also to claim various types of social security benefit to financially help them stay in the host state. See, eg, *Fiorini aka Christini* v *SNCF* (32/75), *ONE* v *Deak* (94/84).

The Court has even accorded the status of workers, although not necessarily all of the benefits, to work seekers in cases including *Lebon* (316/85), *Antonissen* (C-292/89) and *Collins* (C-138/02).

Finally, by way of example, is the extension of the term 'worker' to apply in specific circumstances to students, an interpretation which is not obvious from a reading of the appropriate provisions and took place even before the Directives granting rights of residence were passed by the Council in 1990. See the cases of *Lair* v *Universität Hannover* (39/86) and *Bernini* v *Netherlands Ministry of Education and Science* (C-3/90).

Furthermore, in respect of establishment and services, the Court of Justice ruled that Arts 49 and 56 TFEU (ex 52 and 59 EEC) were capable of giving rise to direct effects, an interpretation which could not be expressly derived from the Articles. The fact that the Court of Justice did not see the need for completing legislation is a liberal interpretation; see the cases of *Reyners* (2/74) and *Van Binsbergen* (33/74).

With regard to the free movement of services, there was originally nothing in the Treaty to suggest its application to education or the receivers of services; but this has been achieved in a number of cases. For example, *Luisi* v *Ministero del Tesauro* (286/82) concerned a prosecution under Italian currency regulations for taking money out to pay for tourist and medical provisions abroad. These were held by the Court of Justice to be payments for services and thus coming under the provisions of the EEC Treaty, payments being a fundamental freedom of the Community (Arts 56 and 57 TFEU (ex 59 and 60 EEC) and 18 TFEU (ex 7 EEC)). *Gravier* v *City of Liège* (293/83) concerned the decision that the fee charged to foreign students for vocational training courses but not to nationals was contrary to EU law. It is to be noted that Directive 2004/38 has consolidated both most of the previous secondary legislation in these areas and the case law developments of the ECJ which built upon the statutory rights.

It can be seen from the above cases that there are good examples that the Court of Justice has interpreted Articles and secondary legislation in a far more liberal manner than a functional view would dictate. Adding to this view now is the interpretation that the ECJ has been giving to the citizenship provisions (Arts 20 and 21 TFEU (ex 17 and 18 EC)) in the cases of *Sala* (C-85/96) and *Grzelczyk* (C-184/99) which have extended Union citizens' rights into the areas of social and welfare law of the Member States.

Question 2

After a number of incidents involving minor offences of public order, which led to convictions for disturbing the peace, the founding member of the Tooting Popular Front, a self-proclaimed neo-Communist revolutionary party, Wolfie Smith and his girlfriend Shirley, both of whom had been unemployed in the UK for many months, decided to seek opportunities for work in Germany.

They were accompanied by Shirley's retired father, Charlie, and mother, Florence, who is mentally disturbed.

Shirley obtained work but Wolfie did not and after seven months the immigration authorities, who now had details of Wolfie's convictions and political associations, ordered the expulsion of Wolfie from Germany as a threat to public security and whose presence was contrary to public policy.

Charlie had claimed retirement pension and Florence had made a claim for a special benefit to attend a mental health clinic. Both were refused on the grounds that they had not contributed to the German social security system and were not German citizens and were thus not entitled to benefits. In addition, a deportation order was issued against Florence on the ground that her mental illness was a threat to public policy and public security. She was given just one week to leave.

Wolfie appealed against his deportation on the grounds that he was a worker and entitled to remain in Germany as a result of his street busking (playing guitar in the street for donations of money from the passing public). Wolfie had also joined a local band and played a series of gigs (about 80 hours in total) before ideological differences led the band to split. Afterwards he applied for a grant to attend music college but was turned down by the German authorities.

Shirley's parents also appealed against the refusal of benefit and Florence's deportation.

In order to help them in their appeals before the local administrative tribunal, before which representation is not compulsory, they obtained the services of Ken, a qualified UK solicitor with a practice in Tooting, who visited them in Germany. The tribunal, however, refused to recognise his right to represent them unless he worked in conjunction with a local lawyer and maintained a local chamber as a professional base whilst in Germany. Ken's protest that the provision of services should not be subject to the same restrictive rules was rejected by the German authorities because they argued he had established in Germany, hence they can impose the same rules on him.

You are asked to consider the position of Wolfie, Shirley's parents and Ken under EU law.

Commentary

This long and involved problem question concerns a number of aspects of the free movement of workers including their rights in the host state, the rights of their relatives and the free movement of professionals. As with many problem questions on this topic, it can be difficult to answer because there are often a considerable number of points to be considered. These include procedural points, rights and benefits to be claimed, rights of members of the family and reasons why deportation would not be appropriate.

A good plan is essential in order to structure this answer.

You should commence by briefly outlining the general approach of the ECJ in this area of law before noting the issues that should be tackled in the answer. Then, identify the problems which must be considered. These can be listed person by person. Wolfie is concerned about the deportation, whether he is a worker or has the status of a worker for other reasons, and then whether there are substantive grounds for the deportation order. Florence and Charlie need to know their rights as relatives of a worker to claim benefits and Florence is concerned about the deportation order issued. Ken wishes to know about his ability to provide services.

The order in which these points are tackled is also important and the procedural points should be dealt with first because these are of first relevance for the persons concerned. This is even though you have not decided whether they are yet grounds for the deportation. Then you can deal with each person in turn or combine the treatment of persons where the issues are the same. Given that Wolfie is so complex you might provide a list of the items you need to tackle in respect of him in the answer or maybe just put these down in your plan. I have provided them here as a list, but a list might not be appropriate in the answer itself. Wolfie's concerns are:

Deportation

Worker in own right?

Providing services?

Established?

Seeking work?

Student?

Member of family?

Cohabitee?

Right to be deported

Past convictions and

Personal conduct

Answer plan

- Outline area of law, ECJ approach, and Art 45 TFEU
- Identify procedural and substantive factual issues and relevant secondary law
- Consider the procedural issues according to legislation and case law
- Consider each substantive issue according to legislation and case law
- The legislation on services and establishment of lawyers must be addressed
- Case law applying to Ken's case must be considered, especially *Gebhard*

Suggested answer

The free movement of persons is catered for in Arts 45–62 TFEU, secondary EU law and the case law of the Court of Justice. In this area of law the Court of Justice has taken a line which has sought to promote and protect the freedoms available to individual workers and to restrict, where possible, the reasons by which the Member States can restrict those freedoms.

Wolfie and Florence are facing deportation, Wolfie immediately and Florence with just one week's notice. Union citizens in such circumstances are provided with rights under Directive 2004/38 Art 30 not to be deported immediately but to be allowed to stay for at least a month. Whether they can stay longer depends on the facts of the case; for example, whether they can stay to argue the substantive grounds of the deportation decision through the courts, which may take longer; see Art 31 of Directive 2004/38 and the cases of *Adoui* and *Cornaille* (115 and 116/81) and *Pecastaing* (98/79). However, they cannot be subject to immediate deportation.

The answer can now consider the substantive grounds in respect of Wolfie. His right to remain in the host state must be considered in the light of the grounds for deportation. If he has no right to stay, then deportation will be within the right of the host state. First of all, it should be considered whether he has the right to be able to stay because he is a worker or self-employed as these categories bring with them more extensive rights than just as a Union citizen, which might provide an alternative right to stay. Is he a worker as a busker? Fundamentally, to be a worker, the definition from *Hoekstra* (75/63) is that the person must be employed. The *Levin* case (53/81) also requires there to be a genuine economic activity. A busker does not seem to satisfy the criteria of a worker laid down in the case of *Lawrie Blum* (66/85). His busking is not at the direction or remuneration of an employer and he receives donations only, therefore he is not a worker.

Does the 80 hours' membership of the band and playing gigs qualify him as a worker? Although the case of *Raulin v Netherlands Ministry of Education and Science* (C-357/89) would seem to support this suggestion, again the criteria of *Lawrie Blum* seem not to be satisfied as he is not employed under a contract and the band split. If he is not classified as a worker, it may then be questioned whether he can be considered as self-employed, either as providing services or establishing in the host state. In order to establish or provide services in a host state, a self-employed person must first be established in another Member State (Art 49 EC). Wolfie was not.

A definition for establishment has been given in *Factortame* (C-221/89) by the ECJ, which considered the actual pursuit of an economic activity through a fixed establishment in another Member State for an indefinite period. Wolfie has no fixed establishment, therefore the status of a self-employed person is denied him. The general concept of self-employed, though, has been given recognition by the ECJ in the cases of *Jany* (C-268/99) and *Ex P Barkoci and Malik* (C-257/99). However, the conclusion must be that he has no status as a self-employed person, especially as he plays no part in the tax and social security systems of the host state. So, he has no right to stay unless it can be argued that he is *seeking work* as considered by the ECJ in the case of *Antonisson* (C-292/89). The guidelines in that case are that, if he is actively seeking and there are genuine chances of him finding work, he should be accorded the status of a worker for that purpose. Given the limited facts it would seem that he is not seeking work, apart from his busking which does not appear to constitute work, therefore on the basis of *Antonisson* and the fact he has been without work for seven months, he has no right to stay and, unless there is an alternative right to stay, can be deported. His application to attend music college might provide him with a very weak claim to be a student and thus benefit under the *Lair* case (39/86), but he was refused the grant and his status is uncertain but he does not have the link required under *Lair* between previous employment, studies and future employment. See Directive 2004/38, Art 7 which provided him with a right of residence in the host state providing he is self-sufficient and which would allow him to attend the college but not to obtain the grant.

Directive 2004/38, Arts 2 and 3 2(b) provide that partners, where in a stable registered partnership and officially recognised by the host state law, may be equated with spouses in the host state. Therefore, if Germany grants nationals rights as partners, they must also allow Wolfie such rights. Another final basis which might be argued to provide Wolfie with a right to stay would be the right as a cohabitee of Shirley as in the *Netherlands* v *Reed* case (59/85). Shirley has obtained work and is therefore a worker. It must be stressed that if this were accepted he does not have the right to stay in his own right but as one of the social advantages which Shirley must be allowed to enjoy under Art 7(2) of Regulation 1612/68 but any rights available to him are available equally, as above, only if those rights are granted to German nationals also.

The grounds for deportation of public policy and public security stated by Germany are those allowed by Art 45(3) TFEU. The grounds for the Member State to deport him, must be considered in the light of this tenuous right to stay. The grounds are further defined in Directive 2004/38, Art 27 which states that they must be based exclusively on the personal conduct of the person concerned. So, simple membership of the Tooting Popular Front should not justify deportation; however, the ECJ in the case of *van Duyn* (41/74) held that association with the aims of an organisation may be sufficient, even if the organisation or its activities are not illegal. Given that Wolfie is the founding member, it may rest on the view of the state of the threat posed by the organisation; however, the Directive requires a serious threat to the fundamental interests of society, so the *van Duyn* case is probably not good law now.

Directive 2004/38, Art 27(1) further provides that the state authorities cannot use past convictions as grounds in themselves to warrant deportation. However, the ECJ held in the case of *Bouchereau* (30/77) that where they are a present threat and point to a future threat they can be employed as evidence. In Wolfie's case there are only past convictions and no present problems so it is unlikely that this ground would be upheld as acceptable.

On balance, whilst an unequivocal answer is difficult, deportation is probably not acceptable despite the fact that his right to stay is weak. However, a reference to the ECJ may confirm a change on this point, especially under the new Directive.

Florence and Charlie's right to remain in the host state are based on their status as ascendants of a worker now under Art 2(2) of Directive 2004/38. However, Florence is also facing deportation. The Member State may argue that Directive 2004/38, Art 27 may allow that profound mental disturbance is a disability which might threaten public security or public policy. Whether Florence's mental disturbance is sufficient to satisfy this requirement would depend on her medical condition which would arguably have to be quite severe. Her mental condition is unlikely, therefore, to justify deportation. Mental health is not specified in Art 29 of Directive 2004/38 and it is argued that now to justify expulsion along these lines, the illness would have to be something both very severe and recognised and listed by the WHO.

The claim for retirement pension for Charlie is straightforward and the case of *Castelli* (261/83) can be cited in support, which provides that benefits in respect of members of the family of a worker are also social advantages under Art 7(2) of Regulation 1612/68 which must be enjoyed by the worker.

As far as the special benefit for Florence to attend the mental health clinic is concerned, there is the case of *Michel S* (76/72) which may be argued but this is only applicable to children of workers under Art 12 of Regulation 1612/68. Arguably the ECJ would also hold this to be a social advantage under Art 7(2).

Finally, the situation with regard to Ken must be considered. It is to be assumed that Ken is seeking the freedom to provide services rather than establishment, as there appears no intention to settle permanently or on a long-term basis. Article 56 TFEU is the applicable Treaty Article which is directly effective but Directive 77/249 specifically concerns the freedom of lawyers to provide services. Whilst under Art 5 of this Directive a Member State may require a lawyer providing services to work in conjunction with a national lawyer, the ECJ has held in the case of *Commission v France* (C-294/89) and *Commission v Germany* (427/85) that this may be imposed only if compulsory representation of clients is required before the court concerned. In Ken's case this is not the position, so he cannot be required to work in conjunction.

The requirements to rent and maintain a local office are excluded by Art 4(1) of the Directive and the ECJ confirmed in the case of *Van Binsbergen* (33/74) and *Klopp* (107/83) that local residence requirements cannot be required of lawyers merely wishing to provide services.

As a result of the more recent *Gebhard* case (C-55/94), the German authorities may be correct in describing the position of Ken as establishment but this can only be judged on the facts. A one-off visit would not qualify but if Ken continued to keep his chambers in Germany, this might. In any event, as a result of the *Säger* (C-76/90) and *Gebhard* cases, now and almost regardless of whether the provision of services or establishment is involved, any rules which hinder or make less attractive the exercise of the fundamental freedoms will be subject to the following four conditions. The rules must be:

(i) non-discriminatory in application;

(ii) justified by imperative reason relating to the public interest;

(iii) suitable to secure the objective sought; and

(iv) proportional.

Whilst this is a matter for the national courts to decide, it is arguable the requirements do not meet the criteria but a reference to the ECJ might be necessary to settle the matter.

Question 3

Lister, a UK citizen, has moved to Denmark to take up employment in the Virtual Reality Computer Company (VRCC) as a technician. He is accompanied by his girlfriend Kristine, also a UK national, who is an expectant mother of twins. The claims she has made for unemployment benefit and maternity payments have been rejected by the authorities in Skive, where they have settled. The grounds given are that she is not a national and has not been resident for the required six months. Her claim that she is dependent on Lister is also rejected as she is not married to him.

Another UK national, Rimmer, has also obtained work as a technician in VRCC. Once settled, he is joined by his cousin, Cat, who is not a Union national. Cat attempts to claim unemployment benefit but is refused. The authorities, now aware of his presence, have issued him with a deportation order which only states that he has no right to remain in Denmark. On a visit to Rimmer's home, a quantity of drugs brought in by Cat was discovered. As a result, Rimmer is also issued with a deportation order, stating that the presence of persons in the possession of drugs is considered to be contrary to public policy.

Advise the parties as to their rights under EU law.

 ## Commentary

This problem question on the free movement of persons concentrates to a large extent on the rights of persons connected to and dependent on the worker. You have to consider the rights of Kristine, the girlfriend of Lister, to stay and claim benefits, and the right of Cat to stay and claim benefits. It would be better to start the answer with a general introduction to this area of law, before moving on to consider the issue of the threatened deportations and thus the procedural rights of Rimmer and Cat. You can then move on to consider the substantive issues in the problem. Do not, however, spend an inordinate amount of time proving that Lister or Rimmer are workers, as it is the rights of the others that are more problematic. You should, of course, state that they are workers but only briefly as this point is not contentious. Avoid also entering into a discussion about how criminal law and procedure would regard the discovery of drugs in the home of Rimmer. Stick to the EU law issues at hand.

Answer plan

- Outline area of law, ECJ approach and **Art 45 TFEU**
- Identify procedural and substantive factual issues and relevant secondary law
- Consider the procedural issues according to legislation and case law
- Consider each substantive issue according to legislation and case law
- The position of a worker's family and non-EU nationals must be considered
- The substantive law on deportation must finally be considered

Suggested answer

The free movement of workers is provided for in Arts 45–48 TFEU, secondary EU law and the case law of the Court of Justice. In this area of law, the Court of Justice has taken a line which has sought to promote and protect the freedoms available to individual workers and to restrict, where possible, the reasons by which the Member States can restrict those freedoms.

The issues arising in this question are the deportation orders issued against Kristine, Cat and Rimmer, the right of Kristine to remain and claim benefits, the right of Cat to remain and claim benefits and the reasons given for deportation of Kristine, Cat and Rimmer.

The rights of those facing deportation should be considered before moving on to consider the substantive rights at issue in the problem as this is of immediate concern to them. Union citizens in such circumstances, and members of the family who are given rights under other EU legislation, are provided with rights under Directive 2004/38 not to be deported immediately but to be allowed to stay for at least a month by Art 30 of Directive 2004/38. Whether they can stay longer depends on the facts of the case. For example, whether they can stay to argue the substantive grounds of the deportation decision through the courts, which may take longer, see Art 9 of Directive of 2004/38 and the cases of *Adoui* and *Cornaille* (115 and 116/81), and *Pecastaing* (98/79). However, they cannot be subject to immediate deportation. The grounds for deportation can be discussed later now that the immediate threat of deportation has been diverted.

The first substantive consideration is that of the right of Kristine to stay in Denmark and claim unemployment and maternity benefits. It should first be noted that, as it is stated in the question that Lister has taken up employment and is a

Union national, it can safely be concluded that he is a worker for the purposes of EU law. This point is more important for Kristine.

First, however, it must be determined whether Kristine has any EU law rights under the free movement of persons.

Kristine could be looking for work and would benefit from limited rights provided under Art 45(3)(b) TFEU, confirmed in the case of *Antonnisson* (C-292/89), that Union nationals have the right to enter a host state and stay for a limited period providing they are actively seeking work and there is a genuine chance of being engaged. Given the facts of the case it is unlikely that this conclusion could be reached; however, if she could prove these requirements, she should be given the right to stay for six months at least.

A second and probably stronger possibility exists under Directive 2004/38, Arts 6 and 7. Whilst Art 6 provides that union citizens have a right of residence for up to three months without condition, Art 7 extends this beyond three months but subject to the EU citizen being covered by adequate sickness insurance, which Lister could provide, but also that they do not become a burden on the state. The facts do not reveal how long they have been in the host state but the claims she is making would seem to undermine the rights to claim the protection under Art 7 of this Directive and it appears unlikely that it is applicable in her favour. However, case law has now determined that a person can be a reasonable burden (*Grzelczyk* C-184/99) which is ultimately up to the national court to decide and that the resources of others is acceptable (*Commission* v *Belgium* C-408/03) which would seem to strengthen Kristine's case to stay.

The EU free movement of workers' provisions provides not only rights for the worker but also rights for the worker's family. Directive 2004/38 provides the details of those who can claim rights by virtue of their relationship to the worker. The spouse and other members of the family are defined in Arts 2 and 3. The Directive extends the rights available to the worker to the spouse and descendants and ascendants regardless of nationality. The descendants can be any nationality and include those under 21 and adult children over 21 where they are dependent on the worker. The new Directive includes non-married partners and this was considered by the Court of Justice in the case of *Netherlands* v *Reed* (59/85). Reed applied for a residence permit in Holland claiming her right to remain was based on her cohabitation with a UK national working in the Netherlands. The Dutch Government refused to recognise this. The Court of Justice was aware that provisions of national laws regarding cohabitees' legal rights could be quite varied. It was unable to overcome the clear intention of Art 10 of Regulation 1612/68 (Article now repealed) which referred to a relationship based on marriage. The Court referred instead to the 'social advantages' guaranteed under Art 7(2) of the Regulation as being capable of including the companionship of a cohabitee which could contribute to integration in the host country. Under the new Directive, Art 3, where such stable and registered partnership relationships amongst nationals were accorded the legal advantages under national law, these could not be denied to nationals of other Member States without being discriminatory and thus breaching Arts 12 and 39 of the EC Treaty (now 18 and 45 TFEU) in addition to the Directive. Directive 2004/38 will strengthen these rights by providing that partners, where officially recognised by the host state law, shall be equated with spouses in the host state (Art 2) and have the same rights to work, education and social assistance.

Therefore, as a cohabitee, or as a partner, Kristine would obtain residence rights to stay but can she claim benefits? There are a number of cases from the Court of Justice which have confirmed that a number of benefits may be claimed by members of the family. See, in respect of unemployment benefit, the case of *ONE v Deak* (94/84). Furthermore, it has been held that Art 7(2) also applies to maternity and childbirth allowances without discrimination; see *Commission v Luxembourg* (C-111/91). Her rights therefore depend on how a national cohabitee would be treated because, if possessing the right to stay, the general prohibition of discrimination under Art 18 TFEU would ensure that she should be treated the same. Providing that unemployment benefit and maternity rights were granted the cohabitees of national workers, it is at least arguable that they would be extended to other Union cohabitees, but a certain result is unclear at this time and a reference to the ECJ would be advisable. The same considerations would seem to apply even under the new Directive.

A consideration of the legal position of Cat also involves a discussion of the rights provided in respect to non-immediate members of a worker's family. He is not a Union national and therefore cannot acquire his own right to stay. Directive 2004/38, Art 3(2) also provides that other family members, who are dependent on the Union citizen with primary right of residence, are to be afforded entry and residence rights but a reference would be advisable to the ECJ to confirm this.

A further argument, which is admittedly slim, to find a right for him to stay is that as cohabitee of Rimmer. Quite whether the Court of Justice would entertain this and whether the facts would allow this conclusion to be drawn are speculative and would certainly need a reference to the Court of Justice under Art 267 TFEU. This situation is covered by Art 2(2) of the new Directive as a registered partnership regarded as the equivalent of marriage in the host state. This can be examined by the host state and a reference may still be required to confirm if this is the correct interpretation of the new Directive. Therefore, at present, there is no clear and direct obligation to allow Cat to remain, let alone to claim benefits. In the case of *Lebon* (316/85), a dependant who had the right to stay to find work could be classed as a worker for this purpose but not to be able to claim benefits. Other members of the family have, however, been able to claim benefits when their right to stay was established; see *Deak* (94/84).

In this case, as the Member State is not obliged to let him stay, it is possibly the case that the possession of drugs would be sufficient excuse for the Member

State to deport him, although the Member State has not given the reasons for the deportation which they are required to do so under Art 30 of Directive 2004/38. The Directive will only apply if Cat has a right to stay in the first place; if not, then deportation cannot be prevented. The deportation for drugs may well depend on the nature of the drugs involved. On balance, his rights to avoid deportation and stay are very weak.

The right to deport Rimmer would be subject to other considerations. Article 27(2) of Directive 2004/38 provides that measures adopted on public policy or security must be based on personal conduct. In this case it appears not to be the personal conduct of Rimmer but those of Cat which have prompted the Member State to order deportation. Thus, as no other reasons are apparent, Denmark would not be justified under EU law in deporting Rimmer.

Question 4

Discuss the view that case law concerning the freedoms of establishment and the right to provide services has blurred the distinction between these two concepts.

Commentary

This question is really asking you to consider the effect of the cases of *Säger* v *Dennemeyer* (C-76/90) and *Gebhard* v *Consiglio dell'Ordine degli Avvocati* (C-55/94) and the more recent cases and legislative moves in this area. However, to make sense of this you must put these in context by defining the establishment and the provision of services and then outlining the original distinction between them, indicating this by way of any case law relating to them. Finally, then, you can consider what effect, if any, the cases and new legislation have had.

You should therefore outline the Treaty applicable to the self-employed. In particular you should consider the national rules, especially professional rules which may be considered acceptable for establishment but not for services and how the latest case law has affected this position.

Answer plan

- Outline Arts 3 TEU and 49–62 TFEU
- Provide basic definitions of establishment and provision of services
- Leading cases *Reyners* and *van Binsbergen*
- Distinguishing the concepts
- The *Säger* and *Gebhard* cases and recent legislative intervention
- Conclusions on blurring

Suggested answer

The EU free movement policies are broadly outlined in Art 3 TEU. Free movement for the self-employed is provided by the freedom of establishment (Arts 49–55 TFEU) and the freedom to provide services (Arts 56–62 TFEU). Both establishment and the provision of services have been held by the Court of Justice to be fundamental policies of the Union and thus to be strongly defended by the Court. A person wishing to take advantage of either must first be established in one of the Member States of the EU. These provisions, like those applying to workers, are in favour of nationals of the Member States. Article 18 TFEU (ex 12 EC) has provided and continues to provide a general legislative base to ensure there is no discrimination on the grounds of nationality for those establishing or providing services, rather than secondary legislation. Clear authority for the no discrimination rule is: *Commission* v *UK (Re: Nationality of Fishermen) (Factortame)* (C-246/89).

What is meant by these two terms? The basic definitions are as follows:

Establishment includes the rights to enter another Member State and stay on a long-term or permanent basis, to take up and pursue activities as self-employed persons and to set up and manage undertakings. The concept suggests either permanent residence in the host state or at least the establishment of a permanent professional base. A definition has been given in *Factortame* by the ECJ: 'the actual pursuit of an economic activity through a fixed establishment in another Member State for an indefinite period'.

The provision of services envisages a temporary state of affairs. Appearance in the host state would only be for a limited period to provide specific services and there would be no permanent personal or professional presence in the host state or a necessity to reside. The concept of services is defined by Art 47(1) TFEU as those 'provided for remuneration, in so far as they are not governed by provisions relating to freedom of movement of goods, capital and persons', ie a distinct concept.

The provision of services can also be effected without having to leave the home country or enter the host country by either the provider or receiver of services as was the case of telephone sales in *Alpine Investments BV* v *Minister of Finance* (384/93). Thus far, it would seem that establishment and services could be distinguished by the duration of the activity and to some extent the type of activity. Even this was, however, undermined at an early stage by case law.

Originally, the Commission was empowered under Treaty Arts 53, 57 and 63 EEC (now 53 and 59 TFEU) to issue Directives to obtain the general objectives set for these two areas. This was addressed by the adoption of Directives to abolish national restrictions and provide for the mutual recognition of qualifications on an occupation by occupation basis; however, this process encouraged the view that the only way in which these rights could be promoted was by Directives and not directly from the Treaty, therefore progress was limited and slow.

Two leading cases, in which Arts 49 and 56 TFEU (ex 52 and 59 EEC) were held to create direct effects by the Court of Justice, radically changed the approach of the Commission in taking steps to achieve free movement. The case of *Reyners v Belgian State* (2/74) involved the attempt by a Dutchman to get access to the Belgium bar. The Government argued that Art 52 EEC (now 49 TFEU) was not directly effective because it was incomplete without the issue of Directives required by Art 57 EEC (now 53 TFEU). The Court of Justice held that the prohibition of discrimination under Art 52 EEC (now 49 TFEU) was directly effective and declared that nationality could be no barrier to appropriately qualified lawyers entering a country to practise. The Directives were simply to facilitate free movement and not to establish it, which had already been done by the end of the initial transition period of the Communities. The *Van Binsbergen* case (33/74) concerned a professionally qualified Dutchman, resident in Belgium, who was refused audience rights before the Dutch courts. The Court of Justice held Art 59 EEC (now 56 TFEU) was directly effective and was not conditional on the issue of a subsequent Directive in respect of the specific professions, nor on a residence requirement. Both establishment and services were therefore directly effective and did not therefore need any Directives to define the conditions upon which they could be taken up.

Distinguishing the concepts of establishment and services

A clear factual distinction is difficult to maintain. For example, the Court of Justice considered that the provision of services which included the setting up of offices on a long-term basis and staffed by nationals of the host state could be held to be establishment even though the legal entity remained in the home state. See *Commission v Germany (Re: Insurance Services)* (205/84). Whilst Art 57(3) TFEU states that services may be provided under the same conditions as are imposed by the State on its own nationals, some rules may not be relevant to the temporary provision of services and not all home rules have been found by the Court of Justice to be suitable or acceptable for the provision of services.

In *Ministère Public v Van Wesemael* (110–111/78), a Belgian was prosecuted under a Belgian law for using a French employment agency and not one registered in Belgium, unless it operated in conjunction with a registered Belgian agency, to obtain the services of a variety artist in Belgium. The Court of Justice held that since the agency was registered in one Member State, it was contrary to EC law for another to restrict its right to provide services in that country.

In *van Binsbergen* it was held that professional rules such as the requirement that advocates must be resident for professional purposes within the jurisdiction of certain courts for the provision of services was not objectively justified and proportionate to the aims.

In *Commission v Germany (Re: Insurance Services)* (205/84) the Court of Justice held that Member States were under a duty not only to eliminate all discrimination based on nationality but also all restrictions based on the free provision of services on the grounds that the provider is established in another Member

State. It also emphasised that all those national rules which apply to the self-employed permanently established in a Member State will not necessarily automatically apply to those 'activities of a temporary character which are carried out by enterprises established in other Member States'. Hence a further difference is introduced that not all national rules would apply to services even though they would still apply to nationals and Union nationals establishing in the host state.

In the case of *Säger* v *Dennemeyer* (C-76/90), the ECJ moved further in the development of a rule which prevents the restriction of services from other Member States but may still persist to limit activities of the home providers of services. Dennemeyer wished to provide patent services in Germany, something requiring a licence whose issue was restricted. His right to obtain a licence was challenged by a German Patent agent but D claimed a breach of Art 49 EC (now 56 TFEU). The rule was non-discriminatory in that it applied to all patent agents regardless of residence. The ECJ held that not just discriminatory rules are prohibited, but any rules which are liable to prohibit or otherwise impede persons providing a service which they already lawfully do in the state of their establishment. To be allowed, such rules must satisfy the criteria that they be justified, with no other rules already protecting the public interest and proportionate. It was suggested by the Court that Member States may not apply the same requirements for establishment as those providing services only, thus maintaining a distinction between these two forms of freedom.

However, when faced with a later case, the ECJ does appear now to have narrowed the difference. In *Gebhard* v *Consiglio dell'Ordine degli Avvocati* (C-55/94), a German lawyer who had established a second chamber in Milan was prevented from using the title Avvocato. No Community law Directive was of help to him. The question was raised as to whether the Italian rules could be imposed on him? In principle and according to the general Treaty provision Art 43 EC (now 49 TFEU), he was required to comply with the rules. The ECJ characterised 'establishment' as the right of a community (now Union) national to participate on a stable and continuous basis in the economic life of a Member State other than his or her own and 'services' by the temporary, precarious and discontinuous nature of the services which is to be determined in the light of its duration, regularity, periodicity and continuity.

Hence, the setting up of chambers in Italy by a German lawyer, still practising in Stuttgart, was held to be establishment. So Gebhard, despite non-permanent presence, was deemed not to be providing services. However, the ECJ held that national measures which hinder or make less attractive the exercise of fundamental freedoms must fulfil four conditions. They must be:

  (i) non-discriminatory in application;

  (ii) justified by imperative reason relating to the public interest;

  (iii) suitable to secure the objective sought; and

  (iv) proportional.

It is left to the national courts to determine whether national rules are applicable. The consequence of this decision is that establishment is now closer to services. Indeed, the general concept of self-employed has been given recognition by the ECJ in the cases of *Jany* (C-268/99) and *Ex P Barkoci and Malik* (C-257/99), without concentrating in particular on which variant was more relevant. It could be argued after this case law that it doesn't matter where or how you practice, either on a temporary or permanent basis, provided qualifications are roughly equivalent. Rules which seek to prevent this must satisfy the criteria or be struck out, at least as far as EU citizens are concerned. Hence then, some rules which can apply to nationals may not be appropriate for both services and establishment now. The distinction has arguably narrowed. Furthermore, there is a growing emphasis on the concept of market access which goes beyond discrimination and is not concerned with the distinction between those providing services and those establishing in the host state. The conclusions to be drawn are that regardless of whether services or establishment, any national rule which constitutes an impediment of market access has been held to come within the free movement rules unless objectively justified. See, for example, *Alpine Investments* (C-384/93).

Finally, note can be taken of recent legislative moves whereby extensive consolidating Directives have been enacted which concern themselves comprehensively with both services and establishment. These are Directive 2006/36 on the Recognition of Professional Qualifications and Directive 2004/38 on the Free Movement of Persons. More recently, the Services Directive 2006/123 further consolidates the rules on services and establishment.

Whilst we are not quite at the position where we could say that the two concepts are all but one now, in that more relaxed rules on the temporary provision of services are appropriate, it is certainly the case that the clear distinction suggested by the original Treaty provision is not so discernable.

Question 5

Two UK nationals, Bob and Vic, decide to go to college in Holland because there are no tuition fees and many courses are in English, so they don't have to learn a foreign language. They have saved up some money from working in the UK and have enough to live on for one to two years depending on how careful they are. On entry to Holland they are questioned as to their intentions and financial position and declare that they are fully self-sufficient. The Dutch authorities advise them that they will be provided with residence permits once they have completed all the necessary forms and registered with the local authorities in the Dutch town of Sneek where they have settled. They enrol on a four-year college course on hotel and pub management which involves some practical training working in bars, restaurants and hotels, but this is not paid. They are not, however, too careful with their money because each weekend they travel to Amsterdam to enjoy the café and nightlife culture of that city. In less than one year their money runs out. Both apply to the Dutch authorities for social security assistance so that they can continue to live in Holland and complete their courses. Both are refused assistance. Now that the authorities are alerted to their situation, they discover that Bob and Vic have not completed the immigration formalities and do not possess a residence permit. The authorities issue them with deportation orders, giving them two weeks to leave the country.

Realising that the situation is grave, Bob is able to persuade a local bar owner to provide him with work for two nights per week (eight hours in total) but which is only paid for in free food and drink. He advises the authorities of this and now claims he has the right to stay as a EU worker and also that Vic can stay too as Bob's live-in lover.

Discuss the rights, if any, that Bob and Vic have under EU law relevant to the above situation.

Commentary

This question moves into the newer developing area of free movement of persons, namely the more general rights of movement of the non-economically active and the rights now provided, if any, under the concept of Union Citizenship. In answering the question itself, your starting point should be a brief discussion of the applicable legislative regime including Treaty and secondary provisions to enter as non worker or student and the general rights under Arts 18, 20 and 21 TFEU (ex 12, 17 and 18 EC). When addressing the facts of the case, as this problem also includes the threat of deportation, this should be considered first, followed by establishing whether Bob and Vic have any right to stay in Holland and then if there is a right to stay, whether the Dutch authorities then can establish any substantive grounds for their expulsion. As usual, any relevant cases should be referred to.

Answer plan

- Outline general rights of entry and residence
- Deal with procedural aspects relating to deportation
- Arts 20–21 TFEU and *Sala* and *Grzelczyk* cases
- Article 45 TFEU and worker status, Regulation 1612/68
- Status of cohabitee (*Reed*) or student (*Lair* and *Brown*)
- Directive 2004/38 and any other relevant case law

Suggested answer

Bob and Vic enter Holland not as workers but as students under Directive 2004/38, Art 7 which provides entry and residence rights for students. They are required and have made a declaration that they have sufficient resources not to become a burden on the host state social assistance system and have comprehensive sickness insurance, as required under Art 7 of the Directive. Furthermore, they have to be enrolled on a vocational course in a recognised educational establishment, which in the absence of contrary facts appears to be the case here. Hence, their entry appears to be in order, although there is the paperwork which will have to be addressed later. For the moment though, their most immediate concern, which is the threat of deportation, can be addressed. Whilst Member States do have rights to deport Union citizens under specific grounds laid down in both Art 45 TFEU and Directive 2004/38, Art 27, the Directive also provides procedural safeguards for those facing deportation. Article 30 provides that any decision to expel must be officially notified and the minimum period given to leave shall not be less than one month. Here the facts are slightly confused as we know they have been in Holland for less than one year and that under Art 10 of the Directive, a residence permit should be granted no later than six months after entry, although this is dependent on the production of the appropriate documents under Art 8. Bob and Vic have not completed the entry paperwork formalities and have not registered as may be required under Art 8. What is clear though, is that in any event, the period of notice for expulsion cannot be less than one month and Bob and Vic have only been given 14 days, so this is in contravention of Art 30 of Directive 2004/38. Furthermore, the failure to complete the paperwork formalities should neither prevent them from undertaking their studies nor result in deportation for that reason alone (see Directive 2004/38, Art 8 and the cases of *R v Pieck* (159/79) and *Watson and Belmann* (118/75)). The latter case is, incidentally, also an authority to say that a person does not need to be paid to be considered as a worker under Art 45 TFEU. However, the threat of early deportation is removed and they may be able to stay longer to argue the substantive merits of the deportation before an independent tribunal according to their individual circumstances (see Art 31 of Directive 2004/38 and the cases of *Adoui and Cornaille* (115 and 116/81) and *Gallagher* (175/94)).

It is now possible to turn to their continued right to remain, having confirmed that they had the right to enter under Directive 2004/38 provided that they were self-sufficient and were engaged in a course of vocational study. They then ran out of money and sought to claim social assistance from the Dutch State. Under a strict application of the Directive, this would seem to remove their right to remain once the condition of Art 8, the necessity for self sufficiency, is no longer satisfied. Recent cases will certainly shed some light on the possible attitude of the ECJ to this case but which may not provide a definitive solution. In *Sala* v *Bayern* (C-85/96), the ECJ had held that where a person was legally resident in a host state, they did not have to produce a residence permit to obtain a state benefit, where no similar requirement was demanded of nationals. This would seem to support Bob and Vic's right for assistance but Sala was previously a worker in Germany and had lived there for 25 years in total. The Court did not expressly recognise her right to reside from the Articles on European Union citizenship (Arts 17 and 18 EC (now 20–21 TFEU)) and her rights were possibly derived from her status as an ex-worker, although ultimately it was for the national court to decide. A closer case is that of *Grzelczyk* (C-184/99) which was decided on the basis of non-discrimination (Art 12 EC (now 18 TFEU)) and the right of residence as a Union Citizen (Art 17 EC (now 20 TFEU)) that the right to social assistance, once a person had fallen out of the scope of the Directive, could not necessarily be denied and that furthermore the right to residence should not automatically be lost. The facts as to the truthfulness of a person's declaration in the *Grzelczyk* case is a matter of fact for the national court to decide as it would be also in Bob and Vic's case. Also Grzelczyk worked during the course of his studies to help finance them, whereas Bob and Vic only worked to obtain experience as a part of the training course. Clearly this is not a foregone conclusion for Bob and Vic and it would also be ultimately up to the national court to decide with the help of an Art 267 TFEU reference to the ECJ. So the decision may go either way, but clearly the ECJ in *Grzelczyk* provided some substance to the rights of Citizenship in Art 17 EC (now 20 TFEU) but whether it is enough to cover a possible lack of good faith by Bob and Vic is uncertain. However, the *Collins* case (C-138/02) demonstrates that the ECJ will not allow non-contributory benefits to be claimed when there is not a sufficient connection to the state, although residence under the terms granted by EU law is still upheld. The more recent cases of C-11–12/06 *Morgan and Bucher* and case C-158/07 *Förster* v *IB-Groep* confirm that Member States are justified in requiring proportionate degrees of integration in the host state before granting benefits. There are, however, further facts relating to Bob and Vic which have to be considered.

In the alternative we can consider whether Bob is to be considered a worker under Art 45 TFEU or a student with the status of worker under the *Lair* case (39/86). He has obtained unpaid work in a bar for eight hours per week. Is this enough to qualify him as a worker and thus to all the social advantages as guaranteed by Art 7(2) of Regulation 1612/68 such as social assistance and the companionship of a cohabitee? It is certainly clear that part-time work and remuneration below the national minimum subsistence level or remuneration in kind will not preclude the status of worker from being applied (see the cases of *Kempf* (139/85), *Lawrie-Blum* (66/85), *Steymann* (196/87) and *Trojani* (C-456/02) which would support the claim for social assistance), it thus will depend on whether the activity undertaken is considered to be a genuine and effective economic activity.

If it is, then there may be an argument under Arts 2 and 3 of Directive 2004/38 if they have registered a partnership or under *The Netherlands* v *Reed* (59/85) that Vic can stay as a cohabitee depending on how same-sex cohabitees are treated in Holland.

If the work undertaken is considered not to be genuine enough to provide long-term rights as in the cases of C-357/89 *Raulin* and C-138/02 *Collins*, another alternative is to consider whether the case of *Lair* (39/86) will help in establishing a link between work and the status of students thus allowing the application still of Regulation 1612/68 or whether the view will be taken that the work was only in support of the studies as in *Brown* (197/86) and thus the status of worker is not to be applied.

Clearly, a difficult decision for the national court and perhaps only a reference to the ECJ will help but it may be suggested that if the Court is trying to support the status of Union citizenship and with it, EU law, then Bob and Vic may well be successful in their claims for assistance. Finally then, you should consider the substantive grounds for deportation, whether personal conduct, etc which is now covered by Arts 27 and 28 of Directive 2004/38 and which, on the facts, appear not to reveal any serious threat to a fundamental interest of society which would warrant their deportation.

Question 6

Discuss the extent to which free movement of persons and citizenship in the EU legal order now allows EU citizens and their families to reside and obtain equal rights in any Member State of the EU.

Commentary

This question asks for a discussion of the rapidly expanding law in this area which includes a consideration not just of the economically active person, but of any EU citizen and members of the family who can be from outside the EU. The question impliedly asks you to consider the extent of the rights provided under EU law and whether these rights also apply in the home state and whether all rights can be enjoyed on a par with nationals in a host state. It therefore requires a knowledge not only of the relevant Treaty and secondary law of the EU, but also the range of recent case decisions of the ECJ which has considerably extended EU law and far exceed any legislative changes to the free movement of persons.

Answer plan

- Outline the concepts of free movement of persons and citizenship
- Define those who can be considered EU citizens and their families
- Broadly outline the rights now provided by the TFEU and secondary legislation
- Consider the extent of the rights which can be obtained in the host state
- Consider the rights of third party national family members
- Consider rights in the home state: the 'wholly internal rule'
- Outline the latest case law in this area

Suggested answer

From the start, the EC (now EU) provided for the free movement of persons for workers and those wishing to establish or provide services in another Member State. These rights were granted in favour of the economically active and, with later secondary legislation such as Regulation 1612/68, rights were also granted to members of that person's family. The legislation also envisaged that those seeking work could also obtain limited rights and this was confirmed by the ECJ in cases such as *Lebon* and *Antonisson* (316/85 and C-292/99). Rights of entry and residence were extended to the non-economically active first by three general Directives in 1990 and then by the Treaty of European Union signed at Maastricht by the introduction of the citizenship provisions to the EC Treaty (Arts 17–22 (now 20–25 TFEU)). Essentially, the rights provided are that the economically active worker or self-employed person who does nothing to offend the public policy or security of the host state has the right, not only to reside and stay in the host state but also to bring with him or her other members of the family and to receive employment, social and tax benefits on an equal basis as nationals of the host state. Members of the family also have extensive rights, whereas a person not economically active has general rights now provided by Arts 20 and 21 TFEU to move and reside in a host state subject to any existing restrictions on the free movement of persons in the EU legal order. This means that they must be adequately insured and do not become a burden on the social security systems of the host Member State.

EU citizenship is defined by reference to each Member State's definition of citizenship as agreed by the Member States in Declaration No 2 on Nationality attached to the original TEU, although no longer present in the Declarations listed by the Lisbon Treaty. This provided that nationality shall be settled solely by reference to the national law of the Member State concerned and was upheld in case C-192/99 *Manjit Kaur,* in which the ECJ held that it is for each Member State to lay down the conditions for the acquisition and loss of nationality. The case of *Chen* (C-200/02) further upholds this position.

Family members are not restricted to citizenship of the Union and may include persons from any country as many cases have previously demonstrated, eg case 94/84 ONE v Deak where the Hungarian son was also able to obtain social security benefits. Recent cases by the ECJ have provided a generous interpretation of the rights provided now. For example, in the *Sala* and *Gryzelczyk* cases(C-85/96 and C-184/99), the ECJ held that citizenship required the Union citizen to be treated equally even where claiming non-contributory benefits providing they were not an unreasonable burden on the host state. In the light of these cases, it was considered that this would mean now that once lawfully resident in a host state, citizenship would require that all rights could be enjoyed on an equal basis with nationals, ie there would be complete equality before the law. However, in case C-132/02 *Collins*, and confirmed in *Ioannidis* (C-258/04), the ECJ has stepped back from confirming this position by following the AG in some of the recent cases in requiring that the EU citizen has some greater degree of connection or genuine link to the state than mere lawful residence to be able to claim all benefits on the same basis as nationals. This position is further confirmed in cases C-11–12/06 *Morgan and Bucher* and case C-158/07 *Förster* v *IB-Groep*. However, as held in *D'Hoop* (C-224/98), any conditions on lawful residence in a host state, which are argued to apply to EU citizens must be applied in a proportionate and non-discriminatory way.

The next point to consider is whether the wholly internal rule still continues to apply so that EU law does not apply to a legal situation which does not involve any cross-border element and thus falls entirely within national law. The early law on this demonstrates how the wholly internal rule appears to give rise to reverse discrimination because nationals are denied rights which EU nationals from another Member State can uphold. In cases 35 and 36/82 *Morson and Jhanjan* v *Netherlands*, the applicants, both Surinamese nationals, claimed the right to stay in Holland with their Dutch national son and daughter working there. It was held by the ECJ that there was no application of Community (now EU) law to the wholly internal situation where national workers had not worked in any other Member State. However, because there was no movement from one Member State to another, Community (now EU) law did not apply and movement from a third country does not qualify.

More recent case law has weakened this position slightly. EU citizens who have moved across one of the Union internal borders and who have either provided or received services in the host state are able to take advantage of all EU law rights in both the host state and the home state when they return. For example, in *Surinder Singh* (C-370/90), an Indian spouse of a British national was able to use EU law to derive a right of residence in the UK on the basis that the spouse had previously exercised the right of free movement by providing services in another Member State but who then re-established herself in the UK. Further, in case C-60/00 *Carpenter*, the ECJ held that even where there was no movement of the third country national spouse, she had the right to remain in the UK because the husband had provided services in another EU Member State. However, the situation has not yet arisen that all EU law rights can be enjoyed in the home state, unless some form of cross-border economic activity triggers those EU law rights. It is at the moment unclear just how minimum the activity needs to be; for example, would supplying or ordering cross-border internet services allow an EU citizen to have a spouse from a third country join them and live in their home state? Only a preliminary ruling reference to the ECJ will adequately clear this up.

It is clear from the recent case law that EU law is now much more generous than was previously considered to be the case. This has also been backed up by a Directive which consolidates the previous legislation and case law and provides new rights. Directive 2004/38 has, for example, extended the concept of family to that of the partner's family, where the partnership would be recognised in the host state as equivalent to marriage and will establish a right of permanent residence after five years for both EU citizens and third country family members. However, the complete equality suggested by the question has not yet been established in EU law.

Question 7

Roger is a Belgian national made involuntarily unemployed in Belgium who decides to spend some time in the UK using his redundancy money. He is questioned on entry to the UK about his intentions, financial state and insurance and is allowed entry. He rents a large room in a guest house, where he is joined by his sister Auriana from Belgium and his cousin Benedicta from Turkey. He wants to stay long term in the UK but after 12 weeks his money was running out. He therefore applied for social security benefit and housing benefit to enable them to move out of the guest room into a house of their own. Both of these applications are refused.

Auriana is 16 and is physically and mentally disabled. She has applied for a place at a special needs school in the town. Roger applies for a non-contributory educational allowance for her which is refused by the local education authority.

Benedicta is 25 years old, has not worked at all previously and has applied for social benefit as a member of Roger's family. This is refused by the local authorities.

All three appeal against the decisions of the authorities on the grounds that they are being discriminated against in comparison with nationals. The local authorities wish to deport them as contrary to public policy because they have become a burden on the state.

Advise the parties of their rights under EU law.

Would your answer be any different if Roger claimed he was entitled to stay because of the services he had regularly received in the UK as a result of his extensive daily use of telephone sex lines?

Commentary

This is a problem question which requires you to explore some of the issues discussed in essay form in Question 6. We are dealing with citizens who on the facts clearly have no basis to claim rights as workers or as self-employed. The legal basis and the extent to which they can enter, remain in lawful residence and claim various social rights in the host state must be considered and whether such claims can lawfully be refused by the host state authorities. Furthermore, the question of whether the host state can deport them must also be addressed. Within the question, the dependency of two family members, one close and one slightly removed needs also to be discussed. Finally, you are invited to consider an alternative scenario, which, depending on your answer to the main question, will require you to discuss whether the new facts affect your conclusions as to whether Roger and his family may remain lawfully in the UK and whether in addition they may be successful in making their claims for social benefits.

Answer plan

- Provide a broad outline of the rights contained in Arts 45–62 TFEU
- Outline the consequences of liberal and functional approaches
- Provide examples of ECJ liberal interpretations of workers and Art 45 TFEU
- Case law on secondary law including *Diatta, Reed* and *Deak* cases
- Consider students and services and establishment case law
- Conclusion as to whether a more liberal than functional approach has persisted

Suggested answer

This question is concerned with the rights of EU citizens under the citizen provisions of the TFEU. Whilst the Treaty provision is rather limited and was not expanded significantly for a number of years, these rights have now been supplemented by secondary legislation, in particular Directive 2004/38 and by expansive interpretations of the ECJ. Certainly the free movement of workers was strongly upheld as one of the fundamental freedoms and rights with the EU legal order, but the status of citizenship has been less clear until recent case law confirmed it as conferring directly effective residence rights on EU Citizens.

The facts of this problem are that Roger, a Belgian national, enters the UK and is questioned about his intentions and financial state and is allowed entry. He is not working, nor seeking work but is renting a house. After 12 weeks, he applies for social security and housing benefit but both are refused.

Roger's 16-year-old sister Auriana, also a Belgian national, joins him as does his Turkish cousin, Benedicta. Auriana wants to go to a special needs school because of her disabilities and receive a grant to do so but the grant is refused. Benedicta who is 25 is not working and applies for social benefit, which is refused.

Deportation threat

All three face deportation on the ground given by the authorities of being a burden on the state.

The relevant law includes the citizenship Arts 2–21 TFEU, Directive 2004/38, Regulation 1612/68, which strictly applies to workers only, has been extended by the ECJ to other categories and the relevant case law of the ECJ.

The first matter to address in respect of all three is the possible deportation. Article 30(3) of Directive 2004/38 provides that even in the event of a deportation order being issued, all three will have a minimum of one month before they can be required to leave the host state. This protection, by virtue of Art 27 also applies to Benedicta, the Turkish national. Furthermore, case law, especially the French prostitutes cases, *Adoui* and *Cornaille* (115 and 116/81) and *Pecastaing* (98/79) will allow them to argue that they should stay longer. In any event, Directive 2004/38, Art 31, requires that they must be allowed to present their case in person. Hence, having secured their temporary right to stay, the national court will have to decide whether they are a sufficiently serious threat along the guidelines of Arts 27 and 28 of Directive 2004/38. Whilst that is very unlikely, their right to resist deportation will ultimately depend on whether they have, in fact , any lawful basis to remain, which will be considered next.

Rights of all of them to stay and claim benefits

A and B's rights appear to very much depend on Roger and it is unlikely that they possess their own rights to stay. B is a non-EU national who on her own has no right under EU persons law to enter and remain on her own. The TFEU and Directive 2004/38 do not expressly take into account the position of persons under 18, and whilst entry under Art 6 of the Directive may be allowed, the degree of disability of A is most likely to be the determining factor for the national authorities. In view of the fact that there is no case law governing this, if it becomes a question in the national court, a reference under Art 267 TFEU would appear to be needed.

Thus, if Roger has no right to stay, it is probable that they also must go. The status of Roger must be determined. Roger is a EU citizen, as defined by Art 20 TFEU. He is thus clearly allowed to enter and reside under Arts 20-21 TFEU. Article 21 TFEU refers obliquely to other rights in secondary law which then further determine his right to stay. Article 5 of the Directive provides the basic right of entry and Art 6 provides, without further formality, a right of residence for at least three months, which has not quite expired. Arguably, until it does so he has an absolute right to stay, but which will not last long, although he does now appear to be out of funds and thus presumably dependent on the state. Again, without clear guidance from the case law, a reference to the ECJ may be necessary.

When the three months expire, his right to remain longer is determined under Arts 7 and 14 of Directive 2004/38 provided he continues to satisfy the criteria of Art 7. He is neither a worker nor self-employed and there are no facts to support the conclusion that he is seeking work and can thus avail himself of Art 7(3), so none of these categories provide the right to remain.

He could stay if he were self-sufficient, as in the *Chen* case (C-200/02), which he was but is arguably no longer. He is, though, lawfully resident in the UK and from the facts not yet a burden on the authorities although he has now made social benefits claims. Whilst remaining lawfully in the UK, he has the right not to be discriminated against as held in the *Sala* and *Grzelczyk* cases (C-85/96 and C-184/99). But he must not be a burden according to Art 7 of the Directive, although, this has been interpreted in *Grzelczyk* as not being an unreasonable burden. It is up to Member State authorities to take a final view on this and the recent cases of C-11–12/06 *Morgan and Bucher* and case C-158/07 *Förster* v *IB-Groep* suggest that the Member States do still retain a discretionary right to refuse benefits to those not establishing a sufficiently close connection or degree of integration in the host state. Roger would appear not to possess that. However, whilst Roger is still for the moment lawfully resident in the UK until his money runs out, we have to consider the right of his relations.

A and B are not ascendant nor descendant members of the family possibly within Art 2 of the Directive but more likely under Art 3(2) as other family members and those whose health requires care by Roger. So yes, there is an arguable right to enter and remain under Arts 2, 3, 5 and 6 of the Directive for up to three months.

Realising their other rights and claims

A seeks to attend a special needs school which could be made under Art 12 of Regulation 1612/68 but strictly that does not apply to non-workers but it might receive a sympathetic interpretation by the ECJ. The various claims for social benefits they have made look less likely to be upheld in view of the later case law of *Collins*, *Bidar* and *Ioannidis* (C-138/02, C-209/03 and C-258/04 and more recently cases of C-11–12/06 *Morgan and Bucher* and case C-158/07 *Förster* v *IB-Groep*) which suggest that a close connection or link to the state is required. There appears to be no such link, therefore it would appear than none of them have any right to the benefits. Finally, Roger is not a worker, so Art 7(2) of the Regulation would also not apply.

There is a really outside argument that A has the right to have a carer under *Baumbast* and *Chen* cases (C-413/99 and C-200/02) but as she is not self-sufficient, this is very unlikely.

The conclusion under the present state of the law is that if they are deemed to be a burden on the state which is unreasonable, as they are likely to be found when their claims for benefits are denied, then it would appear that the host state would be justified in deporting them. A reference to the ECJ would certainly clarify this.

The last part of the question asks, would the answer be different if Roger had used sex lines as services received. No, not if the argument is employed that the situation is wholly internal as with *Morson and Jhanjan* v *Netherlands* (cases 35 and 36/82). Counter to this would be that fact that Roger has moved from Belgium to the UK (see the *Garcia Avello* and *D'Hoop* cases (C-148/02 and C-224/98)). Equally, it might be argued that the renting of premises constitutes receiving services and whilst a repealed Directive 64/221 expressly mentioned receiving services, Directive 2004/38 does not. Indeed, the motive for moving or receiving services may not be important as in *Chen* (C-200/02) but in view of the degree of uncertainty at this stage, an Art 267 TFEU reference would be advised.

The facts of this case are at the edge of case law, hence the uncertainty about the outcome of this case and that at various stages a reference to the ECJ has been advised. It may be that cases will soon resolve some of these issues.

Further reading

Barrett, G, 'Family Matters: European Community Law and Third-country Family Members' (2003) 40(2) CML Rev 369.

Carrera, S, 'What Does Free Movement Mean in an Enlarged EU?' (2005) 11 ELJ 699.

Davies, G, 'The High Water Point of Free Movement of Persons: Ending Benefit Tourism and Rescuing Welfare' (2004) 26 Journal of Social Welfare and Family Law 211.

Dougan, M, 'The Constitutional Dimension to the Case Law on Union Citizenship' (2006) 31 EL Rev 613.

Foster, N, 'Family and Welfare Rights in Europe: The Impact of Recent European Court of Justice Decisions in the Area of the Free Movement of Persons' (2003) 25(3) Journal of Social Welfare and Family Law 291.

Hatzopoulos, V and Do, T, 'The Case Law of the ECJ Concerning the Free Provision Services 2000–2005' (2006) 43 CML Rev 923.

Kocharov, A, 'What Intra-Community Mobility for Third-country Workers?' (2008) 33(6) EL Rev 913.

Kunoy, B, 'A Union of National Citizens: The Origins of the Court's Lack of Avantgardisme in the *Chen* Case' (2006) 43(1) CML Rev 179.

Newdick, C, 'Citizenship, Free Movement and Healthcare: Cementing Individual Rights by Corroding Social Solidarity' (2006) 43 CML Rev 1645.

Spaventa, E, 'From *Gebhard* to *Carpenter*: Towards a (Non-)economic European Constitution' (2004) 41(3) CML Rev 743.

White, R, 'The Citizen's Right to Free Movement' (2005) 16 EBLR 547.

8

Competition and Merger Law

Introduction

Questions on competition law can vary considerably in EU courses depending on the approach of a particular course or lecturer in addressing this topic. It is unlikely that all aspects of competition law are addressed in depth on a general course on EU law, unless competition law is itself the subject of a particular course, half course or 'module' in today's terms. If this is the case, then some of the questions in this chapter will be too general. Even if it is not, one of the problems in this area is the amount of material which it is necessary to cover to do justice to the subject. Some courses will not be concerned with the procedural aspects of competition law in any significant way, whilst others may simply provide an overview of the subject matter without going into detail on any aspect. Many courses will probably provide a discourse on the basic concepts and the main requirements of Arts 101 and 102 TFEU (ex 81 and 82 EC). However, the exam questions set for your particular course should reflect the approach adopted in your course.

A variety of questions on competition law have been provided, ranging from a general overview question, a question which surveys the basic concepts and requirements of Arts 101 and 102 TFEU and the Mergers Regulation, to questions concentrating on specific aspects of competition law including the procedure of competition law investigations and enforcement.

The 2007 Lisbon Treaty made little substantive change to the competition law provisions, which can be found in Arts 101–106 of the amended TFEU. More significant for this chapter is the Competition Regulation 1/2003, which repealed Regulations 17 and 141, and the Merger Regulation, 139/2004, which is itself now under revision for future reform or replacement.

Question 1

Why is competition law policy an integral and necessary part of the European Union?

Commentary

This first question is one which concerns an overview of the topic and its place in the EU legal order.

To answer this you must consider the main objectives of the European Union which are outlined in the Preamble to the TEU Treaty. Then it is suggested you provide a brief overview to the main provisions of competition law and the secondary legislation in order to explain how it is to be pursued in the EU legal order.

Finally, you should consider its relations with other policies of the Union and the reasons why it is considered to be a necessary policy in the Union.

Answer plan

- Outline the main and competition objectives of the EU as contained in the Preamble and Arts 2 and 3 TEU
- Outline the specific competition law objectives and rules (Arts 101–102 TFEU)
- Role of the Commission in competition law enforcement
- Consider the relationship with other community objectives

Suggested answer

The EU as originally established was aimed at the establishment of a common market and the progressive approximation of the economic policies of the Member States. The preamble to the EU Treaty generally sets out these basic objectives.

The general aims include the creation of the Common Market which was to be achieved by abolishing obstacles to the freedom of movement of all the factors of production, namely goods, workers, providers of services and capital. The Treaty also provided for the abolition of customs duties between the Member States and the application of a common customs tariff to imports from third countries. There were to be common policies in the spheres of agriculture and transport, and a system ensuring that competition in the Common Market is not distorted by the activities of cartels or market monopolists. EU competition policy was based both on the extensive American experience of the concentration of power in the market place in too few hands and also, to some extent, on the post-Second World War German legislative experience with large undertakings and cartels. Attitudes were also influenced by the desire to protect emerging and expanding industries and companies and to encourage the rebirth of European industry after the devastation of the Second World War. Thus, one of the fundamental positions of the competition law to be established was that there should be no barriers against the entry to the market of new companies and industries. The broad policy objective of competition law, therefore, which was formulated by the European Economic

Community, was to maintain and encourage competition for the benefit of the Community (now Union) and its citizens.

Competition law was therefore constructed to ensure the maintenance of the Common Market. One of the aims of the internal market is to establish and maintain European-wide competition to stimulate the entire economy of the Community (now Union) for both the domestic and world markets and thus assist European capital in competing in the world market. Competition law is designed to help achieve a single market and the integration of the Union, to encourage economic activity amongst small- and medium-size enterprise and to maximise efficiency by allowing the free flow of goods and resources. At the same time it must be ensured that companies do not become too competitive and are able to eliminate competition, thereby starting to dominate a market, or to cooperate in such a way as to act as one unit to the detriment of consumers and smaller firms in the Union. Competition law may also be regarded therefore as necessary to prevent these undesirable developments from being realised. In order to retain fair competition, more so in a capitalist free market, some form of intervention on the part of the state is required. Action is concentrated on the larger players in the market rather than the small and medium business enterprises.

The specific EU Competition rules are generally designed to intervene to prevent agreements which fix prices or conditions or the supply of products, to prohibit agreements which carve up territories, to prevent abuses of market power which have the effect of removing real competition and by controlling mergers which would also remove competition.

The Preamble to the old EC Treaty stated that the 'removal of existing obstacles calls for concerted action in order to guarantee steady expansion, balanced trade and fair competition'. Whilst these aims are not so prominent in the EU Treaties as revised by the Lisbon Treaty, Art 3(3) TEU refers to a highly competitive social market economy and Art 3(d) TFEU provides an exclusive competence to the Union with the 'establishing of the competition rules necessary for the functioning of the internal market'.

Article 10 EC (now 4(3) TEU) has also been pleaded as a general principle of law supporting the argument that competition law also applies in respect of the Member States and not just undertakings so that they are prohibited from encouraging or requiring acts or conduct by companies which may distort competition in the Community (now Union). Article 12 EC (now 18 TFEU) too has also featured in cases on competition law to ensure equal access to markets and the distribution of goods and services without discrimination.

These basic rules are expanded in three sets of rules; one relating to the activities of legal persons, ie the business undertakings; one relating to anti-dumping measures; and the final one relating to the activities of the Member States.

The Commission is given the task under Art 105 TFEU (ex 85 EC) and Regulation 1/2003 of ensuring that competition in the EU is not distorted by companies setting up their own rules and obstacles to trade, thereby replacing the national rules and obstacles which the EU is trying to abolish by application of the free movement of goods provisions. These rules seek to prevent the creation of artificial barriers to trade on the national boundaries. Competition law is therefore inextricably linked to other Union policy areas especially to the free movement of goods, because it would prove to be impossible to have one without ensuring you have the other. To have prevented the Member States on the one hand from restricting the movement of goods just to allow private companies to do it by their agreements and practices would defeat the objectives of the first policy and, vice versa, to prevent companies from artificially dividing the markets, but to allow the Member States to do so would undermine a competition policy. A further argument for having an effective competition policy is that some multinational companies are in a better position to divide the market than some Member States, because they have the same or greater turnover than the GNP of some of the EU Member States and so need to be subject to international control.

The application of the rules by the Commission and the interpretation of the rules of the Court of Justice have not been done in isolation by looking at the provisions alone, but in the light of the objectives of competition policy. The rules are also applied in the light of the general objectives of the Treaty. In *Commercial Solvents* v *Commission* (6 and 7/73), the Court of Justice held:

> 'The prohibitions in Articles 85 and 86 (now 101 and 102 TFEU) must be interpreted and applied in the light of Article 3(f) (now 3(d) TFEU) of the EEC Treaty, which provides that the activities of the Community shall include the institution of a system ensuring that competition is not distorted, and Article 2 of the Treaty, which gives the Community the task of promoting throughout the Community harmonious development of economic activities.'

The case of *Metro* v *Commission* (26/76) is also a good example, whereby the Commission, in pursuit of a goal, was forced to rely on Art 2 EC to justify particular decisions reached. The agreements in question were deemed to satisfy competition rules because they helped to maintain employment. This latter case serves as an example of where the Commission, in carrying out its tasks in relation to competition law, is also required to balance this policy with other policies such as regional development or concern for unemployment and which may cause it to modify its position on the behaviour of companies. The CFI (now the General Court), is now the primary EU court concerned with competition cases, has also stressed the importance of the competition policy to the Union political and constitutional order in *Courage* v *Crehan* (C-453/99).

The general economic climate also influences the Commission, particularly in respect of merger policy, in that in times of poor economic growth, the Commission may treat mergers as being more acceptable because of the efficiency gains to be achieved and the greater ability the emerging company will have in the world market.

Competition law policy cannot, therefore be pursued alone and it is to be concluded that competition law is an inextricable part of the EU and its policies.

Question 2

The Clear Vision Company (CVC) is a manufacturer of camcorders. It wishes to enter into an exclusive distribution agreement of unlimited duration with two dealers of electrical equipment to distribute its products in the UK and Germany. The German Company 'Foto GmbH' (F) and the UK company, 'Video-camera Ltd' (V) are the chosen companies. There is no connection between the two companies.

The Agreements between CVC and F and CVC and V contain the following clauses:

1. CVC undertake not to supply any other distributor in the UK or Germany.

2. F and V shall follow the Advisory Retail Price structure and price increases of CVC.

3. F and V shall not seek to sell outside of their respective areas and shall pass on sales enquiries from the other area to the other party. They shall not sell to other distributors.

4. F and V shall provide a sales display area according to the annex attached and ensure that only CVC-trained staff are responsible for the sales of CVC camcorders.

The parties to the agreement wish to know whether the terms of their agreement are ones which fall either within or outside a block exemption. If not, you are asked to advise whether the terms do then infringe Art 101 TFEU.

 Commentary

This problem on competition law concentrates on distribution agreements and the **Vertical Restraints Regulation**.

The problem question itself sets out what issues it wants you to discuss. You are asked to determine whether the agreement reached between the parties is one which would, for special reasons, be exempted by a block exemption from the consequences of being contrary to EU competition law. This assumes that the agreement is already one likely to offend EU competition law provisions and it must be determined whether this is correct or incorrect.

It is not clear from a first sight whether the agreement is an exclusive or selective one, as it appears it could be either. This is certainly less important now following the enactment of single vertical agreement exemption (**the Vertical Restraints Regulation 2790/1999**) which replaced three different vertical agreement Regulations (1143/83, 1484/83 and 4087/88). The only question here as to whether Regulation 2790/1999 may apply is whether we are dealing with a vertical agreement. As the problem concerns the agreement with a manufacturer and two distributors, this is clearly satisfied. Before this is considered in detail, a brief general introduction to the Competition law rules would put the issues into context.

Further details on the more general aspects of the question related to Art 101 TFEU can be studied in the answers to the questions below.

Answer plan

- Outline the fundamentals of EU competition policy and law
- Provide details of Art 101 TFEU and in particular Art 101(3) TFEU
- Explain the system and application of block exemptions
- Consider the details of Regulation 2970/99 and apply to the question
- Support conclusions with relevant case law
- Determine whether there is an infringement of Art 101 TFEU

Suggested answer

EU Competition law is one of the fundamental policies of the Union and is mentioned generally in the Arts 3 of both the TEU and TFEU. The principal provisions of the policy are contained in Arts 101 and 102 TFEU (ex 81 and 82 EC). Article 101 TFEU is the Article applicable to this problem because it concerns prohibited agreements and practices and prohibits:

agreements between undertakings, decisions by associations of undertakings, and concerted practices which may affect trade between the Member States, and which have as their object or effect the prevention, restriction or distortion of competition within the internal market.

Article 101(2) TFEU provides that 'any agreements or decisions prohibited pursuant to this Article shall be automatically void'. However, there are ways in which an agreement may be considered to be acceptable.

Article 101(3) TFEU provides that:

the provisions of Paragraph 1 may, however, be declared inapplicable in the case of:

any agreement or category of agreements between undertakings;

any decision or category of decisions by associations of undertakings;

any concerted practice or category of concerted practices;

which contributes to improving the production or distribution of goods or to promoting technical or economic progress, while allowing consumers a fair share of the resulting benefit, and which does not: (a) impose on the undertakings concerned restrictions which are not indispensable to the attainment of these objectives; (b) afford such undertakings the possibility of eliminating competition in respect of a substantial part of the products in question.

Previously, the parties to such agreements were required to make an individual notification to the Commission for exemption. Failure to notify meant that the agreement would be void and the parties would be liable to fines. However, in order to avoid unnecessary work for all involved, common agreements may be exempted from the prohibition in Art 101(1) TFEU by virtue of a block exemption for typical types of agreement, sometimes within certain industries or areas of trade and in the new post-2003 competition regime, individual notification has been scrapped. Block exemptions generally set out types of restriction or provision which do not infringe Art 101(1) TFEU or would be exempted and there is one for vertical distribution agreements under Art 2(1) of Regulation 2970/99. The main thrust of this Regulation is that there is a presumption of legality, ie compliance with Art 101 TFEU, for agreements involving firms whose combined transaction counts for less than 30% of the relevant market share (Arts 3 and 9), unless the agreement itself or parts of it contain so-called 'hard-core restrictions' which would not qualify for exemption under Art 4. As we are not given market share information, we shall have to consider the agreement in further detail. Apart from the fact that the agreements have been entered into for an unlimited duration, which does not satisfy Art 5 of the block exemption and therefore the agreement will not benefit from an exemption, the individual clauses in the agreement would also appear to be unacceptable under the block exemption. Article 4 of Vertical Restraints Regulation 2790/99 states that it does not apply to vertical agreements which contain anti-competitive restrictions such as price fixing or territorial protection. Clauses 2 and 3 would appear to offend these prohibitions. Hence, it is very unlikely that a block exemption will save the agreements from the application of Art 101(3) TFEU. Each of the clauses will therefore have to be considered in turn in the light of Art 101 TFEU and the judgments of the ECJ as they appear to set up a distribution agreement which have been held by the Court of Justice to be acceptable where the restrictions are objectively necessary for the performance of a particular type of contract. Contracts relating to technical products requiring specialist sales staff would be ones which the ECJ has considered compatible with Art 101(1) TFEU; see, for example, the *Metro* cases of 1977 and 1986 (26/76 and 75/84). The actual agreements must not, however, contain clauses which go beyond what is strictly necessary to meet the objectives of a controlled distribution of the product.

Clauses which fix prices or which effect a partitioning of markets between manufacturer and distributor, and are capable of affecting trade between Member States, constitute restrictions on competition contrary to Art 101(1) TFEU. Therefore it is necessary to consider the present scheme by looking at the terms of the agreement on a clause-by-clause basis.

The first clause is a complete refusal to supply and is probably not acceptable; see the *Konica* decision (88/172). If other companies comply with the other terms there should be no reason to refuse to supply them.

The pricing clause is ambiguous. If it tries to fix prices rather than simply recommend, it will not be acceptable; see the *Pronuptia* case (161/84) in which advisory prices were considered by the Court of Justice to be acceptable.

The sales restriction in Clause 3 of the agreement almost certainly amounts to an export ban and it will not be acceptable; see the case of *Consten* and *Grundig* (56 and 58/64), the *Bayer Dental* case (65/86) or the *Konica* decision (88/172).

The final clause appears to be an acceptable condition to ensure quality distribution of specialist products; see the *Metro* cases (26/76 and 75/84) and the *Perfume* cases (253/78, 1–3/79).

Given that two of the clauses appear to offend EU law competition provisions, unless the companies are prepared to amend them to eradicate the aspects which infringe Art 101 TFEU, it is unlikely the agreement will come within the terms for a block exemption or permitted selective distribution agreement according to case law.

A complete answer would then determine whether, in fact, an infringement of Art 101(1) TFEU has taken place. To do this it would be necessary to determine whether there is an agreement between undertakings, decisions by associations of undertakings, or a concerted practice which may affect trade between the Member States, and which have as their object or effect the prevention, restriction or distortion of competition within the internal market. The agreement reached between the companies is express and Clauses 2 and 3 are specifically designed to restrict or distort competition. It is necessary, then, to demonstrate that the agreement has or will potentially affect trade between Member States; see the *Consten* and *Grundig* cases (56 and 58/64) which would indicate that an infringement is most likely. Under the new competition law regime introduced by Regulation 2003/1, it is up to the parties to decide if their agreement complies with or offends Art 101 TFEU. If they consider it complies, they need not take any further action but because Art 101(3) TFEU has now been made directly effective, the agreement can be challenged in the national courts by competitors who consider it infringes Art 101 TFEU or even by the parties themselves (see *Courage* v *Crehan* (453/99)). They will be liable to pay damages if the agreement is held by the national court to infringe Art 101 TFEU. In case of doubt an Art 267 TFEU reference to the ECJ can be made. If it is held to be in breach of Art 101(1) TFEU, the agreement will be void under Art 101(2) TFEU.

Question 3

Branches of two non-EU Member State companies, the Red Dwarf Mining Corporation (RDMC) and Green Giant Mining (GGM) have moved into the EU to exploit the remaining European deposits of tin. In informal meetings of the management of the two companies, which took place before their move into the EU, they decided on a strategy to work the European market to their advantage. They have restricted supplies to customers in and outside the EU to drive up prices and thus profits for their parent companies. So far RDMC have secured 42% of the market and GGM have secured 23%.

Complaints have been made by competitors and customers to the Commission, which is investigating. The companies claim the investigations cannot apply to either companies or agreements from outside the EU.

(a) Advise RDMC and GGM.

(b) Would your answer be any different if RDMC ad GGM formally merge prior to any action being taken?

Commentary

This problem question will involve you in a general consideration of the application of the principal provisions of both **Arts 101 and 102 TFEU (ex 81 and 82 EC)**.

After a general introduction to the area of competition law and highlighting the relevant issues in the case, you should briefly outline the scope of **Arts 101 and 102 TFEU** and determine whether the case concerns an agreement between the parties contrary to EU competition law, or whether it concerns the abuse of a dominant position by the parties. A particular issue which should be considered is the fact that the companies' head offices are based outside the EU and whether this will affect the ability of the Commission to investigate and prosecute a breach of EU law.

Finally, you are required to address the alternative situation in which the companies merge. Given that you are not supplied with any real facts to come to definitive conclusions on this aspect, all you can do is generally describe the EU concern and involvement in mergers.

Answer plan

- Introduce competition policy and law and the issues in the question
- Outline the general scope of **Arts 101 and 102 TFEU**
- Consider with reference to case law, if **Arts 101 or 102 TFEU** have been breached
- Consider joint dominance and the position of companies outside the EU
- The effect of merger must be discussed
- The possible application of the **Mergers Regulation** to joint dominance

Suggested answer

Competition law is one of the fundamental policies of the Union and is generally mentioned in Arts 3 of both the TEU and TFEU. Art 3(d) TFEU refers to the 'establishing of the competition rules necessary for the functioning of the internal market'.

The relevant facts in this case are that the branches of two non-EU Member State companies are pursuing a strategy agreed on outside the EU, which involves the restriction of supply to customers to drive up prices and profits. As a result, it would seem that both companies have secured a sizable share of the EU market. The facts thus involve a consideration of the two principal provisions to combat anti-competitive behaviour, Arts 101 and 102 TFEU (ex 81 and 82 EC).

Article 101 TFEU deals with restrictive practices. Article 101(1) TFEU prohibits agreements between undertakings, decisions by associations of undertakings and concerted practices which may affect trade between the Member States, and which have as their object or effect the prevention, restriction or distortion of competition within the internal market. Article 101(2) TFEU provides that any agreements or decisions prohibited pursuant to this Article shall be automatically void.

Article 102 TFEU applies where individual organisations have a near monopoly position or share an oligopolistic market with a small number of other companies and take unfair advantage of this position to the detriment of the market, other companies and the end consumers. Article 102 TFEU provides that the abuse by one or more undertakings of a dominant market position within the internal market or in a substantial part of which affects trade between Member States is prohibited.

First of all, the possible breach of Art 101 TFEU will be considered. In order for it to be breached, it must be shown that there is a form of agreement or concerted practice which may have affected trade between Member States. It has been demonstrated that no actual agreement is necessary to breach Art 101 TFEU and the Article allows for a concerted practice to suffice. In the case of *ICI v Commission* (Dyestuffs) (48/69) general and uniform increases were witnessed from a small number of leading producers. The Court of Justice defined a concerted practice as a form of coordination between enterprises, that had not yet reached the point of true contract relationship but which had in practice substituted cooperation for the risks of competition. See also the *Sugar Cartel* case (*Suiker Unie v Commission* (40–48/73)) in which the firms responsible for the alleged breach said there was no plan. The ECJ held there did not have to be one. In the *Polypropylene* cases (T-7/89, T-9/89 and T-11/89), the CFI (now the General Court) has held that expressions of intention, even if not in writing, of particular conduct could constitute an agreement of concerted practice. Countering these cases is the

Wood Pulp case (C-89, 104 and 125–129/85) in which the ECJ held that parallel conduct could not be regarded as proof of a concerted practice unless that was the only plausible explanation for the conduct. In the present case, providing there is some indication that an agreed practice is being pursued, it is likely that a concerted practice between undertakings will be established.

Next, it must be demonstrated that the agreement was one which had the object or effect of restriction of competition which may affect trade between Member States. Article 101(1) TFEU focuses on particular practices which would offend competition law. Amongst these are those listed under Art 101(1)(b) and (c) TFEU, which limit markets or supply. In the present case the agreement is clearly one which has this object. In fact, even a potential impact will do; see the *Consten* and *Grundig* cases (56 and 58/64). However, to infringe Art 101 TFEU, the practice complained of must be capable of affecting trade between Member States. The cases of *Consten* and *Grundig* and the *Cement Association* (8/72) are examples of the simple requirements for this to be met. It has to be questioned whether it is probable in law or fact that the agreement in question may have an influence, direct or indirect, actual or potential, on the pattern of trade between Member States. If there is an impact on the pattern of trade, then there is an effect on trade. The restrictions on supply and the consequent price increases would clearly fall into this category; therefore a breach of Art 101(1) TFEU is probable. Note that there is now a useful set of Guidelines issued by the Commission in 2004 which summarises the case law of the ECJ on effect on trade between Member States.

Article 102 TFEU may also be breached if there is an abuse of a dominant position in the EU. Dominance must be established both in terms of the product and geographic market.

The product must be a unique product which is not interchangeable. In the absence of further facts it must be assumed that there is no substitute for the raw metal tin. Is there dominance? We are only told that RDMC has 42% and GGM has 23% of the market in the Community. In *United Brands* (27/76), the share of 45% was considered sufficient but the next competitor had 16% only, a greater difference than here with 42% and 23%. Thus considering each company alone, it would be arguable whether RDMC or GGM would be dominant. Whilst there is no clear word from either the Commission or the Court on this point, the Mergers Regulation states that concentrations whose market share does not exceed 25% would not be considered to impede competition. However, Art 102 TFEU applies to one or more companies and the combined share would be 67% which in a joint action would be a position of dominance (confirmed as possible in *Compagnie Maritime Belge SA* v *Commission* C-395 and 396/96P).

The geographic market is also satisfied as it is the whole of the EU; see the *United Brands* (27/76) and *Tetra Pak* (T-51/89) cases.

It then has to be shown that there is an abuse of dominant position. Limiting production is one of the grounds listed in Art 102 TFEU and refusal to supply was held to be in the *United Brands* case, therefore an abuse can be shown in the present case.

In fact, according to the case of *Compagnie Maritime Belge Transports* before the ECJ (C-395 and 396P/96) an agreement within the meaning of Art 85(1) (now 101 TFEU) may result in undertakings being so linked that they become and act as a collective entity as far as their competitors and customers are concerned and as such a collective dominant position can arise, which can then be abused in the manner already noted.

Finally, trade between Member States must be affected. In the *Commercial Solvents v Commission* case (6 and 7/73) it was held that conduct which has the effect of altering the competitive structure within the Common Market will satisfy the requirement of effect on trade between the Member States. This would be the case with RDMC and GGM. Thus a breach of Art 102 TFEU is also likely to be established.

A significant objection of the two firms is that the companies and the agreements are from outside the EU and they would argue that they cannot be touched by the EU competition law rules. However, the basic position adopted by the EU is that the competition rules apply to all undertakings whose operations or agreements affect trade between Member States and have as their object or effect a restraint on competition in the Union. The *ICI Dyestuffs* case (48–57/69) considered that the unity of conduct in the market between the parent and the subsidiary was the decisive factor in the case. The *Wood Pulp* case (C-89, 104 and 125–129/85) is also instructive. In this case the pricing agreements took place outside the EU but the implementation took place within the EU; therefore, if the agreements led to anti-competitive consequences through the activities of branches, they would infringe Art 101 TFEU.

The fact that the breaches are committed in the Union puts the companies within the territorial jurisdiction of the Treaty and thus the Commission and the General Court, even where the parent companies have no direct physical involvement and the agreements were outside of the EU (*ICI Dyestuffs* case).

In the alternative, it is necessary to consider the effect a merger would have. If the merger takes place outside the EU, as is assumed to be the case here, it may still be a concentration with a Union dimension as far as the new Mergers Regulation 139/04 is concerned; see the Decision of the Commission in *Matsushita/MCA* (IV/M37). Article 1 states that it applies where there is a worldwide turnover of more than €5,000 million and an aggregate EU-wide turnover of each of at least two of the undertakings of more than €250 million. An EU dimension may nevertheless pertain, if:

(a) the combined aggregate worldwide turnover of all the undertakings is more than €2,500 million;

(b) in each of at least three Member States, the combined aggregate turnover of all the undertakings is more than €100 million;

(c) in each of at least three Member States, the aggregate turnover of each of at least two of the undertakings concerned is more than €25 million; and

(d) the aggregate EU-wide turnover of each of at least two of the undertakings concerned is more than €100 million.

This information is not provided in the problem, but if the turnover does not reach these thresholds then the merger is not one of an EU dimension. If they do exceed the thresholds the companies are required under Art 4(1) to inform the Commission. Failure to do so will render them liable to a fine under Art 14. The Commission will determine under Art 2 whether the concentration is compatible with the common market with a view to declaring it compatible or suspending it. This may be difficult to enforce outside the EU but an extra-territorial merger was blocked in the *GE/Honeywell* decision (M2220). However, recourse to Art 102 TFEU may still be necessary to combat the anti-competitive behaviour, but it should be noted that a formal merger might not be required to be subject to the Mergers Regulation and that independent firms may be subject to its rules. In joined cases *France* v *Commission* (C-68/94) and *Société Commerciale des Potasses et de l'Azote (SCPA)* v *Commission* (C-30/95), the ECJ determined that the Mergers Regulation applies also to collective dominance, although as noted above collective dominance short of merger may also be caught under Art 102 TFEU. A reference to the ECJ would be required, however, to be certain about this.

Question 4

Widgets Ltd (W) is a UK manufacturer of the widgets which are fitted into beer cans to ensure that the drink has a frothy head. It holds 40% of the EU market. There are three other European manufacturers of this product, the largest of which is Krimskrams GmbH (K) in Germany, which holds 30% of the EU market. The rest of the EU market, valued at more than €1,000 million, is made up by two other EU companies with less than 10% of the market between them and imports from the USA, Japan, Korea and China.

W and K are the only manufacturers of the machines, which produce the widgets.

Press reports have noted that, following the twice yearly Convention of European Widget Manufacturers (CEWM), prices of the UK and German-built widgets rise, followed shortly by the prices of other manufacturers. The companies stated, in a recent statement, that there was never any form of agreement between them in respect of pricing policy. However, W and K have now decided to merge to consolidate their position in the European and world market for widgets. They have also refused to supply spares for the machines to the non-EU manufacturers.

In the light of the developments, the Commission has commenced an investigation into the actions of the companies to determine whether a breach of EU law has been committed.

Advise the Commission as to the likelihood that the Court of Justice will uphold their claim:

(a) that the companies have breached either Art 101 or 102 TFEU;

(b) that the companies have breached the Mergers Regulation.

Commentary

This is a general problem question on competition law covering aspects of Arts 101 and 102 TFEU (ex 81 and 82 EC) and the Mergers Regulation. It concentrates on the main principles of each of these areas rather than going into precise details of any provision in particular. As with other problem-type questions, the issues to be tackled need to be identified. In this question, this is to some extent already done for you in the question because it asks you to consider whether the companies have breached either Arts 101 or 102 TFEU or the Mergers Regulation 139/04. Thus you can concentrate on whether the main requirements of these elements of Community law have been infringed by the actions of the parties.

Answer plan

- Provide a broad outline of competition policy and law
- Outline the issues in the question
- Outline the general scope of Arts 101 and 10 TFEU and the Mergers Regulation
- Consider with reference to case law, if Arts 101 or 102 TFEU have been breached
- The lawfulness of the merger must be assessed
- Joint dominance must also be considered under the Mergers Regulation

Suggested answer

Competition law in general is designed to ensure there is healthy competition in the EU which will benefit not only the EU market but also consumers. The EU competition law policy seeks to achieve this by outlawing any behaviour which is contrary to this credo. Competition law in the EU therefore attacks concerted action which is anti-competitive and individual actions which abuse market strengths to the detriment of competition. The EU has also enacted legislation to combat anti-competitive mergers with a European dimension.

The issues to be considered in the answer are: the price rises which occur after the meeting of CEWM, the decision to merge and the refusal to supply spares for the machines.

The law applicable to this answer is as follows. Article 101(1) TFEU prohibits agreements between undertakings, decisions by associations of undertakings and concerted practices which may affect trade between the Member States, and which have as their object or effect the prevention, restriction or distortion of competition within the internal market. Article 101(2) TFEU provides that any agreements or decisions prohibited pursuant to this Article shall be automatically void.

Article 102 TFEU provides that the abuse by one or more undertakings of a dominant market position within the internal market or in a substantial part of it, which affects trade between Member States, is prohibited.

The Mergers Regulation 139/04 establishes a division between large mergers with a European dimension, over which the Commission will exercise supervision, and smaller mergers which will fall under the jurisdiction of national authorities.

First of all, the possible breach of Art 101 TFEU will be considered. In order for it to be breached it must be shown that there is an agreement which may have affected trade between Member States.

Whilst the companies have declared that there was no formal agreement between them, it has been demonstrated that no actual agreement is necessary to breach Art 101 TFEU and the Article allows for a concerted practice to suffice. In the case of *ICI* v *Commission* (Dyestuffs) (48/69) general and uniform increases were witnessed from a small number of leading producers. The Court of Justice defined a concerted practice as 'a form of coordination between enterprises, that had not yet reached the point of true contract relationship but which had in practice substituted cooperation for the risks of competition'.

In a particular instance there would be a need to show the similarity of rate and timing of increases and whilst not having to prove the existence of agreements, there is still a requirement to establish that some form of contract existed.

In our case it is the meeting of CEWM that should establish this. See also the *Sugar Cartel* case (*Suiker Unie* v *Commission*) (40–48/73) in which the firms responsible for the alleged breach said there was no plan. The ECJ held there did not have to be one. The *Wood Pulp* cases (C-89, 104 and 125–129/85) would, however, increase the burden on the Commission to demonstrate in this case, that there were no other plausible explanations for the parallel price increase other than by agreement of concerted action.

Thus, if it is considered that a concerted practice is in existence it must be shown that the object or effect of it was to restrict competition. A potential impact will be sufficient for the requirements of the Article; see *Consten* and *Grundig* (56 and 58/64). Price fixing, which was the object of the present activity, clearly offends as it is an example provided by Art 101(1)(a) TFEU; therefore this aspect is established in the present case.

To some extent the same question of an impact on trade is applied to determine whether there has been an effect on trade between Member States. The cases of *Consten* and *Grundig* (56 and 58/64) and the *Cement Association* (8/72) are examples of the simple requirements for this to be met. If there is an impact on the pattern of trade then there is an effect on trade. Clearly price increases will impact on the pattern of trade between Member States.

Article 102 TFEU will be breached if there is an abuse of a dominant position in the EU. Dominance must be established both in terms of the product and geographic market. The Commission has published a Notice on the Definition of the Relevant Market (OJ 1997 C372/5) which provides a summary of the case law and Commission methodology and hence, then, guidelines for determining the relevant markets. The product market is widgets for beer tins. In the *United Brands* case (27/76), it was held it must be a unique product which is not interchangeable. In the absence of any evidence to the contrary, this is the position in the present case. It then has to be considered whether there is dominance. We are informed that the two companies, Widgets and Krimskrams have 40% and 30% respectively of the market in the EU. Taken individually, the market share of 40% held by Widgets might not, in view of the case of *United Brands*, be enough on its own to constitute dominance, especially where the next competitor has 30%. If this is uncertain, then it is even more unlikely that the 30% held by Krimskrams would be enough to constitute market dominance.

However, Art 102 also covers the situation of one or more undertakings which together occupy a dominant position. If the two parties were subject to a joint decision of the Commission, the resultant market share of the two companies of 70% would most probably be held to be a position of dominance.

In fact, according to the case of *Compagnie Maritime Belge Transports* before the ECJ (C-395 and 396P/96) an agreement within the meaning of Art 85(1) EEC (now 101 TFEU) may result in undertakings being so linked that they become and act as a collective entity as far as their competitors and customers are concerned and as such a collective dominant position can arise under Art 102 TFEU (ex 86 EEC), which can then be abused.

The geographic market is also satisfied as it is the whole of the EU; see the *United Brands* and *Tetra Pak* (T-51/89) cases.

The supply of spares for the machines is also a separate market, which in the case at hand, the 100% share of the market by the two companies will establish complete dominance; see the *Hugin* case (22/78). It may however be argued that, in respect of the machines, the refusal to supply only has effects outside the EU, but in the *Commercial Solvents* case (6 and 7/73), where the supply was outside the EU market, the Court of Justice held that this fact did not remove its jurisdiction as the effect would still be prominent in the EU market. See also the *Wood Pulp* case (C-89, 104 and 125–129/85) in this respect.

The abuse which offends the community regime is the price fixing in respect of the widgets and the refusal to supply in respect of the spares, specifically noted in Art 102(a) and (b) TFEU.

The *Continental Can* case (6/72) also suggested that a further form of abuse could be the merger itself but this point can now be addressed under the Merger Regulation 139/04.

The next topic for consideration is the lawfulness of the merger. After merger the companies have 70% of a market for widgets estimated at over €1,000 million and 100% of the machines and spares supply market.

Article 1 of the Mergers Regulation states it applies where there is a worldwide turnover of more than €5,000 million and an aggregate EU-wide turnover of each of at least two of the undertakings of more than €250 million. Article 1(3) provides that a EU dimension may nevertheless pertain, if:

(a) the combined aggregate worldwide turnover of all the undertakings is more than €2,500 million;

(b) in each of at least three Member States, the combined aggregate turnover of all the undertakings is more than €100 million;

(c) in each of at least three Member States, the aggregate turnover of each of at least two of the undertakings concerned is more than €25 million; and

(d) the aggregate EU-wide turnover of each of at least two of the undertakings concerned is more than €100 million.

Whilst we know the share of the EU market we do not know of their share of the world market. If they do exceed the limits of Art 1, Regulation 139/04 requires them to inform the Commission. By failing to inform the Commission, Art 4(1), they can be fined (Art 14).

The Commission will determine under Art 2 whether the concentration is compatible with the internal market. The facts do not reveal whether this merger has taken place. If it has, the Commission may investigate with a view to declaring it compatible or suspending it. If not, the abuse of a collective dominance on the part of the two companies may still breach the Mergers Regulation according to the ECJ in the cases of *France* v *Commission* (C-68/94) and *Société Commerciale des Potasses et de l Azote (SCPA)* v *Commission* (C-30/95) or Art 102 TFEU according to *Compagnie Maritime Belge Transports* (C-395 and 396P/96); however, an application to the General Court (ex CFI) would be necessary to determine this. Collective dominance has been further considered in the *Airtours* case (T-342/99) in which it was held that three conditions must be shown by the Commission. There needs to be market transparency, the tacit coordination must have been maintained over a period of time in pursuit of the common policy and that common policy must be safe from market disturbance. In this problem question, there is insufficient information to assess whether these conditions have been satisfied.

Question 5

On the information of Adam, a former employee of 'Kidstuff' (K), a manufacturer of children's toys, the EU Commission is investigating the possibility that K has entered into forms of agreement with companies in France, Italy and Germany which have resulted in price fixing and market sharing. Suspecting that this is the case, EU Commission officials raid all of the companies involved in an attempt to obtain further information.

When they arrived at the premises of K, they were refused entry for five hours and when finally they were allowed in, company employees were obstructive by not facilitating access to locked filing cabinets and computer programs. The Commission officials returned later and seized a considerable amount of correspondence. The company has later claimed that many of the letters were subject to principles of professional secrecy and legal privilege and should not have been taken and cannot be used in the investigation and decision in respect of their activities.

As a result of the fact that Adam's new employer, a competitor of K, has learned from Commission documents that Adam had tipped off the Commission, he has been dismissed.

With reference to the case law of the Court of Justice, outline the rights and duties of the Commission and the company in the investigation of competition law infringements.

Commentary

This problem on competition law is largely concerned with the application of the new **Regulation 1/2003** which replaced **Regulation 17**, which sets out the powers and duties of the Commission in investigating suspected competition law infringements and is thus concerned with the procedural law of investigations by the Commission. To answer the question you will need to identify the issues and then consider the power of the Commission to raid the premises of companies, the entry rights the Commission has, the ability or power it has to take documents, professional privacy, the duty of secrecy which is imposed on it and the rights of the employee who has lost his job.

Answer plan

- Provide a broad outline of competition policy and enforcement
- Outline the powers provided by **Regulation 1/2003** and relevant case law
- Apply this law to the issues in the question
- Address, particularly, the professional secrecy and legal privilege issues
- Note the possibility of an action for damages by Adam

Suggested answer

Competition law policy in the EU seeks to maintain and encourage competition in the EU for the benefit of the whole Union and for its consumers and citizens. It aims to do this by preventing anti-competitive practices and the abuse of dominant positions by undertakings in the EU. In order to achieve this effectively, the competition rules enacted need to be enforced. In turn, an enforcement agency must be given adequate powers and sanctions by which it can operate to make the policy effective.

Within the original EC Treaty, the Council was empowered under Art 87 (now 103 TFEU) to enact secondary EU legislation to give effect to the principles of law set out in Arts 101 and 102 TFEU (ex 81 and 82 EC), which are the principal provisions to combat anti-competitive behaviour. Article 105 TFEU (ex 85 EC) empowers the Commission to ensure Arts 101 and 102 TFEU are applied and to carry out investigation of suspected infringements of the Treaty Articles. This was substantially supplemented by Council Regulation 17 which has now been replaced with Regulation 1/2003 which contains similar enforcement rights.

Regulation 1/2003 sets out the powers and duties of the Commission in the conduct of investigations of competition law abuses. Articles 1–16 are mainly concerned with the respective powers of the Commission and national authorities, interim measures, cooperation between the Commission and national authorities, and with the procedure of the declarations by the Commission that the agreement either infringes the Treaty articles or is exempt from the Treaty provisions. They are not, therefore, of direct concern in answering this question.

This question is more concerned with Arts 17–21 which concern the powers of the Commission in conducting investigations, Arts 23–28, concerned with sanctions available to the Commission in the case of established infringements and the rights of the parties under investigation.

Articles 17–18 are concerned with requests for information. It generally empowers the Commission to request information to assist its investigations from both the authorities of the Member States and from the undertakings. The owners of undertakings or their representatives are obliged to supply the information requested. If this is not forthcoming the Commission can adopt a formal decision requiring the information to be supplied (Art 18(3)). Penalties may then be imposed for non-compliance with the terms of the Decision.

Article 20 empowers the Commission to undertake all necessary investigations including the right of its officials to examine books, take copies of records and books, ask for oral explanations and enter the premises of the undertakings. This can be undertaken without the consent of the undertaking involved providing it is specifically authorised in advance by the Commission; see the *National Panasonic* case (136/79). Alternatively, a formal Decision may be adopted for a mandatory investigation. There is no need to approach the company in advance and the Commission should not be subjected to a delay before the investigation can take place. The investigations authorised under this provision include the infamous 'Dawn Raids' on the premises of companies under investigation. In *Hoechst* (cases 46/87 and 227/88) the authority to raid was challenged on the grounds that it lacked precision but the ECJ held that it was acceptable providing the Commission indicated clearly its suspicions rather than have to supply full information.

Therefore, in application to the case at hand, the Commission has the right to request information and be given it by the company. It can also obtain the right of entry to the premises of the company and K should not have refused entry, although it has been held that waiting a short time for a lawyer to arrive may be acceptable; see the *National Panasonic* case. Case law has, however, further determined that force cannot be used by Commission officials to gain entry and examine documents, but assistance to gain entry must be obtained via the national authorities; see the cases of *Hoechst v Commission* (46/87 and 227/88), *Dow v Commission* (85/87) and *Orkem v Commission* (374/87). In the last case, it was held by the ECJ that the power to compel the production of information does not extend to requiring the company to admit breaches of the competition rules and thus incriminate itself. In effect, a company can be obstructive but may suffer the penalty of fines being imposed on it under Art 23 which can be up to 1% of the previous year's turnover, where a company has misled the Commission.

In the Decision *Fabbrica Pisana* (80/334) it was held that a duty of the company existed to assist the Commission to find documents and in the situation whereby the company is being obstructive, the Commission has a right to search; see the *Hoechst* case.

Thus, whilst the company may delay the entry to the building, the Commission, if sufficiently prepared with a Decision to enter and search and with the prior cooperation and assistance of the national authorities, will be able to obtain the information it requires. Any failure to comply with the Commission or not to cooperate will render the company liable to a fine under Art 23; confirmed in the *Sugar* case (40–48/73). However, in respect of the rights over the documents, it is a right to take copies and not the documents themselves (Art 20). Therefore, in this case, the Commission may have overstepped the mark and rendered the Decision void. An appeal by the Company should be made to the General Court (previously named the Court of First Instance), under Art 263 TFEU (ex 230 EC).

In the present case the company has also claimed that certain documents are subject to professional secrecy and legal privilege. The type of documents which are subject to legal privilege and professional secrecy have been the subject of case law. Legal privilege is recognised and covers correspondence between the company and an independent lawyer; see the *AM and S* case (155/79). In-house lawyers do not enjoy such privilege, so it depends on the nature of the correspondence. The *Hilti* case (T-30/89) decided that the privilege extends to in-house lawyers' reports of the independent lawyers' findings. In the *Samenwerkende* case (C-36/92 P), a refusal to hand over documents considered to be confidential was held to be unjustified in the light of the existing protections in EU law under which the Commission is required to notify undertakings of the documents they intend to release to the national authorities and thus give the undertakings the chance to seek judicial review to protect these documents. As such then, refusal to supply would be unjustified. In the end the General Court and the European Court of Justice must be the arbiters of what is privileged.

The principle of professional secrecy does not apply to allow a company to protect documents from the Commission but to ensure that information received by the Commission in an investigation is not disclosed to competitors, refer to Arts 27 and 28 and the cases of *Dow Benelux*, *Van Landewyck* (209–215 and 218/78) and *AKZO* (53/85).

Finally, the Commission owes a duty of care to Adam not to disclose his name. An action for damages may be successful under Art 340 TFEU (ex 288 EC). Here the case of *Adams* v *Commission* (145/83) is clearly relevant. It may be that, as in the *Adams* case, there was also a duty of Adam to ensure he could not be identified so that the damages payable may be reduced.

Question 6

'Even though Art 81 [now 101 TFEU] is meant to cover concerted actions as opposed to abusive conduct covered by Art 82 [now 102 TFEU], both provisions need to be interpreted in conjunction with each other.' (Van Bael & Bellis)
    Discuss.

Commentary

This question requires you to consider the relationship of Arts 101 and 102 TFEU (ex 81 and 82 EC) to each other. First of all, you should outline the basic legislative regime under the Treaty and then briefly outline the specific area covered by Arts 101 and 102 TFEU. Then you should address the quotation and consider whether the provisions do need to be interpreted in conjunction with each other or whether they can be regarded as mutually exclusive.

Answer plan

- Outline the broad principles of Competition policy and law
- Outline the scope of Arts 101 and 102 TFEU
- Discuss the relationship and any overlap of the two articles
- Consider the case law of the ECJ which addresses this issue

Suggested answer

EC Competition law is one of the fundamental policies of the Community and is generally mentioned in the Art 3 of both the TEU and the TFEU. Its aims are to prevent anti-competitive behaviour which will distort the competitive balance of the EU market. EU Competition rules are generally designed to intervene to prevent agreements which fix prices or conditions or the supply of products, to prohibit agreements which carve up territories, to prevent abuses of market power which have the effect of removing real competition and by controlling mergers which would also remove competition.

Whilst these aims are not so prominent in the EU Treaties as revised by the Lisbon Treaty, Art 3(3) TEU refers to a highly competitive social market economy and Art 3(d) TFEU provides an exclusive competence to the Union the 'establishing of the competition rules necessary for the functioning of the internal market'.

Two main provisions have been enacted to tackle two different situations. Article 101 TFEU (ex 81 EC) deals with anti-competitive practices arising as a result of agreements or concerted actions of two or more undertakings and Art 102 TFEU (ex 82 EC) concerns the abuse of a position of dominance by one or more undertakings.

Article 101(1) TFEU deals with restrictive practices. It sets out the prohibitions and details of the consequences of the failure to observe the prohibition and provides a framework by which exemptions from the prohibitions can be obtained.

Article 101(1) TFEU prohibits agreements between undertakings, decisions by associations of undertakings, and concerted practices which may affect trade between the Member States, and which have as their object or effect the prevention, restriction or distortion of competition within the internal market.

Article 101(2) TFEU provides that any agreements or decisions prohibited pursuant to this Article shall be automatically void, although there are ways in which an agreement may be held to be acceptable. The terms of an agreement may be acceptable as being consistent with one of the exemptions provided by the Vertical Restraints Regulation 2790/1999.

Article 102 TFEU applies where individual organisations have a near-monopoly position or share an oligopolistic market with a small number of other companies, and who take unfair advantage of this position to the detriment of the market, other companies and to the end consumers. Article 102 TFEU provides that the abuse by one or more undertakings of a dominant market position within the internal market, or in a substantial part of it, which affects trade between Member States, is prohibited. The requirements are therefore a dominant position, abuse of it and the effect between Member States.

At first sight, therefore, there seems to be at least a different focus of the two articles, with Art 101 TFEU aimed at two or more undertakings in collusion and Art 102 TFEU aimed at just a single entity. However, it can be observed in the case of *Ford v Commission* (25 and 26/84) that the unilateral action of one undertaking may still fall foul of Art 101 TFEU, whereas Art 102 TFEU expressly provides that it also applies to the activities of one or more undertakings.

The relationship of Arts 101 and 102 TFEU is highlighted in a case concerned with the difficulties in dealing with the realities of complex commercial cross holdings. In *BAT v Commission* (142 and 156/84), the Court of Justice had to determine whether the Commission decision was correct that the acquisition of a minority holding in a competing company was not an infringement of Arts 81 and 82 (now 101 and 102 TFEU). Two applicant and competitive companies had objected to the decision. The companies, whose activities were the subject of complaint, had remained independent after their agreement to establish cross holdings, so Art 81 (now 101 TFEU) was considered first. The Commission's decision that no anti-competitive object or effect had been established was upheld by the Court. Furthermore, no control by a particular company had been proved, and so there was no case under Art 82 (now 102 TFEU) either. However, the Court of Justice did consider that, although an acquisition itself might not restrict competition, it may lead to influence conduct to restrict or distort competition. Thus, it becomes necessary to consider the application of both Articles in such complex situations.

Prior to the Mergers Regulation 4064/89 and its replacement Regulation 139/04 coming into effect, it was in the area of mergers and acquisitions, or in EU jargon, concentrations, that the relationship of Arts 81 and 82 EC (now 101 and 102 TFEU) with each other had come under closest scrutiny.

Originally the Commission was of the view that Art 81 EC (now 101 TFEU) would not apply to concentrations. Thus, if competition was restricted or distorted by a concentration of companies, Art 82 EC (now 102 TFEU) was the appropriate measure with which to tackle it. This policy was pursued by the Commission in the case of *Continental Can* (6/72) when the Commission tried to remedy an abuse of a dominant position which had been achieved by takeovers and substantial holdings in European companies by an American company. It was the first attempt at merger control in this way by the Commission. It was not successful, mainly because the Commission failed to establish the relevant markets, rather than failed to show abuses by the concentration.

The view of the Court of Justice in the case was, however, instructive in respect of the relationship of Arts 81 and 82 EC (now 1010 and 102 TFEU) and the restrictive approach to the problem adopted by the Commission. The Court of Justice considered that, by refusing to consider the use of Art 81 EC (now 102 TFEU) as well, the Commission had handicapped itself.

The Court of Justice held that:

Articles 85 and 86 [now 101 and 102 TFEU] seek to achieve the same aim on different levels, viz. the maintenance of effective competition within the Common Market. The restraint of competition which is prohibited if it is the result of behaviour falling under Article 85 [now 101 TFEU], cannot be permissible by the fact that such behaviour succeeds under the influence of a dominant undertaking and results in the merger of the undertakings concerned. In the absence of explicit provisions one cannot assume that the Treaty, which prohibits in Article 85 [now 101 TFEU] certain decisions of ordinary associations of undertakings restricting competition without eliminating it, permits in Art 86 [now 102 TFEU] that undertakings after merging into an organic unit, should reach such a dominant position that any serious chance of competition is practically rendered impossible. Such diverse legal treatment would make a breach in the entire competition law which could jeopardise the proper functioning of the Common Market.

Thus, firms could avoid Art 101 TFEU by establishing close connections which did not constitute full merger and thus be caught by Art 102 TFEU. This would allow market partition and a defeat of the aims of the Community.

In any case Arts 101 and 102 TFEU cannot be interpreted in such a way that they contradict each other, because they serve to achieve the same aim. So, depending on the circumstance, it would be wise to consider the possibility of the application of both Arts 101 and 102 TFEU. Following the *Continental Can* case, the Community realised that a new approach was required to tackle the problems of concentrations and after some delay, the first Mergers Regulation (4064/89) was enacted. This has been considered by the ECJ as applicable to situations of collective dominance rather than Art 102 TFEU. See the cases of *France v Commission* (C-68/94) and *Société Commerciale des Potasses et de l Azote (SCPA) v Commission* (C-30/95). Therefore, under certain circumstances it might also be necessary to consider the application of the Merger Regulation (now 139/04) as well. Case law also demonstrates a link between the two main competition law articles in that the ECJ has held that an agreement within the meaning of Art 101 (1) TFEU between legally separate undertakings may nevertheless result in undertakings being so linked that they become and act as a collective entity as far as their competitors and customers are concerned. As such, then, it can lead to a position of collective dominance which is then capable of being abused. See *Compagnie Maritime Belge Transports* (C-395 and 396P/96). Some activities clearly need to be considered in the light of both Arts 101 and 102 TFEU and the Mergers Regulation.

Further reading

Eilmansberger, T, 'How to Distinguish Good from Bad Competition under Article 82: In Search of Clearer and More Coherent Standards for Anti-Competitive Abuses' (2005) 42 CML Rev 49.

Forrester, I, 'Due Process in EC Competition Law Cases: A Distinguished Institution with Flawed Procedures' (2009) 34 EL Rev 817.

Lianos, I, 'Collusion in Vertical Relations under Art 81 EC' (2008) 45 CML Rev 1027.

Monti, G, 'The Scope of Collective Dominance under Article 82' (2001) CML Rev 131.

Reich, N, 'The Courage Doctrine: Encouraging or Discouraging Compensation for Antitrust injuries?' (2005) 42 CML Rev 35.

Slot, PJ, 'A View from the Mountain: 40 Years of Developments in EC Competition Law' (2004) 41(2) CML Rev 443.

Venit, JS, 'Brave New World: The Modernization and Decentralization of Enforcement under Articles 81 and 82 of the EC Treaty' (2003) 40(3) CML Rev 545.

Vickers, J, 'Merger Policy in Europe: Retrospect and Prospect' (2004) 25(7) ECLR 455.

Vogelaar, F, 'European Competition Law Revisited: The "Great Overhaul" of 2004 Analysed' (2005) 32 Legal IEI 105.

9

Sex Discrimination and Equality Law

Introduction

The topic of sex discrimination or gender equality rights in the EU, within the European Union's social policy generally, may not be covered in all EU law courses but it is a topic which has given rise to quite a considerable number of cases, a number of which have become leading cases on general principles of EU law; see, for example, the cases of *Marshall* (152/84) and *von Colson* (14/83), amongst others. It may be surprising that the topic has given rise to so many cases given that there is only very narrow Treaty provision for it and, certainly at first, little secondary legislation. On the other hand, it might be concluded that it is exactly because there is little statutory provision that equal rights have had to be fought for in the courts. Furthermore, the range of rights originally provided by EU legislation in this area was contained within a quite narrow band and largely concerned employment. Although, as the Union has made further legislative moves into the area of social policy and equality rights on a broader front, further equal rights legislation has appeared.

To some extent the questions on the topic of sex discrimination which are considered on EU courses reflect this narrow band of issues, and questions are likely to focus on issues concerned with equal pay and equal treatment, especially in matters relating to retirement and dismissal.

To a more limited extent there may be questions on social security aspects of equal treatment but as this is a more complex area of EU law, there is less likelihood of questions.

The 2007 Lisbon Treaty has reaffirmed the recognition of equality rights in the European Union by the inclusion of equality and non-discrimination provisions in the Charter of Fundamental Rights which is attached to the Treaties via a declaration with legally binding status, excepting the opt-outs for Poland and the UK. A new Art 10 is introduced into the TFEU which provides that the Union in its policies shall aim to combat discriminations including sex and sexual orientation. No specific substantive changes have been introduced, though, by the Treaty and the law remains, at present, as it was in the following answers.

The questions in this chapter have been divided into a general question on the inclusion of sex discrimination provision in the first place, problem questions on aspects of equal pay and equal treatment, an essay question on a specific development in this area of law which considers the overlapping area of pay and pensions and a problem on pregnancy-related matters.

A new consolidating Directive in this area of law (2006/54) has replaced Directives 75/117, 76/207, 86/378 and 97/80 but because all case law was decided under the previous Directives, reference to both old and new Directives and Articles will be made.

Question 1

How can the appearance of gender equality rights in the EU Treaties be explained, when the Union seems to be a vehicle for economic integration rather than a champion for women's rights?

Commentary

This is a general question aimed to address the reason for the inclusion of Articles concerned mainly with the prohibition of discrimination on the grounds of sex within the EU Treaties.

The first part requires you to consider the original aims of the Community (now Union) and the reason for the inclusion of social rights and, in particular, rights concerned with equality. The second part requires you to consider the development of the Community and Union and the development of those rights. Thus, the aspects of this question which are required to be addressed are: the actual provision of rights in the Treaty; the suggestion that the Union is essentially an economic Union; the limited place that social concern had or has in its development; and what the position is now, following the legislative, judicial and policy developments in the area. The eventual provision of rights is best discussed in the light of the attitude displayed by the Court of Justice in case law.

Answer plan

- Outline the original aims and objectives of the European Community
- Consider reasons for the inclusion of a narrow band of social rights
- The development and extension of those equal pay and treatment rights
- The enactment of a series of Directives
- Judicial developments in equality law (*Defrenne* litigation and others)
- The further policy direction of the EU

Suggested answer

The area of sex discrimination law or gender equality rights for women in EU law is a later developer than the other areas of law because of the original, less extensive provision for it in the Treaty than other policy areas, the delays by the Union and, in particular, the Commission in introducing secondary legislation and the delays by the Member States in implementing the principles of equal pay from Art 119 EEC (now 157 TFEU) of the Treaty and equal pay and equal treatment from the secondary legislation. Article 119 EEC (now 157 TFEU) was the sole original Treaty provision for the European Union to concern itself with sex discrimination.

Given that the EEC was, at least, originally, of limited scope, it was clear that the main aim of the Community was undoubtedly the harmonisation of specific aspects of the Member States' economies and principally, at first, the creation of the common or single market. Social policy was at first (and still is by some) not regarded as greatly assisting the achievement of this result. However, it is also suggested that the original reason for including Art 119 (now 157 TFEU) in the EEC Treaty when drafted was not for reasons of social justice, but out of economic considerations. The Article was allegedly included more at the request of the French, whose legislation purported to provide for equality between male and female workers. It was feared that French industry would be at a disadvantage if equal pay were not a principle enforced in the other Member States. Thus, the aim was to ensure similar economic conditions applied in all the Member States. A consideration which supports this view is the fact that Art 119 EEC (now 157 TFEU) originally applied only to equal pay and not to all discrimination on the grounds of sex, although the ECJ has since then considerably expanded its scope in a number of judgments and the Union has now introduced more general anti-discrimination Articles into the Treaties. The range is now much more extensive and includes Arts 2 and 3 TEU, Art 8 TFEU (ex 3 EC), new Art 10 TFEU, Art 19 TFEU (ex 13 EC) (general power to prohibit discrimination across a range of issues), and Art 153 TFEU (ex 137 EC) (equality of men and women in the work environment). Furthermore, the EU has enacted Directives 2000/43 and 2000/78 dealing with other forms of discrimination. The objective to achieve an economic equality between Member States is acknowledged by the ECJ in the second *Defrenne* case (43/75). Additionally, however, in that case the ECJ went on to declare that Art 119 EEC (now 157 TFEU) also forms part of the social objectives of the Community (EU) and therefore emphasised that the Community (EU) was not merely an economic union. The Court of Justice considered that it was at the same time intended, by common action, to ensure social progress and to seek the constant improvement of the living and working conditions of their peoples, as could be observed by considering the Preamble to the Treaty. It concluded that the double aim, which is at once economic and social, shows that the principle of equal pay forms part of the foundations of the Community (EU). This has been followed up more recently in the case of *Deutsche Telekom* v *Vick* (C-324 and 325/96) in which the ECJ pronounced the social aims of Art 119 EEC (now 157 TFEU) prevail over those of the economic aims.

Therefore, whilst the initial concern may have been for economic reasons and originally the economic goals of the Community (EU) were undoubtedly paramount, if not exclusive, continuing concern is arguably more genuinely concerned with social rights and rights of equality in themselves, as demonstrated by developments to date, including the Directives on equal treatment and the considerable body of EU law on the subject. These developments might therefore lead to an amended conclusion to the question. This developing concern was prompted by a desire by the Member States in the European Summit meetings in 1972–3 to demonstrate that the EU was also concerned about social needs and equal rights and the view, adopted by the original Member States, was that it was necessary to get their act together before the new Member States joined in 1973. Requiring greater legislative changes by the new states should work to the advantage of the existing Member States who had, at least on paper, more time to make the necessary adjustments. The reality of this was somewhat different as can be observed by some of the case law on the matter.

Consequently, therefore, the Commission was encouraged to produce proposals for a Social Action Programme. After some considerable delay and somewhat watered down in their final form, an almost inevitable result of the EU legislative process, the following Directives were adopted: Council Directive 75/117, the Equal Pay Directive 1975; Council Directive 76/207, the Equal Treatment Directive; and Directive 79/7, the Social Security Directive. Much later, Directive 86/378 on equal treatment in occupational pensions, Directive 86/613 concerning equal treatment of the self-employed, and Directive 92/85 on pregnancy and maternity rights were adopted. To these can now be added the Parental Leave Directive (96/34), the Burden of Proof in Sex Discrimination Cases Directive (97/80) and the Part-time Workers Directive (97/81); although this latter Directive is not directly aimed to address sex discrimination, it will have this affect as it aims to reduce the inequality between full-time workers and part-time workers, the majority of whom are women. More recently, Directives 75/117, 76/207, 86/378 and 97/80 have been repealed and recast in Directive 2006/54 but without substantive amendment.

However, EU law is characteristically framed in broad general terms and concepts which seemed unsuitable for the provision of individual rights. EU legislation was criticised because of its formality, limited accessibility and distance from those who needed the effective application and enforcement of the provisions, ie women at work. The effect was, at first, that very little knowledge of European Union equal rights law was disseminated beyond the small number of people in direct contact with these laws except where given substantial media publicity after the event as in the leading cases such as the *Marshall* case (152/84), the *Pickstone v Freemans* case ([1988] 3 CMLR 221), the *Drake* case (150/85) and the *Webb v EMO* case (C-32/93). EU law has, however, provided a considerable source of legislative impetus for women's rights in employment in the Member States.

EU law provisions have been dependent largely on individual enforcement for its effectiveness where either governments have failed to take appropriate measures to implement it, or enforce them if implemented, or the European Commission has not taken enforcement actions against the recalcitrant governments. It has largely been on the individual level only that these rights have been successfully established as positive rights for women.

Notable successes such as the *Defrenne* litigation (80/70, 43/75 and 149/77) involving a Belgian Air Stewardess whose action, albeit after a lengthy process, gave the European Court of Justice the opportunity to interpret Art 119 EEC (now 157 TFEU) to include indirect and more subtle forms of discrimination. Another prime example of individual action required to force change is the *Marshall* case.

These cases alone would appear to create more interest in the creation of the enforcement and the development of women's rights than the efforts of many national groups. However, the backing of national agencies to promote equal rights has been fundamental in promoting women's rights, particularly in Belgium and the UK.

An additional very important factor which has helped promote and develop these rights is that the EU legal provisions can be and have been subject to very liberal interpretations by the European Court of Justice, far beyond a literal reading of the Articles; see, for example, the wide interpretation of Art 157 TFEU (ex 119 EEC & 141 EC), including the concept of pay in the *Garland* case (12/81), and the concept of indirect discrimination in the *Jenkins v Kingsgate* (96/80) and *Bilka-Kaufhaus* cases (170/84). The Equal Treatment Directives have also been interpreted generously in cases such as *Marschall* (C-409/95) and *Barber* (C-262/88). The Court has even advanced the cause of equal rights through procedural means so that an effective remedy should be given by the Member States in cases where rights have been breached; see the *von Colson* case (14/83) and *Johnston v RUC* case (222/84). In *Richards* (C-423/04) equal treatment rights were held to apply to secure equal right to pension access for a transgendered woman. More recently the *Mangold* case (C-144/04) provides that non-discrimination as a general principle is one that can be enforced horizontally between individuals, although its potential as a gender equality weapon is yet untested and unconfirmed.

Although sex discrimination rights, of course, apply equally to men and women, they have been regarded as more beneficial, for the most part, for women who were generally more discriminated against. However, the body of case law involving claims by men is increasing.

Women's rights in the EU were considerably strengthened by changes introduced by the Treaty of Amsterdam. The Treaty introduced as one of the goals outlined in Art 2 EC 'equality between men and women' and added a new final sentence to Art 3 EC which read: 'In all the activities referred to in this Article, the Community shall aim to eliminate inequalities, and to promote equality, between men and women'. These are now to be found in Arts 2 and 3 TEU and Art 8 TFEU. Furthermore, a new enabling power was introduced in Art 13 EC (now 19 TFEU) which provides that the Council, acting unanimously, and in consultation with the EP, may take appropriate action to combat discrimination based on sex or sexual orientation, amongst others. Directives have already been enacted under this provision including Directive 2000/78 which provides a framework to prohibit direct or indirect discrimination generally in employment on the grounds of religion or belief, disability, age or sexual orientation. Finally, the EC Treaty was amended by adding two sentences to Art 141 EC (now 157 TFEU) which located within a Treaty base the principles of equal pay for work of equal value and positive discrimination previously contained in Directives only, which meant that they could not previously have given rise to direct effects against other individuals (no horizontal direct effects of Directives – *Marschall*). The *Mangold* judgment, noted above, may though have circumvented that limitation. The Lisbon Treaty has attached the Charter of Fundamental Rights to the Treaties which has further provided for equality rights. Furthermore, Art 10 of the TFEU provides that the Union in its policies shall aim to combat discriminations including sex and sexual orientation.

Measures of positive discrimination have, however, been given a mixed reception by the ECJ and rules of positive discrimination which try to promote the appointment of women to achieve more substantive rather than just formal equality have been subject to exacting criteria to ensure that men are not then discriminated against. See the case of *Marschall* (C-409/95).

Finally, there have been a number of non-legislative or soft law initiatives to promote equality including the most recent, the Roadmap for Equality (2006–2010).

In summary then, although Art 119 provided the only specific mention of equal treatment in the original EEC Treaty, it formed the basis upon which the principle has been expanded into areas beyond equal pay, and has become a fundamental social principle of the Treaty. Whilst the amount of legislation is limited, it has been subject to very liberal interpretations by the Court of Justice far beyond a literal reading of the Articles in cases more often brought by individuals rather than the Commission in Art 258 TFEU actions; see the *Garland*, *Defrenne* and *Marschall* cases.

According to your own view on what the Court of Justice has done or what it should do, your conclusion may range from considering that the Union and in particular, Court of Justice, have contributed significantly in promoting and enforcing equal treatment rights for women, to the views that it has only done what was to be expected or not enough so far.

Question 2

Meg and Nicola work part-time for the telephone call centre of the 'Chaste Direct Bank'. They discover that even though they were working what they considered to be antisocial hours (from 6.00 pm until 12.00 midnight), they were receiving less per hour than their full-time colleagues working during daylight hours. There are 18 female and two male part-time evening workers. The daytime staff are evenly divided between male and female workers. Meg complains to her boss, Mr Branston, that this appears to be discrimination. He explains that it is far easier to get staff for evening work and, in particular, women find this a very suitable way of combining their commitment to a family and being able to earn money. He has very many applicants for the part-time evening work but in contrast far fewer for the daytime work. Soon after, Meg is dismissed on the grounds of displaying a poor attitude. She has found it difficult to obtain alternative employment as Mr Branston has failed to respond to enquiries for a reference for Meg.

Nicola became pregnant but suffered ill health as a result of the pregnancy. She was forced to take time off during the early part of the pregnancy but, after a successful birth she returned to work at the end of her 14 weeks' maternity leave. Her rights to the Sports and Social Club were suspended during her maternity leave. However, since the birth of her baby, the health problems which had first manifested themselves during pregnancy flared up again and, combined with the depression from which Nicola also suffers, has meant she has been absent for 25 days in 12 weeks. She was dismissed because she exceeded the number of days off which could be taken on the grounds of ill health.

The call centre has advertised for a new manager. The shortlist for applications consists of two equally qualified persons only. George is an internal candidate who already works for the company and Posy is an external applicant. 'Chaste Direct' stated its positive discrimination policy for filling job vacancies in the advertisement and as a result has appointed Posy as the new manager. George has protested that he has been discriminated against by the company and threatens to take the matter to court. In response the company issue him with a formal warning that he will be dismissed if he causes any more difficulty. Shortly afterwards another management position is advertised and George applies again but under the name Georgina. Appearing at the interview, George/Georgina states that he intends to undergo a sex change operation. This time there was no equally or better qualified female applicant. George/Georgina, however, was dismissed.

Meg, Nicola and George seek your advice as to their rights, if any, under EU law.

Commentary

This is quite a complex and involved question with a number of points to be addressed. As a general introduction to this problem on discrimination you could state the narrow Treaty base for EU law, but that a number of Directives have been issued and that the Court interprets these rights liberally, to give the maximum protection to the rights provided. Given that this is such a long question, any general treatment must be brief to give you time to deal with the many substantive issues arising.

You must identify the issues which start with part-time pay, an old favourite but nevertheless still frequently appearing in exam questions. This may be an equal pay claim or possibly equal pay for work of equal value. There is a possible objective justification which needs to be discussed. Then include the dismissal of Meg and the failure to give a reference, Nicola's treatment during pregnancy and dismissal afterwards and finally the issues affecting George. These are the failure to be appointed which includes an aspect of positive discrimination and the dismissal. For the purposes of answering the question, at least, you will have to assume that the stated intention of George is genuine. Then with reference to the appropriate statutory provisions first, and case law where relevant, you should suggest the outcome of these issues.

Additionally, you should consider the right to pursue these claims before the national tribunals. It is to be noted that this last issue is particularly important because they are employed by a private employer, which may affect their rights to remedy in the national courts if they are dependent on the direct effects of Directives. However, unless you are advised on a particular course that a full discussion of the procedural aspects of the case must be given, a brief statement of the problems and possible solutions should complete an answer in a question which essentially concerns sex discrimination.

Answer plan

- Introduce **Art 157 TFEU**, the applicable Directives, and the various issues
- Equal pay (*Jenkins*, *Bilka-Kaufhaus* and *Enderby* cases)
- Pregnancy rights (*Lewen*, *Larsson* and *Brown* cases)
- Positive discrimination (*Marschall* and *Badeck* cases)
- Dismissal of George (*P & S* case)
- Procedural difficulties with direct effects

Suggested answer

The area of law applicable to the factual situation in this problem stems originally from a very narrow legislative base in the EEC Treaty. This is Art 119 (now 157 TFEU) which was the sole primary legislative provision for the European Union to concern itself with sex discrimination. It is concerned predominantly with equal pay but also following the Treaty of Amsterdam with positive discrimination. There also exists a growing body of EU law on the subject following the enactment of a number of Directives, on matters of equality between men and women. Case law on these, as with the original Treaty provision, has extended the scope of protection further.

The factual circumstances in this question give rise to a number of issues to be resolved. They are:

part-time pay;

the possible objective justification;

the dismissal of Meg;

the failure to give a reference;

Nicola's treatment during pregnancy and dismissal afterwards; and

the failure to appoint George and his dismissal.

The part-time staff, who are predominantly women, receive less pay per hour than the full-timers. Meg is claiming that she has been indirectly discriminated against compared to full-time workers and despite the fact they are paid the same as male part-time workers, of which there are only two out of 20. It is well-established law that the prohibition of discrimination in pay under Art 157 TFEU applies not only to direct but also to indirect discrimination. The cases of *Jenkins* v *Kingsgate* (96/80) and *Bilka-Kaufhaus* v *Weber* (170/84) confirm that this situation will be regarded as indirect discrimination, when a disadvantage falls on a category which is predominantly female, unless it can be justified objectively. Indirect discrimination in this area is covered in the new consolidating Directive 2006/54 which takes its definition from the earlier general discrimination directives as: where an apparently neutral provision, criterion or practice would put persons of one sex at a particular disadvantage compared with persons of the other sex, unless that provision, criterion or practice is objectively justified by a legitimate aim, and the means of achieving that aim are appropriate and necessary. The *Bilka-Kaufhaus* case provides three guidelines to determine whether a difference in pay is objectively justified. The measure employed must correspond to a real need on the part of the undertaking, be appropriate to achieve the objective and be necessary for that objective. It is in the end a question of fact to be decided by the national court but the ECJ has further held in the case of *Dansk* v *Danfoss* (109/88) that the burden is to be placed on the employer to prove that the difference is justified and that this should be transparent. The reasons put forward in the present case appear to be an objective justification because there is no shortage of applicants for part-time positions compared with full-time daytime positions. However, it is combined with references to marital and family status, which was expressly covered in Art 2 of the Equal Treatment Directive (76/207) that there shall be no discrimination whatsoever on grounds of sex either directly or indirectly by reference in particular to family or marital status, although that particular reference has been omitted from the consolidating Directive 2006/54. This would appear to be unlawful indirect discrimination but if there is a doubt, given the applicants for the positions, a reference under Art 267 TFEU to the ECJ may be necessary to decide the point. There may also be an argument here that Meg has a claim for equal pay for work of equal value. Article 157 TFEU now includes the words 'equal pay for work of equal value', previously restricted to Directive 75/117. In the present case, Meg is comparing her wages with a male worker whose work is arguably of equal or lesser value because it is daytime work and she is working anti-social hours but receives lower wages. She could ask for a job evaluation scheme and should the company refuse to carry out a job evaluation scheme to test this, it can be imposed on them through court proceedings, *Commission v UK* (61/81). Following *Murphy v Irish Telecom* (157/86) and *Enderby v Frenchay* (C-127/92), in which the ECJ held that Art 119 EEC (now 157 TFEU) could be used to make a comparison of work of equal value, this claim has a good chance of success. Article 19 of Directive 2006/54 now removes the need to produce statistical evidence to support a claim of indirect discrimination in pay and that the burden of proof was on the employer to rebut this.

Meg was then dismissed, which appears to be a reaction to her making a complaint and this is specifically covered now in Directive 2006/54, Art 24 which serves to protect complainants from unfair dismissal on the grounds that they have complained. The procedural difficulty that this is a private employer will be considered at the end of this answer.

Finally concerning Meg is the refusal to give a reference. This point is covered by the case of *Coote v Granada* (C-185/97) which held that a refusal to provide a reference would undermine Art 6 of Directive 76/207 but which is contained now in Directive 2006/54, Art 17, under which Member States should take measures to achieve the aims of the Directive and must ensure the rights can be enforced by an individual before the national courts. The ECJ held that Art 6 of Directive 76/207 also covers measures an employer might take as a reaction against legal proceedings of a former employee outside of dismissal.

Turning to Nicola, the suspension of rights during 14 weeks would appear to be a straightforward breach of Art 11 of Directive 92/85 which serves to protect employment rights during pregnancy and maternity (see *Susanne Lewen v Lothar Denda* (C-333/97)). If there was any doubt about this, a reference to the ECJ would be necessary. However, the dismissal for absence outside of the 14-week protected period due to ill health arising from pregnancy would appear to be lawful according to the case law of the ECJ and not protected by either Directive 76/207 or 92/85 and with no change under the new Directive 2006/54. See *Larsson v Dansk Handel and Service* (C-400/95), in which the ECJ confirmed that Directive 76/207 does not prevent dismissals for absences due to illness attributable to pregnancy even where the illness arose during pregnancy and continued during and after maternity. Directive 92/85 does not help as this also only protects against dismissal for the beginning of pregnancy to the end of maternity leave, as confirmed in *Brown v Rentokil* (C-394/96), that absences due to illnesses thereafter are treated in the same way as any other illness and may constitute grounds for dismissal according to provisions of national law. The more recent case of *NW Health Board v McKenna* (C-191/03) confirms that this basis of comparison is acceptable. Hence, the dismissal appears to be lawful.

George was not appointed and suspects the positive discrimination policy has actually discriminated against him. Positive discrimination is now located in Art 157(4) TFEU although the first cases arose under Directive 76/207, Art 2(4), now recast in Art 3 of Directive 2006/54. In the case of *Hellmut Marschall v Land Nordrhein-Westfalen* (C-409/95), the ECJ held that clauses favouring women applicants would only be acceptable if they contained a 'saving clause' which provides that if a particular male candidate has grounds which tilt the balance in his favour, women are not to be given priority. Further, such clauses are acceptable provided the candidates are objectively assessed to determine whether there are any factors tilting the balance in favour of a male candidate but that such criteria employed do not themselves discriminate against women. This position is now supported by the *Badeck* case (C-158/97) which is based on Art 141(4) EC (now 157 TFEU). The facts reveal no such clause in the present case, and unless there is such a clause, it is unlikely that the positive discrimination policy of the bank conforms with EU law.

George was dismissed after stating that he was to undergo a sex change operation. These facts fit within the case of *P v S and Cornwall County Council* (C-13/94) which involved a male-to-female transsexual who was dismissed from employment in an educational establishment after informing the employers he was going to undergo gender reassignment. The ECJ held that this was unlawful discrimination on the grounds of sex because it was 'based, essentially if not exclusively on the sex of the person concerned'. The dismissal would be contrary to Art 24 of Directive 2006/54 which provides that Member States must introduce into their own legal systems such measures as are necessary to enable all persons who consider themselves wronged to pursue their claims by judicial process.

The final aspect concerns the difficulties which might arise in respect of pursuit of the claims in the national tribunals. Any claims made under Art 157 TFEU will be safe in all circumstances because this was held to be directly effective in *Defrenne (No 2)* (43/75), both vertically against the state and horizontally against other individuals. If the Member State has accurately implemented the Directives, then applicants can invoke national law before the national court. However, if they have not been implemented or correctly implemented, the claimants will be unable to rely directly on the Directives because a private employer is involved and there are no horizontal direct effects of Directives; see the *Marshall* case (152/84). The result in such a circumstance would depend on whether the national court could interpret any national law in compliance with EU law, thus following the *von Colson* (14/83) and *Marleasing* cases (C-106/89). If this is not the case, a further possibility exists in that a claim may be made against the state, in accordance with the *Francovich* case (C-6/90), for a failure to implement the Directive with the result that the claimant has suffered damage.

Question 3

In 1989, Margaret set up a Ladies' Hairdressing Salon called 'Thatcher's Cuts'. Her cuts were cheap and popular because her wage costs were kept low by the employment of a large proportion of part-time staff who were paid a third less than full-time employees. All except one of the part-time employees were female. When asked by Sharon and Tracey why this was, Margaret explained that she wanted to attract more male full-time hairdressers. She considered that they were more popular with her clients and higher salaries were needed to fill the posts advertised. She also regarded this as justified to redress the balance positively in favour of men in a profession largely dominated by female hairdressers. Margaret, who was an advocate of private pensions, additionally established a redundancy scheme and an 'opted-out' pension scheme for her employees.

Tracey, a female part-timer, who wanted to work full-time, was unable to obtain a position which was advertised but filled by a man with the same qualifications. In January 2006, Tracey, who had read in a women's magazine that she had rights to equal treatment under European law, mentioned this to Margaret. Margaret, who disliked Europe, dismissed her for impertinence. Tracey went to a solicitor who filed a claim on her behalf in respect of both pay and, in case it was relevant, pensions.

Margaret fell on hard times and in November 2008 had to shut up shop. She closed the salon and made the staff redundant. The amount of the redundancy payments and pensions made were based pro rata on earnings so that full-time ex-employees received 50% higher payments than part-timers. Sharon was made redundant at this time.

Advise Tracey and Sharon as to their rights under EU law, if any, including any procedural difficulties, they may face.

Commentary

This question involves questions of indirect discrimination of part-time workers and a possible objective justification for this. It also includes a policy of positive discrimination which has to be considered to see whether this offends EU law. The most difficult part of this question is that dealing with the redundancy payments and pensions, particularly as claims for equal pensions are subject to a time bar introduced by the *Barber* case (C-262/88).

The answer should be started with a brief statement on the EU legal regime, list the issues which need to be considered and suggest possible solutions based on the legislative provision and case law of the ECJ. The lack of horizontal direct effects of Directives should also be mentioned.

Answer plan

- Introduce **Art 157 TFEU**, the applicable Directives, and the various issues
- Equal pay (*Jenkins*, *Bilka-Kaufhaus*, and *Enderby* cases)
- Positive discrimination (*Marschall* and *Badeck* cases)

- Dismissal of Tracey (**Directive 2006/54**)
- Pensions as pay (*Barber* case)
- Procedural difficulties with direct effects

Suggested answer

The area of law applicable to this question stems originally from a very narrow legislative base in the EEC Treaty. This is Art 119 (now 157 TFEU) which remains the primary legislative provision for the European Union to concern itself with gender equality. It is concerned predominantly with equal pay but also following the Treaty of Amsterdam, with positive discrimination. There also exists a growing body of EU law on the subject following the enactment of a number of Directives, on matters of equality between men and women. Case law on these, as with the original Treaty provision, has extended the scope of protection further.

The factual circumstances in this question give rise to a number of issues to be resolved. They are:

part-time pay;

the possible objective justification;

positive discrimination;

the dismissal of Tracey; and

the redundancy payments and pensions for both Tracey and Sharon.

The part-time staff, who are predominantly women, receive less pay per hour than the full-timers. Sharon and Tracey are concerned that they are suffering discrimination on the grounds of sex contrary to Art 157 TFEU. It appears as if they have been indirectly discriminated against compared to full-time workers and despite the fact that they are paid the same as male part-time workers, of which there is only one. It is well-established law that the prohibition of discrimination in pay under Art 157 TFEU applies not only to direct but also to indirect discrimination. The cases of *Jenkins* v *Kingsgate* (96/80) and *Bilka-Kaufhaus* v *Weber* (170/84) confirm that this situation will be regarded as indirect discrimination, when a disadvantage falls on a category which consists predominantly of one sex, unless it can be justified objectively. Indirect discrimination in this area is covered in the new consolidating Directive 2006/54 which takes its definition from the earlier general discrimination Directives as: where an apparently neutral provision, criterion or practice would put persons of one sex at a particular disadvantage compared with persons of the other sex, unless that provision, criterion or practice is objectively justified by a legitimate aim, and the means of achieving that aim are appropriate and necessary. The *Bilka-Kaufhaus* case provides three guidelines to determine whether a difference in pay is objectively justified. The measure employed must correspond to a real need on the part of the undertaking, be appropriate to achieve the objective and be necessary for that objective. It is in the end a question of fact to be decided by the national court, but the ECJ has further held in the case of *Dansk* v *Danfoss* (109/88) that the burden is to be placed on the employer to prove that the difference is justified and that this should be transparent. Article 19 of Directive 2006/54 now removes the need to produce statistical evidence to support a claim of indirect discrimination in pay and that the burden of proof was on the employer to rebut this. The reasons put forward in the present case are the policy to attract more full-time workers and to carry out a policy of positive discrimination in favour of men. Would these justify the discrimination? Clearly, favouring men above women would not be justified as the discrimination is based expressly on sex. How does the positive discrimination policy affect this? Originally only contained in Directive 76/207 and now Art 3 of Directive 2006/54, positive discrimination is also located in Art 157(4) TFEU although the first cases arose under the Directive. In the case of *Hellmut Marschall* v *Land Nordrhein-Westfalen* (C-409/95), the ECJ held that clauses favouring women applicants would only be acceptable if they contained a 'saving clause' which provides that if a particular male candidate has grounds which tilt the balance in his favour, women are not to be given priority. Further, such clauses are acceptable provided the candidates are objectively assessed to determine whether there are any factors tilting the balance in favour of a male candidate but that such criteria employed do not themselves discriminate against women. This position is now supported by the *Badeck* case (C-158/97). The facts reveal no such clause in the present case, therefore it is unlikely that the positive discrimination policy conforms with EU law. If there is any doubt that this judgment could not be applied in the same manner to determine whether positive discrimination in favour of men offends EU law, then a reference to the ECJ would be needed. It is unlikely that the higher payments would be lawful discrimination and unless there was sufficient safeguards in the system of positive discrimination, this would also be unlikely to satisfy EU law requirements.

Tracey has not been accepted for the full-time position. This aspect would also be covered by Arts 1 and 4 of Directive 2006/54 which provide that there shall be no discrimination whatsoever on the grounds of sex in the conditions, including selection criteria, for access to all jobs or posts, whatever the sector or branch or activity and to all levels of the occupational hierarchy. If the positive discrimination policy offends EU law then the Directive will have been breached.

Tracey was then dismissed, which appears to be a reaction to her making a complaint, and this is specifically covered by Art 24 of Directive 2006/54 which provides that Member States must introduce into their own legal systems such measures as are necessary to enable all persons who consider themselves wronged, to pursue their claims by judicial process, and thus serves to protect complainants from unfair dismissal on the grounds that they have complained. The procedural difficulty that this is a private employer will be considered at the end of this answer.

Turning now to the redundancy payments and pensions which were 50% higher for full-time staff than for the predominantly female part-time workers. Again, unlawful indirect discrimination appears to be present here. Dealing first with the redundancy payments, it has been confirmed in *Barber* v *GRE* (C-262/88) that payments in connection with redundancy are to be considered a part of the concept of pay under Art 157 TFEU. As a consequence, there will be no difficulty with direct effects, if this aspect of the claim becomes material. As pay, therefore, the amount should be equal and if not this is a clear breach of Art 157 TFEU, Sharon would be unlawfully discriminated against.

Any claims in respect of pensions are more problematic because it was originally considered that pensions were so linked to personable age that they would be exempted from the equal treatment regime of the EC by virtue of Art 7 of Directive 79/7. However, the case of *Barber* held that pensions were 'pay' within Art 141 (now 157 TFEU) because they were a part of the employment relationship. The pensions provided by Margaret were opted out from the state scheme, hence then clearly pay according to the ECJ for the purposes of Art 157 TFEU. As such then, a difference in payment for the part-time workers who were predominantly female would unlawfully discriminate against them contrary to Art 157 TFEU.

An additional aspect here is the procedural difficulty of any claim for equal rights in pensions. The *Barber* decision caused severe problems as it was not expected that pensions should be pay because they were linked to retirement and this had been different for men and women, most schemes set up on the basis that women would retire earlier. Actuaries knew they would live longer so they were necessarily different, ie there would be differences based on the different ages in the schemes. As a result of the *Barber* judgment, this would mean that there would be unlawful discrimination not previously thought to be the case, for which huge amounts of compensation, not previously contemplated, would be payable. This would not have been taken account of in the actuarial schemes and the pensions schemes would have had severe difficulties in making payments not previously foreseen. Hence then, ECJ declared Art 141 to be directly effective for pensions only from the date of judgment, ie 17 May 1990.

Hence then, the dates of the pension claim are important in respect of the *Barber* case. The Member States introduced Protocol II to the Maastricht Treaty when it was negotiated, confirming and clarifying the *Barber* judgment that only payments attributable to periods of service after the date of judgment would count for pay under Art 157 TFEU. Hence for Sharon the period is from only 17 May 1990 to her redundancy in November 2008 and not from 1989.

The final aspect concerns the difficulties, which might arise in respect of pursuit of the claims in the national tribunals. Any claims made under Art 157 TFEU will be safe in all circumstances because this was held to be directly effective in *Defrenne* (No 2) (43/75), both vertically and horizontally. If the Member State has accurately implemented the Directives, then applicants can invoke national law before the national court. However, if they have not been implemented or correctly implemented, the claimants will be unable to rely directly on the Directives because a private employer is involved and there are no horizontal direct effects; see the *Marshall* case (152/84). The result in such a circumstance would depend on whether the national court could interpret any national law in compliance with EU law, thus following the *von Colson* (14/83) and *Marleasing* (C-106/89) cases. If this is not the case, a further possibility exists in that a claim may be made against the state, in accordance with the *Francovich* case (C-6/90), for a failure to implement the Directive with the result that the claimant has suffered damage.

Question 4

Whilst the case of *Barber* (C-262/88) may have finally decided that benefits paid in connection with redundancy were to be considered pay within the meaning of Art 141 of the EC Treaty (now Art 157 TFEU), the precise effect of the judgment was far from clear.

Discuss the difficulties raised by this judgment and the solutions found to overcome them.

 ## Commentary

This essay-type question concentrates on a particular difficulty which has developed in the case law of the Court of Justice. This is the interpretation which should be given in respect of payments made in connection with redundancies and whether such payments should be considered as pay within the scope of Art 157 TFEU. The problem had arisen from the fact that redundancy payments and pension payments have been argued and regarded as connected with state pensions and thus a part of the social policy reserved to the Member States, outside the jurisdiction of the EU. The *Barber* case upset this previous position.

In answering this question you need to set out in some detail the facts and decision in the case of *Barber* as the basis to your answer. The words 'finally decided' in the first sentence suggest that there had been previous cases which had considered this but without coming to the conclusions reached in the *Barber* case. You should, therefore, at least summarise the earlier case law development. The statement then suggests that there is some uncertainty about the decision in the words 'the precise effect of the judgment was far from clear'. You should identify the difficulties which have been noted in respect of this judgment and the ensuing problems and the steps that have been taken to overcome them.

Answer plan

- Provide the facts and judgments of the *Barber* case
- Outline scope of **Art 157 TFEU** and the ECJ case law on the meaning of pay
- Discuss the consequences of the *Barber* Judgment for similar claims
- Review the **Maastricht Protocol** and subsequent case law
- Note effect of **Directive 86/378** as replaced by **Directive 2006/54**

Suggested answer

The case of *Barber v Guardian Royal Exchange Assurance Group* (C-262/88) concerned the provision of a non-state pension scheme, known as a contracted-out scheme, as a part of the contract of employment. The contract also stated that the normal pension ages were 65 for men and 60 for women. Early retirement with immediate pension could be made at any time within ten years of pensionable age. Barber was made redundant at the age of 52. The severance terms required that men must be 55 and women 50 to obtain immediate pensions. Ineligible for this, Barber was granted instead a deferred pension and a severance payment, but claimed that because the scheme involved an age differential as to when men and women were able to obtain redundancy pensions (50 for women, 55 for men), it was discrimination contrary to Community (EU) law.

Essentially, the Court of Justice held that benefits paid in connection with redundancy, even though compulsory and even though they reflected considerations of a Member State's social security policy, were a form of payment made after the termination of the contract of employment and therefore covered by Art 119 EC (now 157 TFEU). Article 157 TFEU applies to any consideration, immediate or future, and whether received indirectly as a result of a contract of employment with an employer. This conclusion was reached even though the UK argued the payments reflected considerations of a Member State's social security policy and should be assessed under Art 118 EC (now 156 TFEU) and not within the scope of Art 119 EC (now 157 TFEU). The ECJ held that they were a part of the employment relationship and that redundancy benefits were to be regarded as pay regardless of whether a part of the contract of employment, compulsory under national legislation or paid voluntarily by the employer.

The case follows a number of previous cases which have been considered by the Court of Justice concerning the complicated relationships between pay and contributions to state pensions, state redundancy payment schemes and non-state pension schemes. In *Defrenne (No 1)* (80/70) the ECJ held that contributions made to a state social security scheme were not pay because they were the result of legal requirements imposed by the state. The decisive criterion in that case was the fact that the pension rights in question related wholly to a state social security scheme. In *Barber* the Court of Justice held that contracted-out pensions schemes were not covered by the rule in *Defrenne* and they should be considered under Art 119 EC (now 157 TFEU), even if a substitute for part of the state scheme.

In *Worringham and Humphreys* v *Lloyds Bank* (69/80), the Court of Justice ruled that a contribution to a retirement benefit scheme which is paid by the employer on the employee's behalf by means of an addition to gross salary was pay within the meaning of Art 119 EC (now 157 TFEU) and that amounts which determine other benefits linked to salary were also part of the pay of the employee within the second paragraph of Art 119 EC (now 157 TFEU), even if they were deducted at source by the employer and paid into a pension fund on behalf of the employee.

In *Bilka-Kaufhaus* v *Karin Weber Van Harz* (170/84), it was held that, where payments are made in respect of a non-contributory occupational pension scheme established under contract with the employer, they constitute pay under Art 119 EC (now 157 TFEU).

In *Liefting* v *University of Amsterdam* (22/83), a Dutch statutory social security scheme for civil servants meant that lower employer contributions were paid by the employer to women than men with the consequence that if the women were to make this up themselves, their take-home pay was less. It was argued on the basis of *Defrenne 2* that social security was not pay and therefore was excluded from the scope of Art 119 EC (now 157 TFEU) and the jurisdiction of the Community (EU). The Court of Justice held that the sums provided by the employer become pay if they form part of the gross pay calculation for other benefits and if these are not the same for males and females they will breach Art 119 EC (now 157 TFEU).

However, the case of *Newstead* v *Department of Transport* (192/85) concerned the question of whether a compulsory deduction from the gross pay of male unmarried civil servants towards a widow's pension amounted to a breach of Art 119 EC (now 157 TFEU) and Directives 75/117 and 76/207 (now replaced by 2006/54). The Court of Justice ruled that the requirement to pay was neither a benefit paid to workers nor a contribution paid by the employer to a pension scheme on behalf of the employee; therefore, it falls within the scope of Art 118 EC (now 156 TFEU) not Art 119 EC (now 157 TFEU) because it was argued it affected net and not gross pay and thus distinguishes itself from *Liefting*. This case would now seem to be overruled by the *Barber* case.

Therefore, having decided in the *Barber* case that the pension was pay, the age difference causing deferred pension rights for males was a form of unlawful discrimination.

The deciding factor in the light of these cases is whether the rules of the specific scheme are a part of the employment contract. Schemes which are entirely compulsory state social security schemes are not considered to be part of the employment relationship and are not subject to Art 157 TFEU.

The immediate consequence of the *Barber* judgment was that the employer in the case was required to pay out pensions earlier to men than previously thought necessary. However, the most difficult aspect of the case is the further consequence for all other employers and the calculation for pension schemes which were based on different retirement ages according to the previous legal position. The judgment of the Court reflects that and therefore the ECJ held that, because of the confusion over the exact scope of Art 119 EC (now 157 TFEU), the Member States could not previously have planned clearly on the true basis as now regarded; therefore the judgment could not be retroactive. This would cause too many complications for pension schemes because employers could not have foreseen that Art 119 EC (now 157 TFEU) was applicable to contracted-out pension schemes. Therefore, the Court of Justice held that Art 119 EC (now 157 TFEU) could not be relied on to claim an entitlement to a pension with effect prior to the date of judgment of 17 May 1990, except claims already in the pipeline.

A controversy then arose as to the precise meaning and effect of this ruling. It was uncertain whether *Barber* referred to benefits or pensions received from the date of judgment or whether it referred to benefits to be received in respect of periods of employment, ie earnings, from the date of judgment, the latter being less onerous on employers than the former.

The matter appeared temporarily to be resolved by the issue of a Protocol at Maastricht which states that the benefits arising from occupational social security schemes shall not be considered as remuneration in respect of periods of employment prior to 17 May 1990, with the exception of those who had instigated proceedings prior to that date. This overcame the damaging economic effect on employers in the case of a retroactive application of the ruling of the Court of Justice in *Barber*.

It was not, however, the end of the story. *Barber* sparked off many more cases seeking to establish its exact meaning and consequences, such that the whole area became even more complex and confusing and another legislative intervention was considered necessary to resolve the matter.

The ECJ confirmed in the *Ten Oever* (C-109/91) and *Coloroll* (C-200/91) cases that pension equality is guaranteed only to awards arising from employment after 17/5/1990; however, in *Vroege* v *NCIV Instituut* (C-57/93) and *Fisscher* v *Voorhuis Hengelo BV* (C-128/93), it held the time limit in *Barber* and Protocol 2 does not apply to discrimination in relation to the right to join, ie gain access to, an occupational pension scheme, which is governed by the previous judgment *Bilka-Kaufhaus* (C-170/84), a well-known case, of which employers should have been aware.

In *Neath* v *Hugh Steeper* (C-152/91) different lump sum pension payments for men and women which were the conversion of periodic pension payments were held to be valid. Whilst benefits and payments must be equal this is not the case for the employers' contributions, as other factors other than a simple difference in sex are involved. The amount needed for the lump sum is determined by actuaries who base their figures on the fact that women live longer after retirement, so greater contributions are needed. This becomes a larger lump sum when converted. The ECJ held that the inequality in employers' contributions arising from actuarial factors such as life expectancy, which differed according to sex, was held not to be caught by Art 119 EC (now 157 TFEU).

In view of the *Barber* case law developments, in particular the judgments in *Coloroll* and *Birds Eye Walls* (C-200/91 and C-132/92), that certain pension arrangements escaped the applications of Art 141 EC (now 157 TFEU), the Council decided it was necessary to amend Directive 86/378 by Directive 96/97. This confirms that Directive 86/378, now Art 8(2) of Directive 2006/54, does not apply to occupational schemes where the benefits are financed by contributions paid by workers on a voluntary basis. It also means that pension supplements to bridge the age between the occupational pension age and the statutory pension age are acceptable, where the aim is to make equal or more nearly equal the overall amount of benefit paid to these persons compared to payments to the other sex in the same situation. The *Neath* judgment was also incorporated and the claim by men and women for a flexible pensionable age under the same conditions would not be incompatible with the Directive. It remains, however, a complex area of law.

Question 5

'Strange Fruit', a wholesale fruit merchant, advertise for a full-time permanent secretary and also for a temporary sales post for four months to provide cover for a member of staff on secondment to another workplace. All the existing secretarial positions in the company are part-time appointments.

The two main contenders for the permanent position are Tony and Astrid. Their qualifications are broadly equivalent but Astrid has slightly more experience, but not so much as to make her a clear favourite. In line with their policy of positive discrimination to appoint staff of the minority sex to posts predominantly staffed by the other sex, they decide to appoint Tony. As a part of that policy they have increased Tony's salary by 10% pro rata over and above that paid to the existing part-time secretaries and provided him with a 20% pension enhancement. The appointment is challenged by Astrid and the increased pay and pension payments have been questioned by Karen, an existing secretary. SF argue that their policy conforms with EU law and argue that the pension enhancement is linked to the state pension age and the fact that men generally work to an older age but die younger, so their policy helps to ensure that male employees get to enjoy the fruits of their labour in the shorter period of retirement likely to be available to them. The increased pay is to attract full-time workers, which, it is argued, is more cost-efficient for the employer.

In the interview for the temporary post, the applicant Clare was asked if there were any grounds which would prevent her from fulfilling all the duties of the contract during the busiest fruit sales period of spring and summer. She replied that there were no obstacles and was subsequently appointed, starting work on 1 May. Clare knew she was pregnant at the time of the interview and after just three weeks in work announced that she was due to give birth at the end of June and was taking maternity leave as from 1 June. When she left work one week later, she was dismissed and paid only for the time actually worked.

Advise the various parties of their rights under EU law.

Commentary

This question is included to take account of further case developments. Hence then, I will concentrate on these points and provide summary coverage only of the aspects of the question already covered in sufficient detail by the previous suggested answers. The novel aspects of this question are a revisit to the positive discrimination issue and the dismissal of Clare who applied and was appointed to a temporary position when pregnant but was subsequently dismissed when the pregnancy was revealed.

Answer plan

- Refer to **Art 157 TFEU**, especially **paragraph 4** and **Directive 2006/54**
- Outline issues arising and positive discrimination provisions
- Review case law of *Kalanke*, *Marschall* and *Badeck*
- Equal pay issue cases (*Jenkins*, *Bilka-Kaufhaus* and *Enderby*)
- Pregnant temporary worker dismissal cases (*Webb*, *Mahlberg* and *Tele Danmark*)

Suggested answer

This question is concerned with some of the more recent developments of equality law which has become one of the fundamental policies of EU substantive law. The issues which arise are the appointment of a worker on the basis of the application of a policy of positive discrimination, which then gives rise to Astrid's claim to equal access to employment under Directive 2006/54. It is also concerned with indirect discrimination between full-time and part-time workers and finally the dismissal of a pregnant woman from a temporary contract.

A limited form of positive discrimination is provided in Art 3 of Directive 2006/54 and paragraph (4) of Art 157 TFEU. Article 3 of the Directive provides that the Directive shall be without prejudice to measures to promote equal opportunity for men and women, in particular by removing existing inequalities which affect women's opportunities. It would seem therefore to concern women only but not exclusively, as seen in case law. Hence then, despite the actual words contained within it, it was not limited to women. Article 157(4) TFEU provides:

> With a view to ensuring full equality in practice between men and women in working life, the principle of equal treatment shall not prevent any Member State from maintaining or adopting measures providing for specific advantages in order to make it easier for the under-represented sex to pursue a vocational activity or to prevent or compensate for disadvantages in professional careers.

The Treaty Article is thus aimed to cover both men and women but is specifically addressed to the Member States. It would nevertheless have direct effects. The facts of the present case involve a private employer, therefore the Treaty Article would need to be applied if there were any doubts about the Directive. Article 3 of Directive 2006/54 provides that Member States may maintain or adopt measures within the meaning of Art 141(4) EC (now 157 TFEU) with a view to ensuring full equality in practice between men and women, thus backing up the amended Article in the Treaty.

It has already been observed in the cases of *Kalanke* (C-450/93), *Marschall* (C-409/95) and *Badeck* (C-158/97) that where a policy of positive discrimination is employed it should not automatically favour one sex and that procedures must be included within any such policy to ensure that an objective assessment of the individual candidates is undertaken. This position was made even clearer in the case of *Abrahamsson* (C-407/98) whereby a female was appointed to a university Chair in preference to a male applicant on the basis of a positive discrimination regulation and despite a clear vote in favour of a male applicant (5:3), his qualifications and the overall higher ranking of the male. The university contended that the difference was not so great as to breach the objectivity requirement. However, the ECJ held that EC (EU) law, primary or secondary, does not support appointments based on automatic preference for the underrepresented sex irrespective of whether the qualifications are better or worse and where no objective assessment of each candidate has taken place. Whether that would be enough in Astrid's case to support her claim for unlawful discrimination in access to employment contrary to Arts 1 and 4 of Directive 2006/54, is difficult to say with certainty here in the absence of more detailed facts. A reference to the ECJ may be needed.

What is clear from numerous cases and pronouncements of the ECJ, is that the additional salary for Tony as a full-timer in comparison with the female part-timers could only be accepted as lawful if objectively justified. (See the cases of *Jenkins* (96/80), *Bilka-Kaufhaus* (170/84) and *Enderby* (C-127/92).) Here, there does not appear to be an overwhelming objective reason to support this. The increase in pension is also to be regarded as pay following the *Barber* case (C-262/88) and must therefore also be at the same rate unless similarly objectively justified. It may also be argued that it is up to the pension fund actuaries to determine the pension payments and the amount needed to be paid into the pension fund and not for the employers themselves. Indeed, this will have already been taken into account in calculating payments, thus removing the need for the employer to do so, in which case it appears more like an unlawful discriminatory measure. Again, in the event of uncertainty here, a reference to the ECJ should be made.

The final issue here concerns the dismissal of the pregnant worker from a temporary post. However unjust it might be felt in certain quarters that the employer is suffering unduly in such a circumstance, a line of cases from the ECJ show clearly that the ECJ upholds fully the rights provided now by Directive 2006/54, Art 15 and Directive 92/85, Art 10 in protecting women workers from dismissal whilst pregnant including those on temporary contracts (see the cases of *Webb* (C-32/93), *Mahlberg* (C-207/98), and *Tele Danmark* (C-109/00)). In the last case, the pregnant worker had also not informed the employer of her pregnancy; however, the ECJ held quite clearly that 'Had the Community legislature wished to exclude fixed-term contracts, which represent a substantial proportion of the employment relationships, from the scope of those directives, it would have done so expressly.' The only distinguishing factor would be that in the present case, the employers specifically asked whether there would be any grounds on which the applicant could not fulfil the entire contract. Once again, only a reference to the ECJ on this point would determine whether it would make any difference to alter the previous view of the court. I would suggest it would not, particularly in the light of case C-320/01 *Busch* in which the pregnancy of a worker returning to duty was not revealed to the employer, although there is clearly scope for argument. Overall then, the employer appears to be in breach of EU law provisions for the actions it has undertaken.

Further reading

Bell, M and Waddington, W, 'Reflecting on Inequalities in European Equality Law' (2003) 28(3) EL Rev 349.

Burrows, N and Robinson, M, 'An Assessment of the Recast Equality Laws' (2007) 13 EL Rev 186.

Caracciolo di Torella, E and Masselot, A, 'Pregnancy, Maternity and the Organisation of Family Life: An Attempt to Classify the Case Law of the Court of Justice' (2001) 26 EL Rev 239.

Costello, C and Davies, G, 'The Case Law of the Court of Justice in the Field of Sex Equality Since 2000' (2006) 43 CML Rev 1567.

Masselot, A, 'The State of Gender Equality Law in the European Union' (2007) 13 ELJ 152.

Prechal, S, 'Equality of Treatment, Non-discrimination and Social Policy: Achievements in Three Themes' (2004) 41(2) CML Rev 533.

10

Mixed Subject Questions

Introduction

The questions in this chapter involve a consideration of more than one topic. This may be a combination of procedural actions or a mix of substantive law topics with a procedural action before the Court of Justice. It may well be that questions you will face will be formed in such a way. Inevitably, the mixed question will mean that there is less time that can be spent on each of the possible actions and that the answers will reflect this.

Question 1

'Whilst the doctrine of the supremacy of EU law is a logical if not a necessary inference from the EU Treaties, the same cannot be said of the doctrine of direct effects of EU law.'
  Discuss.

 Commentary

This is a combined topic question which concerns the now well-established doctrines of the supremacy of EU law and direct effects. First of all, both of these legal concepts need to be defined. So, with the above question you need to state clearly and concisely what you understand by the phrases 'the doctrine of the supremacy of EU law' and 'the doctrine of direct effect'. Both of these concepts are ones developed by the Court of Justice in leading cases of EU law including the notable cases of *Van Gend en Loos* (26/62) and *Costa* v *ENEL* (6/64).

You are first asked whether it is the case that it is 'a logical if not a necessary inference' and you have to determine exactly what this cryptic part of the question is demanding for an answer. It suggests the supremacy of EU law is logical, but that it is not a necessary inference from the Treaties. You must address both these contentions. Although the word 'logical' appears first you would be advised to address the part about the inference first, because this refers you to the

Treaty provisions. It also appears to me to make sense to consider whether the Treaties do provide for the supremacy before having to consider the logic of whether EU law is supreme. Then finally, you must decide whether and if so, how the Treaties logically provide for supremacy. Do this by reference to any help from the Treaty Articles and the ECJ view of these in case law. It is worthwhile pointing out now that following the entry into force of the 2007 Lisbon Treaty, supremacy has been acknowledged, albeit somewhat indirectly, in Declaration 17 attached to the amended Treaties.

This particular question is a variation on the question in Chapter 4 on the supremacy of EU law, with a twist in the tail, because in contrast to the position on supremacy, the converse is expressed to be the case with direct effects, ie it cannot be said the doctrine of direct effects is a logical if not a necessary inference. You therefore need to consider whether the doctrine is either logical or necessary.

Answer plan

- Define the doctrine of supremacy of EU law in the light of Treaty provisions
- Consider whether this is necessary or logical in the light of ECJ case law
- Define the doctrine of direct effects
- In the light of the case, consider whether this is either necessary or logical

Suggested answer

The doctrine of the supremacy will be considered first. The doctrine of the supremacy of EU law is one which has been developed by the Court of Justice in a series of cases, the most notable of which are *Van Gend en Loos* (26/62), *Costa v ENEL* (6/64) and the *Simmenthal* (106/77) case.

The question has already hinted that the Treaties do not expressly provide for supremacy, ie there is no Article which clearly states that EU law is supreme and by a direct reading of the Treaty you might not necessarily infer that EU law is supreme. However, whilst there is presently no express statement of supremacy in the Treaty, it can be argued that some of the Articles of the EC Treaty impliedly or logically require supremacy and now subsequent to the entry into force of the Lisbon Treaty, supremacy has been obliquely acknowledged in Declaration 17 attached to the Treaties which provides the opinion of the Commission legal Counsel that previous case law of the ECJ established supremacy.

Thus, a conclusion as to whether EU law supremacy is a logical conclusion to be drawn from the Treaties depends upon a consideration of some of their provisions and the Declaration. For example:

Art 4 (3) TEU (ex 10 EC), the good faith or fidelity clause;

Art 18 TFEU (ex 12 EC), the general prohibition of discrimination on the grounds of nationality;

Art 288 TFEU (ex 249 EC), in respect of the direct applicability of Regulations;

Art 344 TFEU (ex 292 EC), the obligation of Member States to submit only to Treaty dispute resolution; and

Art 260 TFEU (ex 228 EC), the requirement to comply with rulings of the Court of Justice.

Declaration 17 provides that 'The Conference recalls that, in accordance with well settled case law of the Court of Justice of the European Union, the Treaties and the law adopted by the Union on the basis of the Treaties have primacy over the law of Member States, under the conditions laid down by the said case law.'

So you could conclude that EU law logically requires supremacy but cannot state that the Treaties expressly or categorically imposes it except via Declaration 17.

The Court of Justice in the cases of *Van Gend en Loos, Costa v ENEL* and *Simmenthal*, amongst others, has held that EU law supremacy is a logical conclusion to reach. EU law should be supreme because of the transfer of powers from the Member States and, because it has its own law-making machinery, it must have precedence if the EU is going to work.

In the *Van Gend en Loos* case, the Court of Justice held that the Community (now Union) constitutes a new legal order of international law for the benefit of which the States have limited their sovereign rights. Further elaboration of the new legal order in *Van Gend en Loos* was given in the case of *Costa v ENEL*. The Court of Justice stressed the autonomous legal order of Community (EU) Law in contrast with ordinary international treaties. It held that the EEC Treaty has created its own legal system which became an integral part of the legal systems of the Member States and which their courts are bound to apply. Thus, by creating a Community (Union) of unlimited duration which has its own institutions, its own personality, its own legal capacity and more particularly real powers stemming from a limitation of sovereignty or a transfer of powers from the states to the Community (Union), the Member States have limited their sovereign rights and have created a body of law to bind their nationals and themselves. It is impossible, in the light of this, for the states to accord precedence to a unilateral and subsequent measure over a legal system accepted by them. The Court summed up its position:

It follows . . . that the law stemming from the treaty, an independent source of law, could not because of its special and original nature, be overridden by domestic legal provisions, however framed, without being deprived of its character as Community law and without the legal basis of the Community itself being called into question.

Therefore EU law is to be supreme over subsequent national law.

The case of *Simmenthal* (106/77) arises from a conflict between the Italian constitution and Community (EU) law. A lower court was faced with inconsistency between a Community (EU) law provision and a national provision but was aware that a reference to the Italian constitutional court would have the effect of subjecting Community (EU) law to national law, inconsistent with existent Community (EU) case law on the matter in the *Costa v ENEL* case. However, disregarding the national law was contrary to constitutional requirements. The Italian magistrate made a reference to the ECJ and asked whether subsequent national measures which conflict with Community (EU) law must be disregarded without waiting until those measures are formally repealed or declared unconstitutional. The ECJ firstly declared that the doctrine of direct effects of Community (EU) legislation was not dependent on any national constitutional provisions but a source of rights in themselves. Therefore, national courts which are called upon to apply provisions of Community (EU) law are under a duty to give full effect to those provisions including a refusal to apply conflicting national legislation, even if adopted subsequently. The ECJ also ruled that directly effective provisions of Community (EU) law also preclude the valid adoption of new legislative measures to the extent that they would be incompatible with Community (EU) provisions and that any inconsistent national legislation recognised by national legislatures as having legal effect would deny the effectiveness of the obligations undertaken by the Member State and imperil the existence of the Community (EU).

Hence, the Court of Justice in the cases of *Van Gend en Loos*, *Costa v ENEL* and *Simmenthal*, amongst others, has held that EU law supremacy is a logical inference to make from the Treaties.

The second part of the question requires a consideration of whether the doctrine of direct effects of EU law is a logical conclusion or a necessary inference.

Direct effects is the term given to judicial enforcement of rights arising from provisions of EU law which can be upheld in favour of individuals in the courts of the Member States. It describes the right to rely directly on EU law in the absence of national law or in the face of conflicting national law. Direct effects can apply to Articles of the Treaty, Regulations, Directives and Decisions, in fact any binding law in terms of Art 288 TFEU (ex 249 EC) and in some circumstances outside Art 288 TFEU as with international agreements. Certain criteria have to be fulfilled before the ECJ can declare a particular EU law provision to give rise to direct effects. These were determined by the ECJ in a series of cases commencing with the leading EU law case of *Van Gend en Loos* (26/62). In *Van Gend en Loos*, a private legal individual company challenged a new import duty imposed by the Dutch authorities and claimed it was contrary to Arts 12 and 13 EEC (now 30 TFEU). The Dutch authorities in their defence claimed that the obligation was one imposed by the Treaty on the Dutch state alone and could not be invoked by an individual of that state. The Court of Justice held that the institutions of the Community (EU) are endowed with sovereign rights, the exercise of which affects not only Member States but also their citizens and that Community (EU) law was capable of conferring rights on individuals which become part of their legal heritage. The provision must however:

be clear;

be precise;

require no further implementation on the part of the Member State; and

be complete.

There is nothing in the EU Treaties from which it could be logically concluded nor inferred that provisions of EU law could be held to have direct effects in certain circumstances. Whilst Treaty Articles and Regulations are directly applicable this does not mean to say that they can be invoked by individuals and Directives are in any case addressed to the Member States. The criteria by which direct effects may be established are entirely a judicial creation of the Court of Justice. However, it may be stated that direct effects are a logical and necessary inference from the supremacy of EU law. If an EU provision is supreme over inconsistent national law, to deny direct effects where appropriate would be illogical. It is to be inferred, therefore, directly effective law is supreme over national law.

Question 2

How and to what extent are the rights of individuals protected in the EU legal order?

 Commentary

This is a general overview question on the range of actions which are available to individuals to protect their rights in EU law. An underlying aspect of the question is that there are many new laws which have been created by the European Union directly affecting individuals by both bestowing advantages on them but also imposing duties and sometimes infringing their rights. The scope of these laws can be discovered from a review of the Treaties and EU legislation. Yet, the means by which individuals can protect their rights are less obvious. It would be useful to preface your answer with this concern.

In answering the question, you should broadly identify the range of legal activities encompassed by the EU. This can be done by briefly outlining the major areas of EU law included in the Treaty and secondary legislation which may affect individual rights.

Secondly, you should outline the procedures by which these rights can be protected in the EU legal order and where these rights can be protected, ie in which legal forums. It is to be noted that a new **Art 19(1) TEU** requires that 'member states shall provide remedies sufficient to ensure effective legal protection in the fields covered by Union law', but the importance of this in providing protection is yet to be established.

Finally a qualitative element is introduced by the term 'to what extent' which requires you to consider how well or how effectively these rights are protected in reality.

Answer plan

- Generally introduce the EU legal regime and its impact on individuals
- Outline the range of individual protective procedural rights in EU law
- Consider the actions which are heard directly by the ECJ
- Outline the ways individuals can seek protection before the national courts
- Consider the position of fundamental rights protection in the EU legal order
- Refer to the **Art 267 TFEU** reference procedure and conclude on the overall protection

Suggested answer

The European Union now covers vast tracts of the economic and increasingly the social spheres of the Member States' national jurisdictions. The Treaties and secondary law established under the Treaties thus straddle many areas of law and impose very many duties and rights. Individuals in the EU are therefore subject to very many new laws which emerge from both the Council and the Commission in Brussels, and to an increasing extent today have been subject to the influence of the European Parliament in the legislative process. They have created a new source of law, additional to the Member States' own laws and established protections of individual rights. Since the establishment of the EU, Union individuals have become subject to the legislative, executive and judicial authority of the Union. Concerns have then quite rightly been raised about the protections that individuals have in the face of this new legal source of authority, particularly as the democratic protection in the EU from the European Parliament is not as strong at the EU level as National Parliaments and political answerability in the Member States.

Thus, it is necessary first to define how the EU affects the individual and then to outline the legal protections available. The term 'individuals' is taken to mean both natural and legal persons in the Union who are concerned in some way with the substantive and procedural law of the EU.

Essentially, three different aspects need to be considered: the substantive rights under the various chapters of the Treaty; the procedural rights, ie the various actions that can be pursued in the Union courts; and a set of general fundamental rights.

The impact of the EU on individuals will be considered first of all. Individuals are affected by a vast range of substantive laws enacted by the EU. Legislation enacted in any of the areas of EU law can affect the rights of individuals. Legislation can be enacted to regulate agricultural activities, to ensure or standardise product or trading rules, to ensure the free movement of goods, to ensure that competition in the EU is being maintained, or to provide for the free movement of persons, to give just a few examples of the range of areas covered by the EU. This legislation can either promote or infringe individual rights. Whilst for the most part these laws impose duties on the Member States, they can also give rise to corresponding rights of individuals; see as a classic example the *Van Gend en Loos* case (26/62) and the establishment of the doctrine of direct effects by the Court of Justice.

Individuals may, as a result, consider their rights to have been infringed by the institutions of the Union in enacting these rules. Sometimes they can also be affected by the national implementation of EU law by Member States. Thus, individuals may need to be protected against the acts of the Union institutions and the Member States or to challenge Member States where they have failed to implement EU law. Protections need to be considered in the actions both against the Union and the Member States.

The difficulties experienced in pursuing these actions or in terms of the question posed, the extent of the protection, will be considered at the same time.

The main forms of protection are provided by the EU Treaties which outlines a number of actions which, in varying circumstances and subject to differing criteria, may aid an individual in the protection of rights. Actions against the EU can be made under a number of Treaty provisions.

Article 263 TFEU (ex 230 EC) allows a direct challenge against legislative acts of the institutions where they are unlawful and the infringement can be classified under one of the four grounds listed in the Article itself. This action, however, can only be used by individuals in limited circumstances. It cannot be used to challenge Regulations and can only be employed to challenge an act addressed to that person or which is of direct and individual concern to them, and against a regulatory act which is of direct concern to them and does not entail implementing measures. There is a time limit of two months in which actions can be brought following the fifteenth day after publication in the Official Journal.

Article 265 TFEU (ex 232 EC) provides an action against the institutions of the EU for a failure to act but this can only be employed by the potential addressee of the legal act, or those, in view of more recent case law, which are in an analogous position as applicants under Art 263 TFEU, in that they are directly and individually concerned with a potential act. Articles 263 and 265 TFEU are regarded as particularly difficult actions in which individuals are unlikely to succeed. They seem more designed for use by the Member States and the institutions of the Union.

An indirect challenge to an EU Regulation can be made under Art 277 TFEU (ex 241 EC) but this is only available providing a related matter of EU law is already being adjudicated in the Court of Justice and, again, is of limited use to individuals. Of more use, and more likely to be successful to assist individuals, is an action for damages where loss has been suffered as a result of the action or act of the Union and its institutions, which can be made under Art 240 (2) TFEU (ex 288(2) EC). However, where legislative acts are concerned, the damage must be the result of a sufficiently serious breach of a superior rule of law for the protection of an individual or as appears to be developing a sufficiently serious breach of a rule of law intended to confer rights on individuals, something which has been demonstrated in the case law of the Court of Justice to be extremely difficult to prove.

All of the above actions take place before the General Court or the Court of Justice.

As far as the Member States are concerned and the national courts, individuals can defend their rights arising from EU law generally against the inconsistent legislation of the Member States in the national courts or where Member States have failed to implement EU law and seek to prosecute individuals for breaches of national law; see the *Van Gend en Loos* (26/62), *Ratti* (148/78), *von Colson* (14/83), *Francovich* (C-6 and 9/90) and *Factortame* (C-213/89 and 46/93) cases. The latter cases highlight the developments by which individuals can sue a Member State where he or she has suffered damage which was the result of the Member State's breach of EU law. Individuals can also be protected incidentally by EU legislation which has not been complied with by a Member State in an action involving another individual, as in the case of *CIA Security* v *Signalson* (C-194/94). They may also be able to count on the protection horizontally against other individual of general principles of EU law such as discrimination as in the *Mangold* case (C-144/04). The Member States now are specifically required by a new Art 19(1) TEU to 'provide remedies sufficient to ensure effective legal protection in the fields covered by Union law'; however, the importance of this in providing protection is yet to be established.

Individuals can also defend their rights against EU law provisions if these unlawfully affect individual rights by infringing fundamental rights of an individual. Fundamental rights for the protection of individuals can be brought into play in the course of any of the procedural actions to enforce individual rights in substantive areas of EU law. These have been recognised by the Court of Justice because they are contained in many of the Member States' constitutions and also the European Convention for the protection of Human and Fundamental Rights has been held by the Court of Justice to apply in the EU legal order and Art 6(1) and (3) of the Treaty on European Union now obliges the EU to conform to it and to observe the Charter of Fundamental Rights of the European Union attached in a Declaration to the Treaties by the 2007 Lisbon Reform Treaty, which will be binding if it comes into force, although with opt-outs for Poland and the UK.

In support of all of these actions and before the national courts, individuals may, if necessary, request that a reference to the Court of Justice be made using the preliminary ruling procedure of Art 267 TFEU (ex 234 EC). It is through this that leading principles of EU law have been developed by the ECJ and which have greatly enhanced the protection of individual rights in the Union. One only has to consider the cases of *Van Gend en Loos* (26/62) or *Francovich* (C-6 and 9/90) to see how the ECJ has secured the rights of individuals.

In conclusion, the development of direct effects in actions before the national courts may be regarded as far more successful than the use of direct actions before the Court of Justice and potentially more useful, in respect of Member States' breaches, is the action to claim damages from the Member State for loss under the *Francovich*-type actions.

Question 3

On 1 May 2009 the Council adopted a (fictitious) Directive concerned with the protection of young persons in employment. The Directive, inter alia, provides that no person under 18 years old shall be required to work at night, and that any such person who is dismissed by his/her employer for refusing to work at night when requested to do so shall be entitled to 'an appropriate remedy from a national court or tribunal, which may include compensation'. Member States were given one year in which to implement the Directive.

The UK Government was opposed to the Directive on ideological grounds and actually voted against its adoption in the Council, where the Directive, in accordance with the Treaty provision on which it was based, was adopted by a qualified majority vote. For this reason, and because it is concerned by the possibly adverse economic consequences for employers of the Directive, the UK Government has not yet taken any steps to implement the Directive.

Jake, who is 17 years old, has been employed in a Ministry of Defence munitions factory for 12 months. As a consequence of the need to reduce the size of the manufacturing facility and economise on production, Jake has been asked to work at night on the newly established night shift. Not wishing to ruin a happy social life, Jake has refused to do so. As a result he has been threatened with dismissal unless he complies. Advise:

(a) the Commission of what steps it can take against the UK to ensure that the Directive is implemented;

(b) Jake as to whether he can take legal proceedings to uphold his legal position and obtain compensation if dismissed.

Would your advice to Jake differ if the factory where he worked was in private ownership?

For the purposes of this question, you should ignore actual Directive 94/33!

Commentary

This problem question requires you to consider two main judicial procedures. The first one involves a consideration of an Art 258 TFEU (ex 226 EC) action by the Commission against the Member State for a failure to implement the Directive. The second one concentrates on Jake's ability to take action in the national courts using an Art 267 TFEU (ex 234 EC) reference to the ECJ if necessary

Apart from a brief discussion of the procedure involved in the two particular actions, the substantive issues which arise in the problem must also be considered.

First, it is necessary to determine whether there has been a breach by the UK or whether they can rely on any defence for their lack of action. Secondly, it must be determined whether Jake can rely on the direct effects of the Directive and whether there is a remedy he can seek, both to defend himself against the threatened dismissal or to obtain damages from the employer, if dismissed.

You are also asked to consider the situation where the employer is a private employer and this requires a discussion of horizontal direct effects and the consequences for employees of private employers. You should then follow this with suggestions on how these difficulties may be overcome by Jake.

Answer plan

- After a brief consideration of facts, outline the Art 258 TFEU enforcement action
- Consider the chances of success of the Art 258 TFEU action by the Commission
- Consider Jake's ability to rely on the Directive using direct effects
- Apply the *von Colson* and *Marshall II* cases to the compensation claim
- Where the employer is private, indirect effects must be considered
- As an alternative remedy, state liability should be considered

Suggested answer

The UK Government was given, along with the other Member States, one year to implement the Directive. That year expired on 1 May 2010. In the circumstances, the Commission would be entitled to commence a formal Art 258 TFEU action, if behind the scenes persuasion failed to convince the UK that it should implement the Directive in full. Article 258 TFEU states: 'if the Commission considers that a Member State has failed to fulfil an obligation under the Treaties, it shall deliver a reasoned opinion on the matter'. The Commission will inform the Member State and give them the opportunity to answer the allegation or correct its action or inaction before the Art 258 TFEU action continues. Following the reply from the Member State or after a reasonable time where no reply is received, the Commission will then deliver a reasoned opinion which records the reasons for the failure of the Member State. If the Member State should then fail to comply with the reasoned opinion of the Commission within a reasonable time, the Commission then has the discretionary right to bring the matter before the Court of Justice. The judgment of the Court of Justice is merely declaratory but the Member State is required under Art 260 TFEU to take the necessary measures to comply with the judgment.

There would appear to be no defence that could be raised by the UK that would justify its non-compliance as Art 4(3) TEU (ex 10 EC) requires Member States to fulfil all Community law obligations and Art 344 TFEU (ex 292 EC) obliges Member States not to seek other solutions to disputes. The UK should therefore comply and implement the Directive.

If it does not do this, a further action may lie against the UK, by the Commission under Art 258 TFEU, for a breach of Art 260 TFEU. Article 260 TFEU now provides that sanctions can be requested by the Commission in an action to establish that the Member States have failed to comply with a previous judgment of the Court of Justice. Thus, if the UK has still failed to implement the Directive and the further action to establish that it also failed to comply with the Court of Justice has taken place, the UK may be fined by the Court of Justice. It is, however, extremely unlikely that the matter would go so far and it is more likely that the UK will have complied either before the first action or, at least, after the judgment of the Court of Justice in the first action.

Turning to Jake, he is advised to seek an action in a UK industrial tribunal to prevent the employer from dismissing him, basing his right to refuse to work nights on the EU Directive or to commence an action for compensation for unfair dismissal in the event of his dismissal. In order, however, to rely on EU law, it must either have been implemented in the UK, which it has not, or give rise to direct effects.

Directives can give rise to direct effects providing they satisfy the criteria as laid down in *Van Gend en Loos* (26/62) and subsequent cases. The criteria are that in order for a particular provision of EU law to be upheld before a national court in the face of non-implementation or incorrect implementation of national law the provisions:

have to be clear;

have to be precise;

should leave no discretion to the authorities of the Member State;

are unconditional; and

require no further implementation by either the Union or the Member State.

The special concerns of Directives and the time limits given for their implementation were considered in *Publico Ministero v Ratti* (148/78) which concerned the prosecution by the Italian authorities for breaches of national law concerning product labelling. Mr Ratti had complied with two Community (EU) Directives; however, the expiry period for implementation of one of which had not expired.

The Court held he could rely on the one for which the time period had expired provided it satisfied the other requirements, but not for the Directive whose implementation period had not expired. So, when the time period expires an individual can rely on the Directive providing it fulfils the criteria.

In the present case, the obligation states quite clearly that no person under 18 years shall be required to work at night and the time period for implementation of one year has expired, therefore the Directive has direct effects which can be relied on by Jake to avoid dismissal. If, however, he has been dismissed, the Directive provides that an appropriate remedy must be provided. Whilst not as clear as the first part, it has been held in the case of *von Colson* (14/83) and the second *Marshall* ([1986] 1 CMLR 688) case that the Member States' courts are required to ensure that an adequate remedy, in this case compensation, must be awarded. Jake will thus be entitled to receive adequate damages.

The advice to Jake would differ if the factory where he worked was in private ownership because in the case of *Marshall* (152/84), the ECJ held that Directives could not be enforced against other individuals but could only be enforced vertically against the Member State to whom they were addressed, ie there are no horizontal direct effects stemming from the Directive. Therefore, Jake would have to try pleading the principle under *von Colson*. The ECJ held in *von Colson* that, although a Directive may not be horizontally directly effective, the Member States' courts should take the provisions of the Directive into account when applying national law. However, there are no rights in national law, so a national court cannot interpret according to EU law, thus the *Marleasing* (C-106/89) and *Kolpinghuis* (80/86) cases should be applied to state that there are general obligations under Arts 4(3) TEU and 288 TFEU (ex 10 and 249 EC) for the Member States to ensure compliance with EU law. But if the UK court was unable or unwilling to rely on national legislation to interpret he might have to attempt suing the state to obtain damages under the principle established in the *Francovich* (C-6 and 9/90) case for liability arising from the failure to implement a Directive. If an individual suffers damage as a result of the failure of a Member State to implement a Directive, the Member State may be liable to pay damages, providing the Directive itself defined and conferred a right on individuals, the content of which was clear.

This principle appears to be satisfied in the present case. Furthermore, the Court in *Brasserie du Pêcheur* (C-46 and 48/93) held that all manner of breaches of EU law by any of the three arms of state could lead to liability to individuals. Thus it expands the circumstances which might give rise to liability in cases where otherwise there would be no enforceable rights because of either no horizontal direct effect or even no direct effect at all. But the focus has been moved to the seriousness of the breach. *Factortame III* (C-46 and 48/93) introduced the revised criteria that the breach must be analogous to that applied to liability of the EU institutions under Art 340(2) (ex 288(2) EC). This is known as the Shöppenstedt Formula and in order for liability to arise on the part of the Member State, there must have been a sufficiently serious breach of a superior rule of law designed for the protection of individuals. This has provoked further case law to help decide how serious a breach is required for Member States to incur liability. *British Telecom* (C-392/93) takes a less generous view of what constitutes a breach but this can be contrasted with the *Hedley Lomas* case (C-5/94) where a mere infringement will invoke potential liability. Thus, if there is a breach, Member States must compensate according to the principles established in *Francovich*. Finally, damages must be adequate to reflect the loss suffered. It may be concluded that there appears to be sufficient alternative possibilities for Jake to receive some form of compensation against a private employer for their unlawful dismissal.

Question 4

On 20 October 2010, the Council adopted a Regulation, to take effect on 1 January 2011, under which the sales of sugar beet to food and drinks manufacturers were to be subsidised in order to reduce the Community's increasing sugar mountain. Sweetness Ltd is an aspartamine (an artificial sweetener) manufacturer and fears that the business will suffer as a result of this subsidy.

On 10 November 2010, Sweetness Ltd wrote to the Council asking it to withdraw the Regulation on the ground that in adopting the Regulation, the Council had failed to observe the principle of non-discrimination in Art 40(2) TFEU.

On 5 January 2011, the Council replied to Sweetness Ltd saying it understood why Sweetness Ltd was aggrieved but considered there was no alternative but to adopt the Regulation.

The next day Sweetness Ltd wrote to the Commission asking it to bring an action against the Council under Art 263 TFEU. Two weeks later the Commission replied to Sweetness Ltd saying that it did not consider the Council to be in breach of the EC Treaty.

What actions, if any, can Sweetness Ltd take against either the Commission or the Council before the Court of Justice?

 Commentary

This question requires you to consider the possible actions which may be attempted by the applicant arising from the factual circumstances. The problem which can be identified and which has caused Sweetness Ltd to take action is the passing of an EU Regulation which provides subsidies for sugar sales. Thus you need to outline the problem and the possible remedies which may be available and then go through those possible actions in turn, commenting on the chances that the individual may have under each one. In light of the fact that there is very limited factual information supplied, many of the courses of action will be somewhat speculative; however, you should still give at least an outline of the possible courses of action and the problems arising and reasons why the action is likely to be unsuccessful.

Answer plan

- Outline the facts and the range of possible remedial actions
- Consider the **Art 263 TFEU** application to annul the Regulation or letters
- Consider **Art 265 TFEU** actions against the Council and Commission
- Consider the **Art 277 TFEU** incidental challenge to the Regulation
- Consider an action for damages under **Art 340 TFEU** from a breach of **Art 40 TFEU**
- As an alternative, an **Art 267 TFEU** reference from a national court could lie

Suggested answer

The problem, as far as Sweetness Ltd is concerned, is that an EU Regulation has been passed which provides subsidies for the sale of sugar. The effect will be to reduce the price of sugar and thus increase its competitiveness, particularly in relation to manufacturers of artificial sweeteners who will probably lose sales and profits as a result. The informal moves Sweetness has made have been of no success, therefore the possibilities of the following formal actions must be considered.

Before the Court of Justice the possible actions are: a direct challenge to the Regulation as an act of the institutions under Art 263 TFEU (ex 230 EC) or a challenge to the letters written by the Council and Commission; an action under Art 265 TFEU (ex 232) requiring the Council to remove the Regulation; an action under Art 265 TFEU requiring the Commission to take action against the Council; an action under Art 277 TFEU (ex 241 EC), the indirect challenge to EU Regulations; and an action for damages under Art 340(2) TFEU (ex 288(2) EC).

(a) The action under Art 263 TFEU to challenge the Regulation

Overcoming the admissibility hurdle in respect of time limits and *locus standi* are the biggest stumbling blocks with this possibility. Article 263 TFEU imposes a two-month time limit in which actions should be taken. The Regulation was passed on 20 October and the earliest date that a possible challenge could be made is 20 January given that the letter to the Commission was written on 6 January and the reply was written two weeks later. This is three months after the Regulation was enacted and thus outside the time limit; even with the allowance of the Court of Justice from its rules of procedure of a further 15 days, it will still be too late. Thus, an action under Art 263 TFEU will be inadmissible without the need to discuss the difficulties of individuals challenging Regulations.

Sweetness would not be able to challenge the letters written by the Commission and Council under Art 263 TFEU as they are not reviewable acts within the meaning of Art 263 TFEU unless they can be shown to alter the legal position of the Company; see the *Noordwijks Cement Accord* case (8–11/66). On the facts, there is no alteration of the Company's legal position which remains the same.

(b) An action under Art 265 TFEU requiring the Council to act to remove the Regulation

This is also doomed to failure because of the strict *locus standi* requirements imposed by the Treaty. Individuals can only challenge acts which could and should have been addressed to them. As Regulations are normative acts they cannot be addressed to individuals; see *Lord Bethell* v *Commission* (246/81) and *Holzt* v *Council* (134/73). Trying to plead that the matter is nevertheless of direct and individual concern will only help if it can be shown that the Regulation would have directly and individually concerned the applicant (*T Port* (C-68/95)). Regulations do not directly and individually concern individuals. Furthermore, where the Council has written and advised that it has decided to do nothing, this definition of position by the Council would satisfy the terms of Art 265 TFEU even if admissible and the action would be dismissed.

(c) An action under Art 265 TFEU requiring the Commission to take action

An individual cannot force the Commission to take Art 263 TFEU proceedings as the Commission has a discretion under the terms of the Article. Again, the action would fail because Sweetness would be seeking the adoption of an act which they were not entitled to claim; see *Mackprang* v *Commission* (15/71). Even if the action were admissible, the Commission has defined its position and thus brought an end to the proceedings; see the *Lütticke* case (48/65).

(d) A challenge under Art 277 TFEU to annul Community Regulations

This would also be rejected by the ECJ to challenge the Regulation if it was made directly and not in the course of some other proceedings before the Court of Justice (see *Wöhrmann* v *Commission* (31 and 33/62)). This might be done in the course of the final possible action against the Council or Commission for damages.

(e) An action for damages under Art 340(2) TFEU

The Court of Justice is given jurisdiction under Art 268 TFEU (ex 235 EC) to consider actions for damages brought by individuals under Art 340(2) TFEU. However, in order to be successful a number of criteria have been identified which must be fulfilled. These are that an act or omission on the part of the institutions must be shown to have caused damage to the applicants. Furthermore, in cases which involve a legislative act, which necessarily involve a choice of economic policy on the part of the Union, a sufficiently serious breach of a superior rule of law for the protection of individuals must be shown; see the *Schöppenstedt* case (5/71) or now following the *Bergaderm* case (C-352/98P), a rule conferring rights on individuals.

In the present case the rule of law for the protection of individuals is the principle of non-discrimination and there is even a Treaty Article which requires that there be no discrimination between suppliers, *viz* Art 40(2) TFEU which has been pleaded by the applicants. In the Gritz and *Quellmehl* (*Dumortier Frères*) cases (64 and 113/76), the ending of the subsidy was held to be a breach of the principle of non-discrimination because it was retained on starch which was in direct competition.

The next requirement to ascertain is whether the breach is sufficiently serious. Sufficiently serious has been defined as 'manifest and grave' (*HNL* case (83/76)), and further as 'verging on the arbitrary' (*KSH Isoglucose* case (143/77)). A breach of the rule on its own is not enough. In order to determine whether the breach was sufficiently serious a number of criteria must be considered. Things to look at are the nature and the effect of the breach. For example, in the *Gritz* and *Quellmehl* cases the Court looked at the numbers affected, and the extent of the loss suffered and the seriousness of the damage caused, ie is it far beyond the risks normally associated with business? However, in *Mulder* (C-104/89 and 37/90) the presence of a large group of claimants did not defeat a claim although a serious breach still had to be demonstrated and that there was no higher public interest for the Union.

In the *HNL* case, which concerned the requirement to buy milk products rather than soya products, the increase in production costs was limited. The Court of Justice considered whether the company could pass on the increases with little loss of profit; if not, then this points towards serious, but if they can, then it is not sufficiently serious. The damage must go beyond the risks normally associated with business, but in the *KSH Isoglucose* case (143/77) although the damage was beyond normal, including causing the liquidation of some of the companies involved, the breach was not flagrant and therefore not verging on the arbitrary. The damage sustained must also be a direct consequence of an action or omission of the Union.

In the *Sofrimport* case (C-152/88) involving the import of Chilean apples which were on the high seas when the Regulation took effect, the Court of Justice held it will look at the number of people affected, the degree of loss and most importantly whether there is a Union interest involved. The *Sofrimport* case was held to involve a closed group because no other could be similarly affected after the date of the Regulation.

In this case it is unlikely that the breach will go beyond that considered to be inherent business risks given the *KSH Isoglucose* case. In this case the Union interest in reducing the sugar mountain may be considered to outweigh the losses caused.

The action may give an opportunity to challenge the Regulation indirectly, outside the time limits under Art 263 TFEU, because it has breached the principle of non-discrimination under Art 40(2) TFEU, which would satisfy the requirements of Art 277 TFEU. The substantive grounds from Art 263 TFEU are employed. If the Court of Justice, despite the previous expressed view of the Commission, held it to be in breach of the Treaty, it will hold the Regulation to be voidable and inapplicable in the case. So, despite the fact it may be held inapplicable, damages may still not be payable as the breach may still not satisfy the test of being sufficiently serious; see *HNL* v *Council and Commission* (83/76).

The final possibility is that, if there is a national element by which an action was taking place in the national courts, the company may raise the possibility of the Regulation being unlawful and ask for a reference to be made from the national court to the Court of Justice under Art 267 TFEU (ex 234 EC) to question the validity of the Treaty. However, it is still up to the adjudication of the Court of Justice to decide whether the Regulation has breached Art 40 TFEU and the same considerations as have already been noted will apply.

Question 5

Prior to the General Election and in view of increasing concern about the numbers of migrant workers taking up employment in the UK, the Government introduced an Act of Parliament under which it temporarily suspended the right of foreign workers to enter the UK to take up employment. The Act says that it applies regardless of any provision of the European Communities Act 1972. Arturo, an Italian, was appointed to a post in a hospital just before the Act came into force. He was refused entry to the UK to take up his post. He applies to the High Court for a declaration that he is entitled to enter the UK and that the UK legislation is incompatible with EU law. He also complains to the Commission, who notify the UK Government that they consider them to be in breach by having introduced their law in contravention of Art 45 TFEU. The Commission has received many complaints from others in the same situation as Arturo, who have now been told that unless they can take up employment within two weeks their jobs will be readvertised.

Comment on the following issues:

(a) What is necessary on the part of the Commission to bring an action under Art 258 TFEU (ex 226 EC) to an effective conclusion in securing the UK Government's compliance with EU law?

(b) What arguments in defence can be advanced by the UK Government?

(c) What remedies are available to Arturo and how effective are they likely to be in securing his rights?

(d) What additional measures could be requested in the course of proceedings by the Commission and Arturo?

(e) Would your answers to (a) and (c) differ if the UK Government had already been declared to be in breach following Art 258 TFEU proceedings in respect of the new UK law?

Commentary

This is a slightly tricky question in that it is a hybrid question consisting of a problem to be solved but set in a series of questions. As with other questions in this chapter it also covers a number of the judicial actions in the EU legal order. The question also includes the supremacy of EU law in the UK legal order. During these aspects, the structure you need to have for your answer has been pretty much set by the question itself.

You should start with a brief overview of the factual issues arising from the text of the question which needs to be addressed and then in turn each of the questions posed should be answered. Inevitably, as you are being asked to provide information on a number of topics your answers will be brief, for the most part. Thus, the Commission enforcement action should be outlined, followed by the possible defences of the UK Government. Arturo's own possible remedies should then be outlined and a view taken as to how effective you think the various actions and remedies are. Point (d) asks you to suggest additional measures. This implies interim measures. Finally, you are asked to address a slight alternative whereby the Commission has already been successful in obtaining a declaration from the ECJ that the UK is in breach of its Treaty obligation. You are asked to consider whether this would make a difference to either the Commission or Arturo.

Answer plan

- Outline the factual issues arising and the legal provisions involved
- Consider the efficacy of the Art 258 TFEU enforcement action by the Commission
- Assess Arturo's remedies in view of the deliberate breach of EU law
- An action for damages under state liability must be considered
- Consider interim measures in the Commission's and Arturo's actions
- To conclude, assess whether a prior Art 258 TFEU action will make a difference

Suggested answer

There is a UK national statute stating that no more foreign workers will be accepted into the UK which appears to be in breach of the UK EU law obligation of Art 45 TFEU (ex 39 EC). It also states that it applies regardless of the ECA 1972, which then is seeking to protect itself from interpretation or construction by the ECA 1972. Arturo has been appointed to a position before the Act came into force but was refused entry to the UK. He has applied to a national court for a declaration that the UK is in breach of EU law and has complained to the Commission to encourage them to take action.

(a) The Art 258 TFEU 226 action by the Commission

The Commission as a part of its duties under Art 17 TEU (ex 211 EC) should guard the Treaty. There would certainly be an Art 258 TFEU action open to the

Commission against the UK for failing to comply with its EU law obligations under Arts 4(3) TEU and 45 TFEU (ex 10 and 39 EC).

Basically there are four stages of an Art 258 TFEU action:

1. Suspicion of the infringement and informal proceedings by the Commission.

2. Informing the Member State by formal notice and asking it to submit its observations.

3. The formal issue of a reasoned opinion containing legal arguments, after the Commission has considered there is a breach.

4. If the Commission considers that the Member State is not in compliance the matter would be submitted to the ECJ which would eventually be concluded by a judgment of the ECJ.

In view of the serious and blatant nature of the breach by the UK in this case, it is all but certain that the ECJ would declare a breach of EU law by the UK (see *Commission v UK (Re: Nationality of Fishermen)* (C-246/89)). A Member State is under a duty under Art 260 TFEU (ex 228 EC) to comply with the judgment of the ECJ but if the Member State fails to comply and breaches this duty, it can only be remedied by another Art 258 TFEU action to try to get the Member State to comply.

The drawbacks of such action are that an Art 258 TFEU process from start of judicial proceedings before the ECJ to judgment can take anything from 18 months to two or three years or longer depending on the outcome and how quickly the Member State responds and reacts to the various stages of the procedure or the judgment. In total with both actions, it could take five years and potentially longer. However, at the end of this process this time, the Member State can be fined by the ECJ for a breach of its obligations. The Commission action under Art 258 TFEU will be effective in the long run, if not in the short term, as most Member States do comply with the judgment of the ECJ and so far fines have been needed to be levied in a few cases, eg *Commission v Greece* (C-387/97), *Commission v Spain* (C-278/01) and *Commission v France* (C-304/02). So the action is ultimately likely to secure compliance with EU law.

(b) Arguments of UK Government

Under the TFEU, there are no specific rules which could be seized on by the UK and only general arguments to defend an alleged breach of an EU law obligation. These have been comprehensively rebutted by the ECJ in its case law. All sorts of argument have been put forward in the past. Few seem particularly relevant here. Perhaps, a defence from international law of economic necessity but this was rejected in *Commission v Italy* (Art Treasures case) (48/71). The only real defence to succeed is that there was no breach on the facts or where the defence fits into exemptions allowed in the Treaty, eg Art 45(3) or (4) (ex 39(3) or (4) EC). This does not appear to be the case here.

(c) What remedies are available to Arturo?

He may notify the Commission in the hope that they take action, which he has already done but, possibly more effective, are actions he can take on his own behalf.

First of all, he can seek to rely on the direct effects of Art 45 TFEU, which we know previously from the *Van Duyn* case (41/74) does give rise to direct effects.

Arturo has already commenced an action in the UK courts by an application to the High Court in which he is challenging the UK rules. If the UK court is reluctant to recognise the direct effects, he should request a reference to the ECJ under Art 267 TFEU (ex 234 EC). However, both the attempt to rely on direct effects and getting a reference to the ECJ depend on the cooperation of the high court in recognising the supremacy of EU law over UK law and applying it in the face of the UK Act which states it is not subject to the ECA interpretation. The question here would be whether the UK court would follow EU law or national law. If the Court follows the lead of the House of Lords in *Factortame* ([1991] 1 AC 603) or the more recent case of *R Jackson v AG* [2006] AC 262, the answer should be yes, in which case direct effects would be recognised and Arturo would be able to rely on them to secure entry to the UK and his post in the UK. If the court is not prepared to follow EU law and acts in accordance with the obiter by Lord Denning in the case of *McCarthy's v Smith* ([1979] ICR 785), then Arturo will have trouble. In this case, Denning considered that with regard to an express or intentional repudiation of the Treaty or expressly acting inconsistently, the courts would be bound to follow the express and clear intent of Parliament to repudiate the Treaty or a section of it by the subsequent Act, in which case Arturo would be obliged to request that national law be interpreted according to EU law along *von Colson* (14/83) guidelines and, if this is also refused, he should request an Art 267 TFEU reference. However, the reality would be that if the court was inclined to apply UK law in preference to EU law, then it would not be likely to want to make an Art 267 TFEU reference and the matter ends there for Arturo. It would really be down to the judges' views in the UK court and as this has not yet been tested in a UK court, it would be pure speculation.

If direct effects were not recognised and upheld, Arturo is likely to lose his job and would thus be put in a position of having suffered loss. There would then be the question of whether Arturo and other persons in a similar position to him could recover damages from the UK authorities. The case of *Francovich* (C-6 and 9/90) would be then applicable here. This referred to the failure to implement a Directive which gave rise to liability to give damages. But a difference here exists, it is not the absence of any implementing measures but that a national law is in conflict. Does *Francovich* apply to such situations? Yes, and it is arguably a stronger case where there has been a breach of a Treaty Article, as confirmed by *Brasserie du Pecheur* and *Factortame III* cases (C-46 and 48/93) that an action for damages lies against all breaches by a state of community law obligations but subject an action to further criteria. The breach must be analogous to that applied to liability of the EU institutions under Art 340(2) TFEU (ex 288(2) EC). This is known as the Shöppenstedt Formula and in order for liability to arise on the part of the Member State, there must have been a sufficiently serious breach of a superior rule of law designed for the protection of individuals. In our case, the breach is quite blatant and it is argued that all the criteria are satisfied here. The breach would seem to be sufficiently serious (see the *Hedley Lomas* case C-5/94).

What at the end of the day does this secure for Arturo? The national courts must entertain this action or make a reference to the ECJ if in doubt. Certainly the new Act does not preclude the national courts from following EC law with regard to a *Francovich* action and it is likely, therefore, that Arturo would be successful in obtaining compensation, but not the job.

The answer from the EU perspective would be that the UK court should disapply the application of the UK law, with or without an interim order from the ECJ, whilst the substantive action is going on, to determine whether the UK law is contrary to EU law. This would of course be answered that it is not.

(d) Additional measures

Interim measures could be asked for by the Commission in its action under Art 279 TFEU (ex 243 EC). The ECJ may prescribe any necessary interim measures in any case before it. They have been used in Art 258 TFEU actions in the past. See in particular *Commission* v *UK* (*Re: Nationality of Fishermen*) (*Factortame*) (246/90R). The interim measures then would be the order to suspend the national legislation in doubt.

The same would count in Arturo's case. If a reference was being made to the Court of Justice, then interim measures, ie an injunction to suspend the allegedly unlawful measures by the UK Government, could be requested.

(e) Prior **Art 258 TFEU** proceedings

If there had already been a successful Art 258 TFEU action by the Commission, then the subsequent Commission action to secure compliance would certainly be at least two years further ahead so it would speed up the eventual compliance by the UK. However, it would not affect the inevitable result.

Again, whilst probably not affecting the result, from the EU point of view with Arturo, it would certainly make clear to the national courts what the outcome should be.

The final conclusion is that both actions are likely to be effective but that the national court action and Art 267 TFEU reference is potentially quicker, unless there is outright intransigence on the part of the UK judiciary and they refuse to either apply EU law or make a reference to the ECJ. Thus far, however, the UK judges have not been given the opportunity to do this.

Bibliography

A limited and selective list of standard texts only on EU law is provided here. For more extensive reading, consult the texts listed.

Amato, G and Ehlermann, C-D (eds), *EC Competition Law: A Critical Assessment* (Oxford: Hart Press, 2007).

Barnard, C, *The Substantive Law of the EU* 3rd edn (Oxford: Oxford University Press, 2010).

Barnard, C, *EC Employment Law* 3rd edn (Oxford: Oxford University Press, 2006).

Chalmers, C, Davies, G and Monti, G, *European Union Law* 2nd edn (Cambridge: Cambridge University Press, 2010).

Fairhurst, J, *Law of the European Union* 8th edn (Harlow: Pearson Press, 2010).

Foster, N, *Foster on EU Law* 2nd edn (Oxford: Oxford University Press, 2009).

Foster, N, *Directions on EU Law* 2nd edn (Oxford: Oxford University Press, 2010).

Foster, N (ed), *EU Treaties and Legislation* 21st edn (Oxford: Oxford University Press, 2010).

Furse, M, *Competition Law of the EC and UK* 6th edn (Oxford: Oxford University Press, 2008).

Hartley, T, *The Foundations of European Community Law* 7th edn (Oxford: Clarendon Press, 2010).

Horspool, M and Humphreys, M, *European Union Law* 6th edn (Oxford: Oxford University Press, 2010).

Jones, A and Sufrin, B, *EC Competition Law* 3rd edn (Oxford: Oxford University Press, 2007).

Steiner, J, Woods, L and Twigg-Flesner, C, *EU Law* 10th edn (Oxford: Oxford University Press, 2009).

Szyszczak, E and Cygan, A, *Understanding EU Law* 2nd edn (London: Sweet & Maxwell, 2008).

Tridimas, T, *The General Principles of EC Law* 2nd edn (Oxford: Oxford University Press, 2006).

Ward, A, *A Critical Introduction to European Law* 3rd edn (Cambridge: Cambridge University Press , 2009).

Ward, A, *Judicial Review and the Rights of Private Parties in EU Law* 2nd edn (Oxford: Oxford University Press, 2007).

Weatherill, S, *Cases and Materials on EU Law* 9th edn (Oxford: Oxford University Press, 2010).

Index

E